novum pocket

Helen Garden

No Going Back …

Rudi's Story

novum pocket

© 2024 novum publishing

ISBN 978-3-903468-44-3
Cover photo:
Tatyana Tomsickova I Dreamstime.com
Cover design, layout & typesetting:
novum publishing
Author's photo: Helen Garden

www.novum-publishing.co.uk

Print product with financial
climate contribution
ClimatePartner.com/16547-2311-1001

Dedicated to Joan Garden

From Riches to Rags

Author's Note

My husband Hedley had been saying to me for years that he really should write a book about his childhood experiences. But for someone who is still unable to spell, this always seemed a daunting and frankly, an impossible task. One day he decided to jot down the odd memory or two as they came to him and one thing led to another and we started putting the memories into some sort of order which resulted in the basis for this book. After many, many hours, weeks, and months spent chewing over, dissecting and fine tuning his childhood recollections and perception of events, and through much laughter and healing tears, I have woven a story around the circumstances which shaped his childhood. Although some aspects of his mother, Joan's character are accurate, what she was actually thinking at the time and her reasoning behind her behaviour, is pure fiction as it is something that we will never know. Joan's escapades really did take place although the names of some characters in the story have been changed.

Contents

Chapter One 9

Chapter Two 23

Chapter Three 50

Chapter Four 71

Chapter Five 100

Chapter Six 125

Chapter Seven 158

Chapter Eight 181

Chapter Nine 219

Chapter Ten 245

Chapter Eleven 275

Chapter Twelve 311

Chapter Thirteen 333

Chapter Fourteen 360

Chapter Fifteen 363

Rudi

My mother was a scream. She was enormous! When she entered a room, you knew! Most of the time she saw the funny side of things, a glass half full kind of person. She enjoyed playing practical jokes on people whether she knew them or not. I loved it when she was playful and I was a co-conspirator in her pranks. It made me feel as tall as a tree. Important. Valued. 'Do it again' I would chortle, doubling over with glee. And I would think up ways to make her laugh. Sometimes it worked. A lot of the time it didn't.

Not everyone saw her the way I did of course. She had a smooth sultry air about her with a crown of dark brown hair and matching large eyes, cupid bow lips and a face that could have adorned the covers of the best fashion magazines. She oozed self confidence and poise and possessed a vivacious and animated spirit revealing none of her deep down insecurity and providing a smoke screen for some of the nastiness and malice that would surface in later years. She relished turning heads when walking into a room and people were drawn to her like moths to a flame especially the men. I mean, she was a beautiful woman. Even I could tell and I was only five.

My father, well, he was just never around. One of my earliest memories of him was when I hid in the back of his car and he heard me giggling when we were way down the road. Needless to say he wasn't happy (I think he was off to see his lady friend so my timing wasn't perfect) and was so cross he turned the car around and drove me back home with a scowl on his face, driving so fast over the potholes that I was flung about in the back like a rag doll. I didn't dare protest.

My father was born and brought up in Yorkshire where he said he played junior cricket for Yorkshire Cricket Club. He came out to South Africa in 1936 at the age of 21 and lived in Johannesburg where he met and married my mother in the early 1940s. My parents took up positions managing the Rand Club, a prestigious gentleman's club in the centre of Johannesburg City that was founded by Cecil John Rhodes in 1887. In 1938 the England cricket team (or Marylebone Cricket Club (MCC) — the name under which England teams toured at the time, were touring South Africa and as my father knew fellow Yorkshireman and now England cricketer, Len Hutton, he invited the team to visit the Rand Club. It was during these years at the club that my sister Jennifer was born in 1947 followed by myself six years later in 1953. I was about three months old when the family moved to Margate on the Natal South Coast.

Owning his own hotel was something my father had always dreamed of and the death of his father in England and the subsequent inheritance that would come his way, gave him precisely the opportunity to do so. My father though had big ideas. He didn't want a small hotel. That wouldn't do at all. It had to be big enough to make a statement and despite my mother's objection that he should 'build something smaller and more manageable Ian!' he built an eight floor, 40-room hotel which was the biggest hotel south of Durban at that time. He had formed a partnership with a local man by the name of

Guy King. They named the hotel the 'Kingsview'. The building company that was commissioned to do the construction was owned and run by Ronnie Baker. Ronnie and his wife Pat would grow to become good friends of my parents over the years and little did I know that they would have such a major role to play and be such a positive influence in my life in the future.

Margate was a typically South African quiet, sleepy seaside town with many homes in later years being bought up by rich businessmen from Johannesburg and surrounds for holiday and second homes many of which were locked up and vacant for the majority of the year. The town itself boasted a cinema where all the latest movies of the day were shown, a couple of small hotels which did very well during the holiday season, thank you very much, and brought a much needed vibrancy to the town when it overflowed with sunburnt, up country visitors, one or two shops selling typical tourist wares like fishing nets, buckets and spades, inflatable beach balls and kids brightly coloured plastic sunglasses and not forgetting the ice creams which were so synonymous with trips to the coast; a pharmacy and one supermarket which had the monopoly of the town at the time and could charge exorbitant prices. There was also a petrol garage, a baker who made the best Chelsea buns in the world, a butcher, a greengrocer and a police station. There was also The Corner Café which was a central point for the locals to meet up over a cuppa and discuss everything and nothing. The school that I would go to was a little further out of town.

My very young years were spent living in two interconnecting rondavels (traditional round African huts made of stone with a conical thatched roof) which were situated just up the road from where my father's hotel was being built at the time. The rondavel on the left was my parents 'bedroom and the one on the other side was shared by my sister and I. The building that connected the two was used as the living area, with a kitchenette that was 'not big enough to swing a cat' as my mom always used to say. I was a bit puzzled from where she was going to get a cat in a swing. The remainder of the space was dominated by a large grey sofa and a table and four chairs where we would eat our meals.

Once the hotel was completed both my father and mother would head off early to go to work and I often didn't see my father for days. And of course with all the logistics of running a hotel, it's not your normal nine to five either. Both my parents were out entertaining guests most evenings and my sister and I were left with the maid. I was eventually sent to play school for the morning when I was about four. The teacher's name was Miss Jermont and she was French and very nice. I can remember that there was an outbuilding that was used as a toilet and it had a row of small tin buckets hanging from hooks that had been knocked into the wall at willy height which we used to wee in. I used to enjoy the sound that it made when I weed against the side of the empty bucket and made sure that I used it as often as I could.

We lived in the rondavels for a number of years before my parents bought a house in neighbouring Ramsgate. These were happy years. Our house was a large and rambling building with big rooms and high ceilings, and windows that were so large they seemed like walls of glass.

There was a garage where my father could park his precious Opel Kapitan and my sister and I each had our own bedroom. I used to love it when my mother was in a playful mood and she would sometimes come into my room in the evenings before bed. She would knock on the door and say in a posh voice, 'can I enter your castle, me lord?' and bow to me with a flourish and we used to burst into fits of laughter and roll around on the bed. Or she would open the door and say 'Where is Rudi? I'm sure he is here somewhere'. Then muttering to herself, she would proceed to look for me purposefully and with much seriousness, under the bed, behind the curtains, in the cupboard or even in my chest of drawers calling all the time 'Rudi where are you?' And I would howl with laughter holding my stomach. Then she would tickle me until I was gasping for breath, then climb up next to me on the bed and we would settle down to read. It was always Davey Crockett, my favourite story. But I especially loved it when she remembered to come and say goodnight to me on the evenings when she was having one of her '*fun raising*' parties. She would always be at her best and would waft into my bedroom looking all pretty and sparkling and her face would light up with a vibrant smile. She would tuck me in and with a big kiss tell me I was her special boy. I used to snuggle down with a warm glow and a smile, the smell of her perfume lingering long after she had left the room. But more often than not, after reminding her throughout the day and waiting and waiting for her to come, determined to stay awake, I would fall asleep and wake up the next morning realising that she had not come and feeling let down and dejected.

My gran, who wasn't my mother's real mother but had looked after her from the age of 14 and whom I knew as Granny Kidd, came to live with us and she had a room down the passage at the other end of the hall. I couldn't understand what she said half the time because she was Scottish, like the terrier, and she spoke funny.

The house itself was set in an acre of garden with large flower beds, loads of fruit trees which included a couple of guava, mango and banana trees of various sizes and a big round pond with slate edging that was home to about five beautiful vibrantly orange koi. The garden was attended to every day by a garden 'boy' by the name of Jabulani, (which means happy in case you don't know) and he regarded it as his domain. It was his pride and joy. There was not a weed in sight, I don't think they dared to show their green heads and he cut the grass and trimmed the flower beds with the precision and accuracy of a barber and would not hesitate to tell me off if I happened to accidentally stand on one of his precious plants. He was always cheerful though and would arrive at work every day, whistling tunelessly through his teeth and the comforting rhythmic swishing of his grass broom on the paving outside my bedroom window, greeted me most mornings. We also had a cook by the name of Charlie and a maid called Ester who used to boss me around a bit.

'Rudi, come and have a look. We have a surprise for you.' Mom's sing-song voice echoed down the passage one day. 'This must be a good surprise' I told myself 'as mom was using her special voice'. I ran down the hall excitedly and there sitting on the step was a new addition to the family, a dog. My mother loved animals. Not cats

14

so much, because she said black cats normally belong to witches and bring bad luck. Dogs however, were her favourite. She belonged to the local animal rescue society and hosted a lot of '*fun raising*' tea parties in the garden. But I couldn't quite see how having fun helped the dogs. She said you could always rely on a dog. They were loyal and didn't judge you, which was confusing. I mean, she had shown me a picture of a judge once, a stern looking man wearing a big red coat and white hair which she told me was a wig. I suppose that he hadn't washed his hair that morning and wanted to cover it up. I imagined a dog sitting at a desk wearing a red coat with a white curly wig on his head, black glasses perched on his nose. This made me smile.

He was a smiley dog of unknown origin, that mom said was a 'pavement special', small with short coarse hair and a hairy chin that resembled a beard. We called him Happy (after Jabulani) and he was to become my best friend. Happy took to following me wherever I went and even though my parents did not like me to bring him indoors, I used to sneak him into my bedroom and hide with him under my bed. Happy of course was up for any game and would just wriggle his bottom and lick me in a frenzy. One day I was playing around the fishpond, walking along the slate edging pretending I was walking along a rope like they do in the circus and I slipped and fell into the water. The water wasn't deep but it was a bit green and slimy and I wanted to cry but Happy raced over barking madly and jumped into the water. I think he was wanting to save me. I gave him a big hug and together with help from a concerned Jabulani, we climbed out of the pond.

Jabulani felt honoured to have our dog named after him and with dignified regularity he used to ensure that his blankets were aired and returned just so to his bed at the end of the day and that his water bowl was always filled to the brim. I would sometimes hear him clicking his tongue and muttering to himself in irritation when he came across Happy's water bowl full of big black ants that were common to the area and with careful concentration he would replace the water. He took his doggie duties very seriously.

Our big garden was often the setting for tea parties of some sort or another, like the '*fun raising*' ones for the dogs. I sat myself down on a selected spot on the top step of the verandah out of the way, where I was 'seen but not heard', Happy lounging contentedly by my feet, overlooking the activity before me. There were a number of tables set out on the lawn each covered with a white table cloth, laden with all sorts of delicious food: Small cakes delicately iced and set out prettily on three -tier stands and little beautifully cut finger sandwiches arranged artfully on my mother's best blue and white china. I did ask her once why the sandwiches were so small and she said that she wanted them to look nice and to make a good impression, whatever that meant. So maybe when she sometimes gave me my sandwiches at lunchtime, two chunky slices of bread and cheese with tomato sauce oozing out onto my fingers, she didn't need to make them with any impression at all, that's why they were so big. But I didn't mind because the tea party sandwiches were so small they surely couldn't be enough to feed a five-year-old, especially one with 'hollow legs' as my mother used to say when I asked for seconds.

There was much gaiety and laughter, with big blue umbrellas fluttering in the breeze, the tinkling of teaspoons, the wonderful smell of sausage rolls fresh out of the oven and the ladies in their wide multi-coloured skirts, a kaleidoscope of colour. I loved to watch my mom at these parties. She was never snappy and nasty like she could be with me sometimes. This was her happy self coming out to play. She was at her best, a bright butterfly flitting all over the place, ensuring everyone was comfortable with tea in hand, serving cake and accepting compliments with grace and a smile for everyone including me. She would ruffle my hair and hand me a piece of cake on one of her special plates. I basked in the attention and felt on cloud nine.

Later on towards evening, tall ice cold glass jugs of juice with cut up pieces of cucumber and strawberries floating like petals in the liquid, were brought outside and served in long crystal glasses. Mom said it wasn't for children as there was gin in there. This was puzzling as Jim was one of her friends, but perhaps he had helped her make it. Never the less, it looked very pretty. The husbands normally arrived in time for *Jim's* drink and the tea parties used to go on late into the night. My dad was often absent from these gatherings as he was usually at work. Sometimes he came home late in the evening when things were in full swing with loud music and dancing in the sitting room where the furniture had been moved to one side. He would more often than not join in the fun although sometimes he was disgruntled and spent the evening sitting in a chair drinking Jim's drink until everyone had gone home.

Often I would wake at night to hear my mother's high pitched angry voice and my father's lower tone raised in reply, heavy footsteps and doors slamming. When I got up one morning after a night filled with noise and shouting, my mother was sitting with her head in her hands at the kitchen table. 'Mom!' I said 'whatever is the matter?' pulling her hands away from her face. Her eyes were red and swollen and she looked as if she hadn't slept. 'Oh it's nothing,' she replied in her pretend happy voice, 'just a bit of a headache that's all.' But I knew it wasn't that. My father would be long gone. These arguments seemed to occur quite often even when there were no tea parties. I didn't like the shouting and used to put my hands over my ears and burrow under the bedclothes to try and block out the noise.

We all went out to Dr Johnston's house (he was the local doctor) one evening to watch the fireworks. It was so funny because my dad lit a jumping jack and it jumped into a box of fireworks and they all went off at the same time. There were fireworks going off in all directions making a huge noise. Everyone screamed and I ran indoors to tell mum and saw her and Dr Johnston kissing in the kitchen. Yuck! *Really!* They jumped apart when they saw me. I didn't want to miss the fireworks so I just grabbed her hand and dragged her outside to see the spectacle.

On the way home in the car I said, 'I saw mom and Dr Johnston kissing in the kitchen. It was yuck!'

There was lots of shouting that night too. Somehow I felt I was to blame.

#

It wasn't long after Happy's arrival that I started school for the first time. I was quite looking forward to meeting some boys my age to play with but I didn't really want to leave Happy all day. Sitting on the bed in my parents' room, I watched mom getting ready to take me into town to be fitted for a school uniform. I don't know why she had to put all that stuff on her face, although I must say that she did look very pretty in her bright red dress and lipstick to match. She didn't normally dress in her best just to go to town so I felt that she was dressing up especially for me. I was excited because it would just be the two of us out together. It made me feel special.

School uniforms were sold at the small local haberdashery shop which was situated towards the end of the main road on the right hand side past the butcher. I felt very important getting into the car with my mother looking so radiant. Driving into town she was excited and bubbly and sang her favourite song at the top of her voice, a large smile on her face. Her enthusiasm was infectious and soon we were tapping feet and swaying together to the music. I'm not too sure how she drove the car at the same time though.

'Let's call into the café and have some tea before we get your uniform Rudi, I'm awfully parched. It must be all that singing.' She winked at me and prodded me in the ribs. I grinned back. This was a treat!

The café was half full when we got there as it was still too early for the lunchtime rush. She stopped to look around at the tables as if searching for someone, then made her way to a table at the back of the room that gave us a good view of the comings and goings and away from the big glass windows that looked out onto the road. I followed. I would have preferred to sit by the window so that I could watch what was going on outside. But I didn't say so.

Mom said I could have a milkshake which was my absolute favourite and as a special treat. I could have a raisin bun as well. She ordered tea for herself and pulled out her compact and checked herself in the mirror touching up her bright red lipstick a bit. My milkshake when it arrived was bright pink and frothy. I took a giant sip and my eyes watered because it was so cold. I devoured my raisin bun but sipped the milkshake trying to make it last as long as I could.

Mom was fidgety. She kept looking at her watch and glancing around and looking expectantly towards the door each time it opened. She fiddled with her hair, took out her compact and looked at her face in the mirror once more. I thought that was silly because how could it have changed so much from ten minutes ago? She pulled at the shoulder strap of her dress and bit the side of her lip. 'I think I will have another cup of tea,' she said after a while in a pretend jolly voice. When the tea arrived she poured herself a cup and continued to look about. Eventually the tea grew cold in the cup. The longer we were there the quieter she became. The animation was gone from her face and was replaced with a look of dejection and familiar lines appeared on her forehead. She had been so happy a minute ago.

'Are ... are we still going to get my school uniform?' I hesitantly asked. She didn't reply and I knew better than to ask again. She got to her feet abruptly as if she had come to a decision, gathered her bag and marched out of the café. I scrambled up, hurrying to follow her as she walked with a determined stride to the haberdashery shop.

We were finished in no time at all. My mother thrust a shirt and pair of shorts into my hands and led the way to the change room where I started to get undressed fumbling with the buttons on my shirt. 'Hurry up, Rudi!' she snapped 'I don't have all day'. With the purchases made, we set off back to the car although I struggled to keep pace with her brisk stride.

There was no singing on the journey home. There was no talking either. I glanced briefly across at her hoping that she would give me one of her special smiles then I would know that I hadn't upset her, but her mouth was set firmly and her red nails were drumming a constant rhythm on the steering wheel. Feeling let down and anxious, I slid down in my seat and didn't say a word.

#

My first day at school was quite enjoyable and after the first week I felt like I had been there forever. As Jennifer had been at school for a while she took me under her wing and made sure that I got there safely. The school bus, which we caught together every day used to stop outside a small shop down the road from our house. So it wasn't too far to walk to the bus stop each day.

One day when I arrived home from school, my mother was at home which was unusual and I saw from her face that she wasn't in a good mood.

'We are going to be moving to the Regent Hotel in Margate where I have got work.' she said, 'Granny Kidd will be going to a retirement home in Pietermaritzburg where she will be cared for and we can visit her there' mom continued not looking at me, 'Unfortunately Happy is going to have to stay with your dad.' Bursting into tears, I ran out the room to find Happy. I had no idea why we were having to move. All I could think about was that I didn't want to be separated from my best friend. Little did I realise at the time, but this marked the end of my parents' marriage and the beginning of a journey of upheaval and trauma in my life.

CHAPTER TWO

Joan

I first saw him across the room talking to an acquaint-ance. Yes … ok … I *know* it sounds like a cliché, but it really happened that way. I decided there and then that I had to have him. My mother had always told me that if you want something badly enough then you will go out and get it no matter what. So I made a beeline for him. Well … wouldn't you?

Ian wasn't the tallest of men but he possessed a charm that was captivating and inscrutable and I could never quite put my finger on what I found so attractive about him. To put it simply … I was captivated. I felt adored, and he looked at me as if I was the most treasured person in the world and nothing else mattered and I didn't ever want to let him go. I would have gone with him to the ends of the earth if he had asked me. I had always thought that if I could find a man to love me, then I would be happy. But I came to realise over time that it doesn't take a man's love to be happy.

My father left my mother for pastures new when I was a baby so I never knew him although I always keenly felt the hole he left. My mother remarried twice after that, her third marriage was to my stepfather when I was six. We lived in Rhodesia, which is now Zimbabwe, on a farm out Hartley way called Hilltop. I enjoyed life on the farm but it was marred by constant disagreements and shouting arguments between my mother and my stepfather. To say that I had a difficult relationship with my mother would not be exaggerating, honestly. I always seemed to get in her way and she would irritably tell me to 'go and find something to occupy yourself or I will give you work to do'. I so longed for the easy friendship with her that my friends seemed to have with their mothers. But I guess, because she was unhappy, she became angry and bitter and took it out on me, although I didn't understand that at the time. I tried to stay out of her way for the most part and spent a lot of time in my room or on the large wrap around verandah with the dogs.

When I was fourteen my mother contracted malaria which turned into blackwater fever and she died not long afterwards. I used to go to her bedroom to spend some time with her in the afternoon after school and I both longed to be there and dreaded it at the same time. She was demanding and disagreeable and the time spent with her left me feeling wretched and depressed. After she died my stepfather felt unable to care for me so I was sent to Johannesburg to stay with a good friend of my mother's Rachel Kidd whom I called Aunt Rachel. I was devastated and felt abandoned by the adults in my life.

'Dear child,' said Aunt Rachel with tears in her eyes as I stepped off the train at Johannesburg station. She wrapped me in a warm embrace that immediately brought tears to my own eyes and I gulped and fell into her softness and sobbed. 'Come child,' she said again as she let me go. 'Let's get you warmed up with a cup of tea and then we will be on our way'. Her soft Scottish accent wrapped around me like a familiar cloak as she took my hand in one of hers, grabbed my suitcase with the other and started towards the station exit.

Aunt Rachel lived just outside the suburb of Hillbrow in the centre of Johannesburg. It was the in place to be at the time, with many new high rise buildings and beautiful apartments for those that could afford it. It was renowned for its vibrant cosmopolitan nightlife and I would spend many a night there in future years.

I collapsed onto the bed once Aunt Rachel had shown me to my room. I felt exhausted. I heard a soft knock at the door and realised that I must have dozed off. Aunt Rachel entered the room holding a tray on which was a large mug of soup and two thinly buttered slices of brown bread and placed it on the table next to the bed.

'You try and eat a bit, love,' she said 'then go wash your face and hands and come to the sitting room so that we can chat. No rush now mind. You take your time'.

She left the room before I could thank her, closing the door quietly behind her. Her kindness brought a lump to my throat and my eyes filled with tears once more. Taking a deep breath I tucked into the soup and bread suddenly realising how hungry I was. After a visit to the bathroom at my aunt's bidding I went downstairs to the sitting room. Aunt Rachel patted the sofa next to her indicating for me to sit.

'Now then child, we need to discuss your future education,' she said softly, looking at me 'You are only 14-years-old and I promised your mother that I would see to it that you are properly educated and equipped to go out into the world. So this is what I have decided would be best for you. And I hope you will agree. There is a lovely convent up the road run by nuns and they would be very happy to welcome you there to complete your schooling. How do you feel about that?' I hadn't given much thought to my education since the death of my mother and to be honest I didn't get along too well with school work. I much preferred drama and acting, which mom had done in the past and encouraged my interest in it. It was fun. But I knew that I would have to go to school anyway. I was only 14 and didn't really have a say in the matter. I tried to smile at her

'Whatever you think is best Aunt Rachel. When would I start?'

'Well, I think we need some time to get you organised with a uniform and odds and ends first. So let's say Monday next week?'

And so it was arranged.

School was nothing like I had expected. Even though I felt rather grown up and lady like in my new navy blue pinafore, white shirt with crisp collar, black stockings, well, especially the stockings, and black patent leather shoes, I still felt uncertain and out of place, not knowing what kind of reception I would get from the other girls. I had joined the school midway through the term and as I walked into class that first day full of apprehension I could feel twenty pairs of eyes following me step by step to my new desk. But as it turned out, I needn't have worried. The girls weren't too bad at all.

I was pleasantly surprised to find that I didn't have to grapple with much arithmetic, history and geography. Instead there were subjects like domestic science, sewing and cookery classes, deportment, elocution lessons, etiquette and manners and how to walk correctly. Even the basics of flower arrangement. Best of all there was a room where there were about 10 typewriters and twice a week we were given lessons on how to type. You even had to learn where all the letters were on the keyboard so that you could type without looking at your hands. I thought it was awesome.

I settled in right away. I loved the elocution and etiquette lessons and we were taught how to behave correctly in company by following the 'Rule of Three' which was 'smile, chat, and charm'. When it came to deportment and how to walk correctly, I felt that I was on the stage and I strode out, head held high with my hands on my hips and huge smile on my face, and swaggered across the room, putting one foot carefully in front of the other as we had been taught. I was in my element. This did not make me popular with the other girls as they accused me of showing off and being snooty and stuck up. But I didn't care! I had found something that made me feel good about myself and that was enough for me.

Life with Aunt Rachel was quiet and predictable and I know she did her best. She insisted that I write regularly to my stepfather as she said it was the right thing to do. After explaining to me that he had sent me to live with her because he thought it would be the best thing for me I felt slightly better. I missed the farm and still felt the loss of my mother and the abandonment of my stepfather deeply and I struggled with anger that would boil up inside me unexpectedly. Sometimes I would flare up and snap at Aunt Rachel nastily then feel bad afterwards. Well, she did *fuss* so! I felt hemmed in somehow, always with that feeling of wanting more. It was as if I was missing out on something, but not understanding what. But despite all this we settled into a comfortable routine together which benefitted us both.

I barely noticed the following two years go by, I was so absorbed in my school and all that it offered. Deep down I was still very insecure but the activities at school helped my self confidence grow and sometimes I could portray an air of composure and poise that deep down, I didn't feel at all. But I told myself it was like acting a part on a stage. It helped me to cope.

When I left school, I got a job in a large department store in the centre of Johannesburg. The placement was arranged by the nuns and I was told how lucky I was to be recommended for the position. I dressed neatly in a black skirt and white buttoned blouse that first day, and nervously made my way to the office of Miss Walters, as I had been told, on the second floor of the store.

'Enter,' I heard a raspy voice. I opened the door and entered a small office dominated by a large heavy wooden desk. Dwarfed by the desk and seated behind an untidy pile of paperwork was, I presumed, Miss Walters. She was a small woman, with iron grey hair, black rimmed glasses behind which were piercing eyes and a complexion covered in a mesh of fine lines. Her voice was gravelly, a condition not helped by the cigarette held loosely between her fingers. It made me want to clear my throat.

'You are late,' she accused, 'and kindly tuck in your shirt. I will not have my staff creating a bad impression. You will be neat at all times. You will be punctual at all times. Is that clearly understood?'

'Ye … yes ma'am,' I said anxiously

'You will address me as Miss Walters.'

'Yes ma' … I mean Yes, Miss Walters,' I stammered. Clearly this was not a good start.

'I have given you this position as a direct favour to Sister Thomas as she has spoken highly of you and asssured me that you have exceptional qualities which we could use.' She said looking at me sternly over the top of her black rimmed spectacles that were perched on her nose. 'With this in mind, I have placed you in the perfume department to start with, where you will be working directly under Marge Green who will take you under her wing. You will commence work at nine sharp every day except Sunday, and work until five in the afternoon with an hour for lunch. You are to ensure that you are neat and tidy at all times and your uniform is immaculate. I trust that you will not let me or Sister Thomas down. Do you have any questions?'

'No questions, Miss Walters' I said, letting out a breath I did not know I was holding.

'Very well then,' she sniffed 'follow me.' And she led the way out of her office, down the back stairs and entered the ground floor of the department store where the perfume counter was located. After introducing me to Marge Green she turned and with a curt nod, walked back through the store to proceed with her daily check of the employees and display counters before the doors opened for the day. I noticed a sudden bustle of activity as the employees fussed with their displays as she made her way between the counters.

'Don't mind her,' Marge whispered to me softly, with a reassuring hand on my arm, 'her bark is worse than her bite'

Marge Green was a lot older than I, possibly about 40 although it was hard to tell because everyone looked old to me. I was after all just sixteen, well nearly seventeen, and anyone over 30 to me, was ancient. But in saying that, she was beautifully dressed, with perfect hair and nails that I couldn't help admiring. She was very chatty and helped me enormously with learning the ins and outs of customer service, guidance when it came to selling perfume and tips in identifying the different fragrances that were on sale. She said that as long as we are punctual, smart and treat the customers with respect, Miss Walters will be happy.

I enjoyed my work at the perfume counter. Marge taught me everything she knew and with her help I started to relax and to develop a rapport with the customers. I always greeted them with a charming smile and did my best to make them feel special and at ease. I chatted easily with them and enjoyed the banter I received in return. The men in particular were very complimentary and sometimes there were two or three waiting for me to help them select a particular perfume. It felt good to be admired and I would laugh gaily and enjoy the attention under their enthralled gaze whilst Marge would roll her eyes at me. I kept all that I had learnt at school, (the Rule of Three) how to make a good impression, the way to carry yourself, the way to converse with people correctly and charmingly, in the forefront of my mind until it became second nature. It was all a game really.

I had been working there for a couple of years when a tall, pleasant looking gentleman approached the perfume counter and handed me his business card. 'My name is Fritz Cohen and I run a modelling agency' he said 'I would be very happy if you could make an appointment for an interview with our agency. I think we might have a position for you.' I was flattered and thanked him, putting the card inside my handbag, my heart thumping in my chest.

'Well,' said Marge with raised eyebrows, 'you have got to find out what this is all about. It could be your chance.'

I agreed with her. I mean, what an opportunity, don't you think? Who wouldn't want to be involved in fashion and saunter around wearing beautiful clothes, even if they weren't your own? I felt a swell of excitement!

Could I really do this?

I made the telephone call as soon as I had the opportunity to do so and secured an appointment for the following Thursday morning. I arranged for some time off work, although I didn't tell them why. Thursday morning was upon me before I knew it. After a restless night's sleep, spent tormenting myself with visions of making a fool of myself and feeling totally inadequate, I dragged myself out of bed and went through to the kitchen to make a cup of tea. Aunt Rachel was already up with the kettle on the boil.

'I see we have both had an unsettled night and I'm not even the one going for the interview today,' she said with a wry smile.

I wish everyone could have an Aunt Rachel like mine. I know that she wasn't entirely happy with my appointment today and was feeling uncomfortable with the prospect of me getting involved in the fashion industry. 'You must always remember what you have been taught. It's important to be well mannered and respectable and always present yourself as a lady of class. You are a young lady now after all,' she told me earnestly.

I hugged her and told her not to worry and planting a kiss on her forehead I went through to the bedroom to get myself ready. I dressed with care in my best blue frock with the white collar and four large buttons affixed to the front down to the waist. I tried to pin my hair in the way that Marge had taught me, fixing it with a large slide to finish it off. I don't think I did too bad a job. Pleased with how I looked with my matching navy shoes and handbag and carrying my white gloves I headed out towards the bus stop trying to quell my nerves.

I entered the large imposing lobby of the building where the agency's offices were housed, taking in the expanse of marble floor and beautiful matching staircase with ornate polished wooden rail leading up to the floor above. An enormous glistening chandelier was hanging suspended from the ceiling and I gazed at it in awe as I made my way to the reception desk and asked to see Fritz Cohen. I was instructed to make my way to the first floor and there would be someone to meet me there. Clutching my bag, taking a deep breath and putting my shoulders back, I mounted the steps boldly, head held high and was shown into a room where there were about eight other young girls sitting in chairs along the wall. One look at them and my confidence vanished. Most were dressed in the very latest fashion. Some were quite smart but others seemed to be somewhat garish and flashy with overdone make up. A bit brassy perhaps, I thought. 'Tacky', Aunt Rachel would have said! The girls were chatting easily amongst themselves and seemed to know one another having been there before apparently. They all seemed so worldly to me. My heart sank. Feeling out of place and self conscious and trying to hide the scuff marks on my shoes, I sat down as unobtrusively as I could manage and listened to their chatter with growing unease.

To my consternation, I was the first to be called into the studio. Fritz leapt to his feet when I entered and taking me by surprise, he took both my hands in his and planted a kiss on each cheek, before showing me to the vacant chair next to his and introducing me to the other gentleman in the room.

The interview lasted less than half an hour and I walked out of there feeling on top of the world. I was about to enter a profession that I had only seen in magazines and the glamour and theatre of it all, appealed to me.

Modelling wasn't nearly as glamorous as I had imagined. It was rigorous. It was repetitive. Training day after day until it became second nature to walk tall, chin held high with shoulders relaxed and a smooth stride. It was dragging myself out of bed like a zombie very early in the morning and getting to the studio or venue for the day before the city was awake. It was on the go, changing from outfit to outfit, rushing off to the seamstress to repair the odd tear or loose button, touching up make-up and ensuring all along that I remained composed. It was back to back schedules of really early mornings and late nights, working under hot lights in remote locations and plastering a smile on my face no matter how tired I felt. It was learning how to smoke for the first time when given a cigarette by one of the girls during a much needed break. It was being introduced to cocktails, to late night dancing at the many clubs we frequented, to gritty morning eyes, bird cage mouth and a throbbing head.

It was brutal.

It was exhausting.

I *loved* it.

I soon discovered another side to myself which I didn't know I had. Modelling had taught me that I could be anyone I chose to be. I just had to hold my head up high and be that person that was confident, charming and attractive. I have been told that I possessed a certain '*je ne sais quai'* which I used to the full, enjoying a captivating audience, teasing the men and charming the women. I took full advantage of my allure knowing that men were attracted to me and enjoying the attention and the feeling of power that it gave me. I flirted endlessly thoroughly enjoying myself and oblivious to the raised eyebrows.

I know Aunt Rachel worried about me but I was having such a wonderful time that I dismissed her concern with a shrug. She was not altogether happy with my modelling at all anyway and in particular the late nights spent with 'those girls who were a bad influence'. So she was very relieved when I met Ian.

It was during one of the many functions that I attended that I was introduced to him. 'I noticed you the moment you walked through the door,' he said in his distinctive voice, taking a step back and throwing out his arm in my direction 'How could I not when perfection walks into a room?' His intense blue eyes held mine and I felt an instant connection and for once couldn't think of anything to say. I felt like the tongue-tied schoolgirl I had once been and to my dismay, I realised that I was blushing and tried to turn away. I mean ... *really*! How *embarrassing*!

He reached for my hand as if it was the most natural thing in the world. 'Let's get out of here,' he said. So we did.

Our courtship was head spinning and intense. Ian was older than me by at least ten years and he had a way about him that was full of authority, masterful even, a 'man of the world'. I was awakened to feelings that I didn't know I possessed. I felt cocooned in his ability to create a feeling of trust in me, as if he would never let me down. So I trusted him.

We were married after a whirlwind courtship just after I turned twenty one. Yes, I know … It is young isn't it, but that is what we *did* those days.

Ian and I had never discussed whether I would carry on with my modelling once we were married. I just presumed that I would. Well why *wouldn't* I? So it came as a surprise when he said one day soon after we got back from honeymoon, 'I've spoken with the board at the club about arranging a position and they have agreed to create a 'front of house' post for you,' he said, his hand softly feeling my arm.

'Oh!' I looked at him puzzled, 'But I have modelling assignments next week that I am committed to and in any case, I am not wanting to stop my work. I'm sure they will find someone else for the position,' I replied airily looking down at his hand with a slight frown as it tightened on my arm.

'My wife is not going to parade up and down, dressed in outrageous outfits for the entertainment of strangers.' His penetrating gaze never left my face. I wasn't aware that he felt that way about my modelling as he had always seemed supportive. I was proud of what I had achieved and I bristled with the sting of his words.

'But I don't *want* to give up my career,' I retorted, my voice rising angrily, 'my work means a lot to me. I have signed a contract until the end of next year which I intend to complete.' Feeling the heat rising up my neck under his gaze I furiously turned and walked off but not before I had seen the disapproval on his face and I could tell that this was going to be an ongoing battle.

Our relationship would continue to be mercurial. It would seesaw from intense arguments, which would flare up unexpectedly as I never knew when to hold my tongue quite frankly, to passionate and emotional reconciliations which left me feeling bewildered and unsettled. These clashes however, were normally caused by our disagreements over the time I spent at work.

As it turned out, I spent the following couple of years modelling on and off. Ian seemed to have accepted the idea and our disagreements became less frequent. During one of my breaks we set off on a trip to Rhodesia together to visit my stepfather on the farm in Hartley and to introduce him to Ian. We spent a relaxing couple of weeks there and as this was the first time I had seen my stepfather since I left at the age of fourteen, I must say that I enjoyed his company.

Soon after arriving home from our long break I realised that the decision to give up modelling had been taken out of my hands. I discovered that I was pregnant. Ian was thrilled although possibly more so by the fact that I would now be forced to be at home than the fact that he was going to be a father.

I did *not* enjoy being pregnant. The early stages were plagued by nausea and vomiting so that I felt wretched and sometimes it was one in the afternoon before I would venture into the shower and change out of my pyjamas. But then the nausea was replaced by feeling ungainly, bloated and unattractive, with swollen ankles and a lethargy that I struggled to cope with. I felt as if my body had been invaded, which it had really. I couldn't wait for the nine months to go by when I would have my body back. I pictured myself serenely holding my content sleeping baby in my arms after a feed, dressed in a new frock to show off my once again slim figure. Ian looked on proudly with his arm around my shoulders, a perfect picture of family togetherness.

The reality of course was quite different. I don't think I took naturally to motherhood. Really, I had nothing to compare it with of course. Aunt Rachel had never had children and my mother was not the mothering kind. When Jennifer was born, I was in awe of this tiny being that I had created and I was filled with such hope and resolve for the future. I was going to be the *perfect* mother. You wait and see!

But with a demanding baby that cried constantly that I struggled to placate no matter what I tried, feeling hormonal and grumpy, and so dreadfully *exhausted* that all I wanted to do was sleep, I felt like a failure. I spent my days in a haze of changing nappies, boiling bottles to sterilise them, making up milk formula, walking up and down pacifying Jennifer in an effort to get her to sleep, then starting all over again. I was lying to friends about how I was coping wishing that they would just leave me alone and bursting into tears at the slightest thing. I found the constant demands hugely challenging and my confidence hit an all- time low. Ian of course, besides hardly being at home, left it all to me. I had never felt so alone.

Jennifer was just past her second birthday when the subject of me working at the club rose its head once more. I had been thinking about getting back to work but as yet hadn't broached the subject with Ian as I just did not have the energy for any more arguments to be honest. So when he suggested that I come help out in the club I jumped at the chance. I found that I had missed the camaraderie and fun that I got from working, I missed the banter, I missed the feeling of accomplishment that it gave me and I missed the admiration I used to get. But most of all, I missed my old enthusiastic fun loving *self*.

I settled into work at the club as easily as slipping on a glove. I just seemed to fit. With plenty of staff willing to take over babysitting duties when needed, I was able to get stuck in right away, learning the ropes. Mary Kelly, the housekeeper, was the only other woman working there apart from the African cleaners, and we became quite good friends and would spend many an afternoon having a good natter.

It was rejuvenating settling myself into the everyday running of the club and familiarising myself with some of its quaint rules. I loved looking the part and choosing the perfect outfit to wear every day, together with having meticulously manicured nails and perfect make up and hair. It was very important to me to look good so I spent time planning my wardrobe and perfecting my look. I realised that I would be in the spotlight and I wanted to look my best. It not only boosted my confidence but it also helped me feel in control. I revelled in the mature conversation, wise quips and adult banter and gave as good as I got. I felt *alive* again.

Despite giving up my modelling career and working closely with Ian at the club, our relationship was still fraught with conflicts and fiery clashes although this time it seemed to be my behaviour that was the catalyst. Ian was not comfortable with the attention that I was attracting from club members and really, all I was doing was the 'Rule of Three' as I had been taught. The fact that I enjoyed feeling attractive and being surrounded by attentive, appreciative men in dinner suits was a bonus and a much needed boost to my ego. I must say I did rather *encourage* the attention and flirted outrageously. It *was* harmless fun ... well, wasn't it? But Ian of course was not happy.

Regardless of the conflicts within our marriage I fell pregnant once more and gave birth to a son almost six years after the birth of Jennifer. Rudi was a gentle and placid baby, with a sunny nature and big smile that lit up the room. He rarely cried and could be left to amuse himself for hours on end. So his entry into our lives was smooth and relatively unchallenging. It was during this pregnancy that we received news that Ian's father had passed away in England and subsequently left Ian a substantial amount of money. The idea to build his own hotel was now becoming more than a dream and after much planning and talking late into the night we decided to take the bull by the horns and put his plan into action. We chose to relocate to the seaside town of Margate on the south coast of Natal. As Margate was a popular holiday destination, and as Ian had friends there, we decided that it was a great place for our hotel.

I was looking forward to the move to Margate. It felt like a new beginning for us and I was hoping that we would be able to rekindle some of the passion and connection that we had once enjoyed. I realised that it had been difficult to combine our family life, with the running of the club, especially since the birth of Jennifer and now Rudi. Although why I thought it would be any easier running a forty bedroom hotel, heaven alone knows! But, it was Ian's dream and I became caught up in the magic. As you do!

We rented two interconnecting rondavels situated in the road above where Ian's hotel was being built. We were pretty comfortable there even though it was rather small and for the first year of our stay there I was at home with the children. Rudi was only three months when we moved so he was not mobile which made things easier in a way and Jennifer went to the local school. I employed a maid who would help out with Rudi once I was needed back at the hotel. To be honest, I couldn't wait to get back to work and it wasn't a year later that the construction was completed.

Ian and I had been like passing ships in the night so I was very happy to be back in the thick of things and to feel that I was giving him support and contributing to the running of the business. Every day I would head off to work eager to see what the day would bring. As time went on and the day to day management was running smoothly, we focused a lot more on entertaining, either at the hotel with the guests or at home for more intimate gatherings. By this stage we had moved to a large four bedroom house in neighbouring Ramsgate. I was really excited, as this was our first real home and I was keen to put my stamp on it. We invited Aunt Rachel to live with us as she hadn't been well and I felt we could care for her. Well we certainly had the space and the staff. And in any case I missed her calming presence.

The following couple of years that we were establishing the business were hard work but satisfying. It was difficult to find suitably skilled workers to employ and it was a constant struggle to train new staff and keep those that we had already trained, happily working. Africans were notoriously well known for their relaxed attitudes especially around punctuality. They did not seem to take it seriously, so it was always challenging.

But despite the everyday difficulties the hotel was fully booked from the first month of opening which was very encouraging.

Rudi was growing quickly and continued to be very easy going, quiet and undemanding and quite happy pottering around on his own. I think in retrospect that his placid nature made it easier for me to neglect him in future years as he was always quietly in the background and never complained. I knew that I wasn't spending as much time with him as I should, but I was busy and distracted and sometimes got home so tired that I just couldn't face it. Esther the maid was there to take care of both the children on a day to day basis anyway so I really didn't give much thought to making time to be with either of them. But in his very early years I used to enjoy going into his bedroom in the evenings and play games and read Davey Crockett to him which he adored. On the evenings when I was entertaining he used to love it even more when I popped in to see him before bed, but not before reminding me throughout the day and making me promise that I would come. Often I didn't. Yes … I know, it *did* make me feel bad. But not bad enough to make him a priority over having fun. I never stopped to think how he was feeling. I did feel a bit guilty though, so thought I would get him a dog. It was a cute little thing and his delight appeased my conscience somewhat.

Towards the end of 1957 I was heartened to see that we were almost at full occupancy for the holiday period. December was our peak season as it is summer and schools are normally closed until mid-January, so we were looking forward to a bumper holiday season with great anticipation. The hotel was looking magical adorned in

Christmas splendour and I was feeling really proud of what we had achieved.

We received news mid-December that there had been a shark attack in Karridene which is a town about 30 minutes from Margate and two days later there was another attack off the neighbouring town of Uvongo. To our horror, this attack was fatal. This was awful news and we were hugely concerned. Two days before Christmas there was another fatal shark attack this time off our hometown beach followed by two further attacks during the following days. The impact on our hotel was immediate and we had a flurry of cancellations to the point where bookings dried up completely.

There were a further four fatal attacks in the area up until May 1958. This had a devastating effect on the tourism industry on the whole of the coast and Margate in particular. Almost instantly the Kingsview was empty. We continued to suffer from this huge setback for the rest of the year and into the following summer season. The financial impact hit us hard, with unoccupied rooms, excess staff that we had to lay off as we couldn't afford to pay them, an all but empty bookings register, and planned entertainment that had to be cancelled. At the same time, we needed to keep the hotel running with a skeleton workforce in the hope that we would get some bookings over the coming months. We coped as best we could, offering holiday specials, having themed dinner dances on Saturday evenings and movie evenings once a week to try and draw in numbers. But due to the lack of income combined with our distraction over our personal problems, the Kingsview would never fully recover.

Despite the reduction in bookings we continued to entertain. It was important to me to be the best at everything I did and I wanted to establish a reputation as a great hostess. I spent more time away from hotel activities and immersed myself in entertaining friends at home and organising many fund raising functions. Ian and I had become well known and respected in the area and I wanted to be seen as stylish and sophisticated and my lavish functions to be the talk of the town. Entertaining was like a stage to me and I felt alive. In the early days Ian was there by my side playing the host and helping to greet guests as they arrived. I valued his encouragement and support and I think half the time I was wanting him to tell me how great I was, which he never did of course. As time went on he attended less and less, mostly with the excuse that he was busy. When he did arrive home later in the evenings, depending on his mood, he would either join in the fun or he would sit in a corner and morosely drink, saying very little but I could always feel his eyes following my movements.

'So you must be the renowned Joan Garden?' a voice said behind me. I turned, a smile on my face and looked into a pair of serious brown eyes. 'Michael Johnston,' he said holding out his hand, not taking his eyes off my face. I knew that Michael Johnston was our local medical doctor although I had never met him. He was popular and well liked by his patients and was an active member of the community. With his impish sense of humour and rather beguiling softly spoken manner, he was easy company.

He had a head of dark wavy hair that hung over his eyes giving him a rakish look.

'I am so pleased to meet you at last. I have heard a lot about you,' I said taking his outstretched hand and feeling glad that I had worn my new green outfit that showed off my figure to perfection.

'All good I hope?'

'Well … no, not exactly' I said with a wink 'some of it I couldn't repeat!'

He threw back his head and laughed. 'My reputation precedes me it seems.'

I spent a lot of the evening chatting to Michael and an easy friendship was formed. We just seemed to click. I knew he was married, so feeling a bit uncomfortable, I invited both him and his wife to all future functions. This did not deter him and he would seek me out whenever he arrived and at times almost took on the role of host in the absence of Ian. I began to look forward each time to his arrival and feeling a bit of a traitor, took extra care with my appearance. Our friendship did take the edge off the hurt that I was feeling caused by the discord in my marriage. It just felt a bit easier to cope.

#

Ian was having an affair. I just knew it. I *knew* it! Felt it deep down. I mean all the signs were there: The months of late nights stumbling into bed reeking of alcohol and cigarette smoke intermingled with the whiff of perfume; the extra care he took with his appearance before he left the house in the mornings; the beach sand that I was always finding in his trouser pockets; always avoiding my gaze and sidestepping my questions; the excuses, always the excuses. I felt sickened.

When did he have the *time*, for heaven's sake!

Could there possibly be an innocent explanation?

'Do you think you will be able to join us this evening, Ian?' I glanced at him in the mirror whilst giving myself a final misty spray of Blue Grass, the perfume that I loved so much. Hoping to entice him, I had bought a stunning off the shoulder cocktail dress in the most gorgeous dark red satin which hugged my curves most seductively. I felt like a million dollars and I knew I looked amazing.

'It's one of our bigger events and I would so like you to be there. I think it will be fun,' I said, trying to entice him. This was one of our more important fund-raising events that I had been working hard at organising for some time. It had taken a lot of preparation and skill and there were many prominent people including the mayor of Margate who would be attending.

'Well, I can't promise anything. Hopefully the day will go smoothly,' he said noncommittally, not meeting my eyes as he made his way out the door. I sighed. He knew how much it meant to me to have him there. I turned away and with a sinking feeling realised that that is the best I can hope for.

By seven o'clock there was still no sign of Ian. The party ... because that is what it had turned into ... was in full swing. I poured myself a large gin and tonic and took a good couple of swift gulps glancing around the room. As a rule, I never drank when I hosted big events such as this, as I liked to have my wits about me, to be in control. After another mouthful, I took a deep breath, flicked my hair away from my face and wandered outside to join the guests.

After spotting Michael, I drained my glass and wove my way to where he was standing. I was starting to feel relaxed. 'Sort of fuzzy around the edges', I muttered to myself smiling. I felt lighter inside as if the hurt had receded into the distance somehow. Beginning to enjoy myself, I thought, 'So what if Ian didn't make it tonight! I can cope without him! In fact I can do better without him!' And it didn't matter so much any more. So I poured myself another drink. Well! Wouldn't you?

And so the pattern started.

Initially, I would have my first drink possibly after lunch whilst I was helping to prepare canapés for entertaining later on in the afternoon. 'Just a small one to help me relax,' I would say to myself. Sometimes that one was enough of a lift and I became busy and distracted and before I knew it the function was well on its way and I hadn't thought of having another drink. Sometimes it wasn't enough. Sometimes when I dragged myself out of bed at midday with a throbbing head and a heaving stomach I would have a 'reg marker' just to take the edge off and set me up for the day. Sometimes I would need more than one.

I don't know if Ian made it to the function that night. I remember very little to be honest other than spilling my drink all over one of the guests. Can't think for the life of me who it was now. Although I do remember stumbling through to the bedroom and falling across the bed laughing my head off over I don't know what. I woke up in the morning to see Ian's side of the bed empty and was surprised to realise that I was still fully dressed. After soaking in a long hot bath and gulping down loads of water I felt reasonably normal and wandered through to the living room to start my day.

Over the following months, my friendship with Michael was becoming increasingly important to me and I found that I confided in him about my troubled marriage more and more. As our friendship deepened, it became clear to me that he too was unhappy at home and I felt that we were kindred spirits.

'I am having a get together with some fireworks this evening,' he said one day, 'and I would really like you all to come. There will be a quite a few people there but at least we will be able to see one another.' I couldn't wait as I hadn't seen or spoken to Michael in over a week. It was a large gathering of locals and I knew most of the people there. It was relaxing not to have to play hostess for a change. Fortified by a couple of gins before we arrived, I brazenly flirted with Michael and after a while managed to lure him into the kitchen.

'Oh, I've missed you so much,' I said throwing myself into his arms and lifting my face to his. He bent his head to mine and we kissed passionately, his arms feeling my body. My need for him was so overpowering and consuming that it didn't bother me that this was his home and his wife was possibly in the next room. It didn't bother me that my husband was outside with twenty other people one of whom could walk in on us at any minute. It didn't bother me that in my haste to get here this evening I had shouted angrily at Rudi to hurry up when all he wanted was to show me his drawing. Michael dominated my thoughts so much that it was all-consuming.

We met frequently, hardly bothering to be discreet and our time together was filled with an intensity and urgency that was intoxicating.

I mean … I have a hundred excuses for my behaviour of course!

No, a thousand excuses!

The gin.

Feeling let down by Ian.

The stress of the business.

The *thrill* of feeling enticing, alluring and wanted once more.

Getting even?

All of the above.

There were many passionate, unrestrained snatched moments which we both relished and which continued until the rumours became too much to deny. To put it plainly, we were reckless.

That night Ian and I had our worst fight yet! I hadn't realised that Rudi had seen us kissing in the kitchen until he cheerfully announced it in the car on the way home. I was so angry with him. I don't know what I had expected, but the confrontation with Ian was an eruption of angry accusations on both sides and we agreed to part ways.

'Michael, I've done it!' I said breathless with excitement on the phone to him some days later. 'Ian and I have agreed to divorce and I am moving out.' There was a hollow silence on the end of the line.

'Oh … have you spoken to Ian already?' he responded hesitantly, 'when did you do that? Where are you going? You know I can't say anything to Susan yet as she is still unwell.' There was a hint of panic in his voice as he peppered me with questions.

'I've got a position at the Regent Hotel as receptionist and the children and I will stay there until you and I find our own place together.' frowning slightly at his reticence. 'I mean, you know that this was our plan as we have already discussed it. I am just so relieved that everything is now out in the open!' I finished eagerly waiting for his response and heard him draw in his breath.

'Joan, I didn't realise that this would be happening quite so soon,' I heard him say tentatively. 'You know we agreed to keep things quiet until I was ready to tell her,' he said pleadingly. 'You know how fragile she is. I think we need to cool things down a bit for a while and once you are settled at the Regent I will come and visit you.'

'Oh Michael, Susan will be *fine*, she's stronger than she makes out to be. I mean she must know by now surely. This will all work out for the best you will see. *Do* hurry up. I can't *wait* to see you' I said hoping to convince him that he was worrying for no reason and at the same time choosing to ignore the fluttering of unease that I felt at his words. The last thing I wanted was for him to start having doubts.

CHAPTER THREE

Rudi

The first time I bunked school I was in year two. I made a jolly good job of it too, even if I do say so myself.

We had now moved to the Regent Hotel where mom worked as receptionist at the front desk. I didn't like it there. First of all, I missed Happy. Secondly, there was no garden to play in, and thirdly, we all lived in one room! I mean in comparison to the Ramsgate house, I really thought we had come down in the world! The room was small with three old iron beds, one each for my sister and I and the big one was for mom. And of course being the youngest and having no say in matters of importance, I had to have the lumpy one! There was an ugly brown chest of drawers under the window which my sister and I used to store our clothes and a wardrobe against one wall leading to the bathroom for mom to use. It was very cramped. 'There isn't enough room in here to swing a cat,' I said to mom with a cheeky grin remembering her words. She turned and glared at me. I knew that look and smartly wiped the smile off my face realising dispiritedly that once again I'd said the wrong thing.

Jennifer and I walked to school every day which was up the road from where the Regent was situated. But I had decided that I didn't like school and would much rather stay at home. So I had come up with a plan.

'I'm really needing to go to the toilet,' I said to my sister one day, grimacing and holding my tummy as if in pain as we were walking to school. 'Carry on without me' and I turned and hurried back down the hill. When I came to the front of the hotel I made sure that the reception desk was clear and then ran quickly upstairs to a spare room that I knew was unoccupied and closed the door as quietly as I could. The room was dimly lit, the only light coming from between the half closed curtains on the window. There was a double bed in the centre of the room and a large carved wardrobe against the far wall. I opened the wardrobe carefully and climbed in pulling the door closed behind me. Sitting with my knees drawn up to my chin, I hugged my legs waiting for my breathing to settle. I was determined that I was not going to go to school even if I had to sit here all day.

There was a noisy clatter as the cleaners came into the room with their mops and buckets and I stayed extra still hardly daring to breath, hoping that they wouldn't need to open the wardrobe for any reason. It was quite dark and musty in there and I'm sure I felt something crawling up my back which made me feel all itchy. So it was with a sigh of relief when I heard them leave the room and with shaky legs I pushed open the door and climbed out. I wandered over to the window and looked out. Directly across the road I saw the Kingsview Hotel. This surprised me because mom had told me that the Kingsview had gone under as there wasn't enough money to keep it going and that was why both her and my dad were not working there any more. But it couldn't have gone under the ground because there it was in front of me! As bold as brass! It was all closed up with boards on some of the windows and lots of papers and leaves had been blown by the wind onto the wide open verandah that ran the length of the building. I sighed not really understanding and turning away from the window and I sat on the floor with my back against the wall.

Even though it did get a bit boring sitting there doing nothing, I was still determined to stay there. When I thought it was sometime near lunch, I came out of my hiding place and feeling very pleased with myself, I made my way downstairs to the dining room as if I had just come home from school.

As the day had been such a success I thought I would do the same the next day with some changes. I mean, I had got away with it hadn't I? I didn't really want to spend another day in a cupboard so I made another plan. The following day I got dressed in my school uniform as usual and left the hotel with Jennifer to begin our walk to school. 'I'm going to go another way to school today,' I said to her, 'I will see you there.' So I turned around and went up another road, peering through the hedge to make sure that she had gone around the corner, then I hurried back to the hotel car park. There I grabbed my fishing rod which I had hidden in some bushes and made my way down to the beach being careful to stay out of sight.

The tide was out, exposing the rock pools, some of which had clusters of mussels and limpid dangling from the sides like bunches of grapes, and there was a wide wavy border of seashells and driftwood halfway up the sand that had been left behind by the retreating water. I clambered over the warm rocks and sat down and put my feet in a pool of water watching the tiny fish nibble at my toes.

This was so much better than being at school. School had become a struggle for me and because it was a struggle, I didn't want to be there. I didn't realise it then, but apart from the fact that I couldn't see very well, I also discovered in later life that I was dyslexic. Dyslexia wasn't a known condition in the nineteen fifties and sixties so it was never picked up of course. So I fumbled through school, labelled with being either lazy or a dunce. The problem with my sight would only be discovered a number of years later.

I spent a lovely morning fishing off the rocks and playing on the beach until I thought it was time to leave. I gathered my things, taking care to brush all the sand off my clothes and feet and made my way home. I stashed my fishing rod back into the bushes and sauntered into the dining room as before. No one questioned me.

It all came to an abrupt end a couple of days later of course. I was tucking into my lunch in the hotel dining room when mom came in and sat at my table.

'I had a phone call from Mr Stead today,' she said

My heart flipped in my chest but I looked at her boldly

'He said that you haven't been at school all week.'

'I don't want to go to school. I don't like it,' I said with a determined voice.

'Well, unfortunately you have to go. From tomorrow Jennifer will walk with you and take you to your classroom.'

I just nodded and looked down continuing to eat. My food had lost its taste.

#

We had been staying at the Regent Hotel for about four weeks when my mother found a small cottage just up the road to rent. I was excited about the move because I would have my own room again and, more importantly I was hoping that Happy could come and stay. I had really been missing him. He had gone to live with my father who was now running the Metropole Hotel in Shelley Beach and I hadn't seen him since we had left Ramsgate.

I had made a friend at school. His name was Freddie van den Berg. We did everything together and if he could have done my school work for me, he would have. We were inseparable and often spent time together at the weekends as well, wandering down to the beach to potter around in the rock pools or playing in the garden. Freddie had been given some of the new South African rand coins by his dad which I thought was awesome. These coins couldn't be used yet as they would only be official sometime next year apparently. But there were posters in the shop showing what the new rand coins were going to look like. I had never handled money before and I thought I must ask mom if I could have pocket money every week like Freddie. But she never did give me any.

I saw Dr Johnston today. It wasn't the first time I had seen him since we had moved out of our big house. He had come to the hotel to see mom a couple of times. After his visits she was often agitated and upset and would have a lot of Jim's drink 'just to help calm her nerves' she told me. I learned to keep out of her way when she was like this having realised that the sharp end of her tongue was something best avoided.

On this occasion he came to the cottage to visit her after she had finished work. I was careful not to look at him as I didn't want to see them kissing. But they didn't thank goodness, so at least I wouldn't get into trouble again. But they were arguing in loud whispers.

'Go to your rooms both of you and find something busy to do,' mom told Jennifer and I, waving her hand at us as if to hurry us up, a cigarette dangling from her fingers. We both scurried away making sure we were as quiet as possible in order to overhear anything of interest.

But Dr Johnston did not stay long and later on that evening when I ventured out of my room, I could see by mom's face that she was not happy.

'I've had enough of blasted men and their blasted promises,' she said vehemently as I entered the room, 'go to the kitchen and make sure that there is lots of ice in the freezer for me and dish yourself up some dinner from the pot on the stove,' she said abruptly, her lips set in a straight line 'then off you go to bed.' I could tell that she had been drinking Jim's drink as her cheeks were red and she had shiny eyes. So I knew what the ice was for. I also knew not to argue so I did as she asked and took myself off to bed.

The next morning dawned bright and sunny and I was looking forward to the afternoon as Freddy and I had made a plan to go to the beach as it was low tide. I didn't hear any of the usual breakfast activity in the kitchen so I dressed in my school uniform quickly and went to investigate. The room was in chaos. Our dishes from last night's supper were in the sink that was full of scummy water with big yellow fat globules floating on the surface and around the rim of the sink and there was a pot on the stove with the lid half off, still containing the remains of our mince supper. Dirty cups and glasses were strewn across the counter and the kitchen table was covered in an array of empty bottles, glasses and dirty plates full of cigarette ends and ash intermingled with rice and mince from last night's meal. 'Where was the maid? 'I wondered.

I went to find mom and discovered that she was still in bed. I tried to shake her awake but she just groaned so I thought it better to leave her and went back to the kitchen. Finding a clean bowl in the cupboard I dished myself up some breakfast cereal and as there was no milk, I ate it dry. Then adding my dirty bowl to the stack of others in the sink, I took myself off to school trying to remain cheerful for the day so that no one would question me.

The thought of Freddy seeing my mother as she was and the state of the house troubled me, so I told him that I had to stay at home and do chores, which was just an excuse.

'Mom ... *Mom*!' I shook her arm. She was sitting on the chair in the lounge in the half light of the closed curtains, her elbows on her knees. I had arrived back from school to even more chaos at home. Mom had clearly been in bed for most of the day and there was stuff all over the place. She looked diminished, fragile even and she turned towards me with unfocused eyes. 'There's nothing in the fridge to eat,' I said

'I'm not well today. Go down to the hotel and get some lunch and tell them I am sick,' she told me in a scratchy voice.

After changing out of my school uniform, I ran off down the road to the hotel and spoke to a lady in the office, telling her than mom was sick. She rolled her eyes and shook her head, but then seeing my face she said quickly, 'It's ok Rudi, it's not your fault. Thank you for letting me know anyway' kindly patting my head. I knew that this was not the first time that mom had been off work sick.

We had lived in our cottage for a couple of months now and I had been constantly nagging my mom to allow Happy to come and live with us. So it was a couple of days later that she said to me that I would be going to live with Happy and my father at the Metropole Hotel in Shelley Beach. She was moving to Pietermaritzburg with my sister to be near Granny Kidd. It didn't worry me too much that mom and Jennifer were leaving me behind. I was so excited about seeing my dog. Happy must have been excited too because when he saw me he jumped straight into my lap and didn't stop wagging his tail and licking me for ages.

The Metropole was a large white double storey hotel overlooking the Indian Ocean. There was an expanse of lawn in front of the building with four stone steps leading off straight onto the beach. The sand was coarse and light in colour and the long straight beach seemed to stretch for miles into the distance. There was a big natural tidal pool to the left of the hotel where I used to swim as it was much calmer there. Happy and I spent many pleasant hours fishing for small bream from the tidal pool, although he was quite clever and never went deeper than his tummy. My Dad never worried about allowing me to go off on my own to the beach. I was six now after all! I think he was just glad to get me out of his hair.

We lived in an annex to the hotel which was not attached to the main building but which did have a small kitchen and bathroom. I ate in the hotel dining room every day. I always kept a bit of food to one side and put it into a napkin to take back to Happy. The kitchen staff also saved scraps for me to take to him as he was really popular with everyone as he was always friendly and well behaved.

During my time with my Dad, I continued to go to school in Margate. I was content. Freddy and I spent time together after school or at weekends whenever we could and were always accompanied by a very boisterous Happy.

One day it all changed. 'Rudi, I have to take you to live with your mom in Pietermaritzburg,' Dad said one day. 'Unfortunately, Happy can't go with you so I have arranged for him to stay with Freddy's family.' I looked at him wide eyed and feeling devastated, I burst into tears. I was losing Happy all over again!

'I don't want to go to Pietermaritzburg!' I wailed not having the faintest idea where Pietermaritzburg was.

'You can see Happy again when you come back,' said my father trying to pacify me. But little did I know that I wouldn't be back for a very long time. There was nothing that I could do and the next day I was packed off in the car to Pietermaritzburg.

Life was very different for me living in Pietermaritzburg. My mom had been unhappy at the Regent Hotel in Margate she told me, but she found work quite easily at the Ansonia Hotel in Pietermaritzburg. It was in Longmarket Street which I think was one of the main streets of the town and rather busy. Certainly a lot busier than what I had been used to. It was in the centre of the city after all. At the back of the hotel there was a set of two rooms which would be our home. I was sharing once more with my sister and my mom had her own room. We would eat all our meals in the hotel dining room which was a long sunny room with large windows looking out over the busy street.

It wasn't long after getting to Pietermaritzburg that my mom told me that I would be going to school there. The school which was across the road from the Ansonia, was a convent run by nuns. It was an old school set in established grounds with ornate stately low buildings and small leaded glass windows. There was also a chapel that had a large stained glass window in the front and when the sun shone through, it made the most magical dancing colours play across the room. I had seen boys and girls in the playground there and wondered whether that was the school that I would go to. Jennifer was already there and she reassured me that it was ok. Although she was twelve already she wouldn't be with me in the younger group at school and I was feeling a bit apprehensive.

I was placed in a class with about twenty other boys and girls who all seemed to be settled in and friendly with one another. I felt very uncomfortable and out of place as I had joined the school in the middle of the term and it was difficult to catch up with the different subjects. The nuns were very strict and if you didn't answer a question correctly or if you gave them backchat, then you would get a swift smack across the knuckles with a ruler. They were scary! Jennifer used to call the one nun Lettuce because apparently she always used to say 'Let us pray' so from then on, all the nuns were Lettuce to me in my head. Mom said that nuns were 'none of this and none of that' which I didn't really understand.

I hated school. I would take ages to get myself out of bed in the morning, sluggishly finding my uniform and getting dressed slowly and with great effort. Marie, who was an Indian maid employed by my mother to look after me, would always bluster in and try and hurry me up. I would make my way to the dining room with leaden feet. I dawdled over breakfast stirring my porridge around and around in my bowl not feeling very hungry and unable to settle the tension in my tummy. Then I would shuffle back to my room supposedly to clean my teeth which I would only sometimes do. There was no one to check and I couldn't be bothered half the time. Then I'd just sit on my bed until Marie came looking for me.

I spent my time at school wishing the day would be over and counting down until the bell rang at the end of the lessons when I would breathe a sigh of relief. Marie would meet me at the school gate and walk me home and see to it that I had lunch and had completed any homework that needed doing. I didn't see much of my mother as she was mostly working although sometimes I would come home from school and she was sleeping so I presumed that she worked at night as well.

I don't think we stayed very long in Pietermaritzburg because the next thing, mom said that we were going to move to Durban where she had got another job at the Savoy. I was just so happy that I was not going to have to go to this school any more that the move didn't bother me.

We were back to sharing one room. The Savoy Hotel in Berea Road was not a posh five-star hotel like it's counterparts of the same name. It was a fairly basic but nice three star establishment that was on a busy main road that ran west out of the city of Durban. It was the main watering hole for many of the locals and served a decent Sunday lunch. It was also built in the colonial style with low wrap around verandas overlooking the city on which clusters of rattan chairs with glass tables were randomly scattered. The bedroom that all three of us once more shared was at the back of the hotel, with the only window opening onto a courtyard facing the kitchens. The air was always thick with the smell of cooking oil and fried breakfasts. Our three beds were in a row against the back wall, with two of them pushed together with no gap in between as there wasn't enough space in the room. There was only one wardrobe for the three of us but we just had to make do.

Once again, I was sent off to school not long after we arrived in Durban. Another school, and another struggle. I found that I was far behind with my schoolwork and needed to catch up with quite a bit. It was also difficult getting used to the ways of another school with a different syllabus. However, the teachers seemed to be very patient so I did feel more relaxed there.

I hadn't seen much of my mother since we lived together at the cottage in Margate, which was months ago now. During our short stay in Pietermaritzburg, I hardly saw her as Marie attended to all my needs and now in Durban she was either at work or in bed. I didn't understand where my fun-loving mother had gone. She never chatted like she used to when she was happy or read to me any more. And she certainly never smiled. She was even looking grey and tired. And then I found out why. She took me aside one day and said, 'I have to go into hospital to have an operation on my lung,' she told me. 'Dr Blankenburg is going to be looking after you whilst I am there and Jennifer will go and stay with your father.'

'But I don't know Dr Blankenburg!' I looked at her in horror, my stomach turning over in anxiety.

Dr Blankenburg, it turns out was the doctor that my mother consulted about her lung problem. I can only think that she had probably charmed him into taking care of me whilst she was in hospital, which was very good of him. He lived with his wife Carol in a large colonial double storey home above the city of Durban not too far from the Savoy. I shared a bedroom with Richard who was one of their sons and who was a bit younger than me.

I soon settled into a routine of sorts and found that I enjoyed the stability. It felt solid and reliable. Mrs Blankenburg used to fetch me from school every day and take me back to the house and make me lunch. She would sit down with me at the kitchen table and chat about my day at school and how I was coping. She would then spend time in the afternoon helping me with my homework. Despite all her efforts though, school continued to be troublesome. But best of all she used to read stories to me together with her son Richard in the evenings before bed. I felt part of a family and was very happy and secure during my stay there.

Mrs Blankenburg took me to visit my mother in hospital one day. As we entered the hospital there were people sitting in black chairs with big wheels, some of them just parked waiting and the others being pushed about from place to place. I thought that was fun and I wanted to have a go but Mrs Blankenburg said that they were special chairs called wheelchairs for people who were unable to walk.

We walked down lots of passages with very shiny floors and lots of doors leading off to rooms with beds in them. It was very quiet.

'Where's mom?' I felt that I had to whisper.

'She's just in the end room around the next corner,' reassured Mrs Blankenburg.

I pushed open the door and peeped around into the room. And there was mom lying in bed in a haze of cigarette smoke, looking the same but happy. I ran in and gave her a hug. She looked cheerful.

'At least I have someone to talk to now because I have been talking to the trees but they don't listen to me,' she said with a laugh and pointed out the window at the tree tops.

'I'll leave you both to chat and come back in a little while to fetch you,' Mrs Blankenburg said.

I spent a lovely time telling mom all about what I had been up to whilst living with the Blankenburgs although I was careful not to show that I was really happy there. It made me feel uncomfortable somehow.

Leaving the hospital I was overwhelmed by confusion and longing. I was loving life with the Blankenburgs and wanted to stay there forever but at the same time I felt it was wrong to feel like that. What about my mom?

As it turned out my mother was away for three months which was an awful long time. And for the first time, I found that I missed her.

Out of the blue one day when I had just got home from school, there was a knock on the door ... .and there was my mother. 'Rudi,' she called holding out her arms to me. I leapt into her embrace and held her as if I would never let her go. Looking into her face I could see how much better she was looking, with pink cheeks, sparkling eyes and a huge smile on her face that I hadn't seen for months. She had also put on some weight which really suited her and her dress no longer hung on her. Her hair was looking full and she had even put some lipstick on. I think I have my mom back!

Back to the Savoy Hotel we went and Jennifer joined us a week later after having spent some time staying with my father. My mother was in good form once more. It didn't last long. Over time there were arguments and disagreements between my mother and the manager of the hotel which escalated day by day. I didn't know what the problems were. I was a kid and adults in those days didn't talk openly to children about things as they do today. But generally she was a lot happier and enjoyed to joke about like she used to do when we lived in Ramsgate.

One evening Mom came into the room and announced, 'We are going to go and live in East London and we are going to go by ship. Don't you think that will be fun?' she looked excited and happy, so I was too. So before I knew it, we were on the move again.

I was very excited to be going on a big ship and could hardly contain myself when a couple of days later we had packed up our clothes once more and climbed into the waiting taxi to head down to Durban docks. And there she was.the Pendennis Castle. The Union Castle Shipping Line ran a regular route between Durban and Southampton in the 1960s and it was a typical way of travel in those days. Standing on the dockside the ship looked huge. The sides were grey and high like a building and dark smoke poured out of a big black and orange funnel that was positioned in the centre of the ship. There were steps, which my mother told me was called the gangway, running up the side which we had to climb up to get on board. The gangway felt rather rickety and moved a bit when we were treading up the stairs. I could see the water through the slats and it looked awfully far down. There was a light breeze that blew across the harbour which smelled warm with a hint of diesel oil. The gangway ended at a large opening that you had to step over to get into the ship. I remember my mother gaily laughing and being helped across into the ship by a sailor in his white uniform and smart hat on his head. She told me that he was the captain. She looked so pretty and happy in her flowery yellow dress that my heart lifted.

We followed a sailor along a passage and down some steep metal steps where he showed us to our cabin. My eyes lit up at the sight of the double bunk fixed to the one wall. Directly opposite was another single bed and there was a round window called a porthole on the far wall. The window didn't open though because then all the water would come in. I raced over to look out and saw the sea just below with the rest of the harbour stretching out towards the bluff.

Left to my own devices, I spent much of the following two days exploring the ship and spending time in the swimming pool which I had discovered. How cool is that to have a pool on a ship!

The first evening on the ship my mother said she was going to take me up to the bridge. 'Wow! I thought. A bridge and a swimming pool on the ship.' The captain met us at the bottom of some more difficult steep metal steps and led the way to a room high up overlooking the front of the ship. I looked around puzzled and said, 'But where's the bridge?' The captain explained that this room was called the bridge and it was where all the instruments were and from where he and his crew steered the ship. Then outside the bridge on the deck, he slowed the ship down to a 'dead crawl' and using a big light he sent a signal to the shore. Mom said that we were off the coast of Margate and she had arranged with him to signal Uncle Ronnie at his house on the hill. Only my mother with all her charm could arrange that!

We arrived in East London early in the morning and waited for the gangway to be erected against the side of the ship. It did look steeper than before and it was a lot more difficult finding my footing going down than coming up somehow. But I managed without too much fuss. We climbed into a waiting taxi and made our way slowly out of the harbour area. East London is not a very big town and we were soon in the middle of the main street. There were crowds of people out on the pavement and the taxi driver said they were waiting for the troops to march down the street. We came to a small beachfront hotel where my mother was going to work and which would now be our home.

Right next door to the hotel was an army barracks which was home to The Kaffrarian Rifles regiment. From my bedroom window I used to enjoy watching the troops leave the barracks every day, all smartly marching in unison out onto the street, wearing brown uniforms and matching caps with rifles in hand. Sometimes there was even a marching band that used to noisily make its way up the road then sometime later it would come back down again along the same route.

I was sent off to school once again and really I can't remember much of my time at school in East London. No excuse though because I was eight now after all! But I do recall one day when we were all given small South African flags on a stick because we were now a republic. Whatever that means?

Living back at the seaside, I really missed Freddie. But, as always, I was left to occupy myself and took to wandering down to the harbour watching the ships and pottering about on the small beach that was on the one side of the pier. The pier was built of concrete and was quite narrow and rounded at the tip. Halfway up the pier wall there was a narrow brick lip about eight inches wide which was low enough to climb onto when the tide was out. It ran all the way around the pier to the harbour side.

One day when I was on the beach I climbed onto the ledge. It was cold and wet under my bare feet as I moved along walking sideways with my back against the wall, facing the sea. It was a bit slippery, but I kept going slowly, past the rounded point where the ledge came to an end. It was then that I discovered how far I had come. Leaning back against the stone wall and realising how high I was from the water in the harbour below, I had a moment of panic. I knew that I would have to go back the way I came. I stifled a sob and taking a deep breath I made my way slowly back along the ledge, trying to ignore my shaky legs. It seemed to take much longer going back. Once I got near the end I jumped off the ledge onto the warm sand and sat down wanting to cry with relief. I had been really scared out there, but what scared me the most was the realisation that if I had fallen into the sea, nobody would have known. It made me feel very alone.

I decided that I wouldn't mention anything to my mother.

My mother had a friend that she met in the hotel and his name was Mark. He liked to go fishing and he asked me one day if I would like to go with him to fish off the rocks near the pier. I jumped at the chance as my fishing rod had been left in Margate when we moved to Pietermaritzburg. We set off one afternoon when the tide was out once I had come home from school. I was looking forward to fishing with Mark because, although he was very old, I think about thirty, he had told me that the spot on the rocks that we are going to is a favourite with the local fishermen. Mark was not only old, he was big too. Mom used to call him 'the thirsty boy' when he wasn't around to hear. I was just glad that I wasn't thirsty like him otherwise I would also be big and round.

We made our way across the sand next to the pier and onto the rocks that ran down to the water. Mark was breathing heavily behind me as I scampered onto the rocks and the next minute I heard a thud and a clatter as his bait box hit the rocks, flying open and spilling sinkers and hooks all over the place. He had slipped and fallen onto his back and was unable to get back up again. I had to run all the way back to the hotel to fetch someone to help him up. Needless to say, that was the end of my fishing.

Ronnie Baker who I called Uncle Ronnie, was a friend of mom's who often spent time with both my parents when we lived in Ramsgate. He was in East London on business and came to visit us one day. I liked Uncle Ronnie as he had always been kind to me. He took me to one side and gave me some pocket money which was so exciting as I could now go and buy some sweets which was such a treat.

During my time in East London we moved to another hotel further up into town. I can only presume that my mother found work there once more. Overall she seemed much happier than she had been previously when we lived in Durban and Pietermaritzburg.

'I've had a phone call from an old friend of mine and he has offered me a modelling job so we are off on the train tomorrow to Johannesburg,' she excitedly told me out of the blue one day. We had been living in East London for about six months by this time. I was fairly settled although still struggling at school and had made a couple of friends. I really didn't feel like another move, but again, taken in by her excitement, I smothered my unease.

The following day after packing our belongings once more (we didn't have much, and it seemed to get less and less) we headed off to the station to catch the train to Durban where we would change to the Johannesburg line.

Travelling on the train was so exciting. I'm not sure what I liked better, the ship or the train! The three of us had our own compartment. There was a sliding door that was the entrance and directly opposite that was a window looking out. On either side of the space were long green benches where we would sit during the daytime. In the middle under the window was a table and if you lifted up the lid, there was a washbasin underneath with its own tap. How cool is that! The toilets were down the corridor and there was even a carriage which had rows of tables and chairs where we would go to eat our meals. After exploring the cabin and settling in I felt the train start to move off out of the station and soon we were out in the countryside and gathering speed. I enjoyed looking out the open window when the train went around a corner so I could count the carriages, not minding the black smoky air that blew in my face and into the carriage.

It seemed like no time at all before it started to get dark outside. A man came into the cabin to get our beds ready for the night. He pulled out a bunk bed that had been folded up against the wall, and set it up above the one green bench and attached a small ladder to the side. He then brought in white sheets with a blue stripe along the top which was made up of the letters SAR repeated in a long line and some grey blankets which he rolled out onto each bed. As soon as he had finished and had left the cabin I climbed up the ladder and lay down on the top bunk, the roof of the cabin no more than a foot from my head and the rhythmic clackity-clack of the train lulling me to sleep.

CHAPTER FOUR

Joan

He let me down!

In the end, he let me down. He let me down like everyone else had done before in my life. Michael had been so full of promises and resolve about our future, assuring me of his commitment and love, telling me that I was the best thing that had happened to him in his life, that we were meant to be together.

Did he mean any of it?

I mean *any of it?*

I was shattered!

#

I was sorry that I had to leave my house in Ramsgate but I held onto the thought that Michael and I would eventually find a place of our own together. I had enjoyed the status of being Joan Garden of the Kingsview, of being respected and important in the community. Somebody who people wanted to be around, somebody who drew crowds and held attention, somebody who everyone wanted to be seen with and would go out of their way to ensure they were included on invitations.

Somebody who was admired.

My life with Ian, together with running the Kingsview as a well respected and prominent couple, had provided the opportunity for me to become all those things. And I had used it to the full. Unfortunately, as was the case so often in extra marital affairs in those years, the female was always to blame. Even though Ian had been having an affair of his own, our friends and business colleagues turned their back on me and I became the scapegoat. That is how it seemed to work. I was not welcomed into society any longer and any friends I thought I had at the time, turned their backs on me.

I was always aware that once Michael and I were together and our affair had been exposed that my status in the community would be affected. I was quite happy with this believing that my irresistible charm and appeal would overcome any disgrace or shame that I had been labelled with. Although the truth was that it really flawed me one day last week when I was in town and a couple of people who I thought were my friends, completely ignored me when I bumped into them outside the bank. I went into the stationers to buy some envelopes and Ivy at the till neither greeted me nor looked me in the eye when she served me, but the open contempt I saw in her face was enough to have me hurrying out of there as fast as I could. I vowed never to go back. The encounters left me feeling vulnerable and exposed and only the thought of a future with Michael by my side kept me going.

#

I arrived at the Regent Hotel in Margate with the children and was shown to our new temporary living quarters … just one room. It was on the first floor so that was a blessing as at least there will be a bit of a breeze, a relief from the intense heat. But that was the only blessing. The room was small and cramped. I didn't know how I was going to cope living there for the next couple of weeks with all three of us in one room. Feeling deflated and irritated, I unpacked the clothes that I had brought with me, using the wardrobe for my belongings, and managing to squeeze Jennifer and Rudi's things into the chest of drawers. The storage was rather inadequate but it would just have to do for the meantime. Sighing, I pushed closed the last drawer and sat back on my haunches feeling suddenly tired.

'There isn't enough room in here to swing a cat,' piped Rudi cheekily. I didn't have the energy to reply so I just turned and glared at him. For heaven's sake! That's all I need right now is being reminded about how small the room is when I'm struggling to adjust to it myself.

Hauling myself to my feet I changed into a black skirt and white blouse bringing back memories of my first day of work at the department store all those years ago now. How young I had been then. How innocent. How *naïve!*

This position as receptionist was a far cry from running the Kingsview and I would miss the glamour and prestige that came with owning our own hotel. But the Kingsview was no more. Ian and I were no more. I felt a pang of regret for what was, although whether it was from losing the hotel or losing Ian I wasn't quite sure. Both probably. Since the shark attacks the tourist industry on the South Coast had all but collapsed and we had really struggled to get any bookings during the following couple of years. Despite offering numerous specials both during the holidays and during off peak times, our rooms remained mostly unoccupied and the Kingsview never recovered. Coupled with the distraction of our personal problems where neither of us were focused on the business, failure was inevitable. In the end the decision was taken out of our hands as there was just no money coming in and we were forced to close.

Ian, as I so rightly suspected, was also having an affair although it had been going on for some time. And as in all cases, I was the last to know. Did I have the right to feel betrayed? Probably not considering my own behaviour although I made the excuse to myself that I was driven to it by his neglect. Did I have regrets … ? I'm not sure. The innocent young girl that Ian had married had grown into a sophisticated temptress that Ian struggled to control and as a result our already combative relationship spiralled uncontrollably downward. I enjoyed the intrigue and the divergence of discovering someone new and I relished the attention. I do regret losing the lifestyle that I was used to, but clung to the thought that with Michael I will eventually return to my status in the community.

As I was now employed, I would no longer have the privilege of dictating my own hours and would have to work according to a roster at the convenience of the hotel. But in any case, this was just temporary until Michael and I found a home of our own. This thought motivated me and smoothing my skirt down, I made my way briskly to the front desk of the hotel to report for my shift.

The first day seemed very long. I would be working alone for most of the time on each shift as the Regent wasn't a big hotel. After spending the morning rearranging the reception area and clearing out a couple of cupboards I sat down and lit a cigarette. My mind kept wandering to Michael. He had promised to phone sometime later this morning and I was looking forward to his call.

Looking at my watch I was dismayed to see that it was already after one.

Where is he?

I just hope that he had managed to speak to Susan so that we can go forward with our plans.

Why is he taking so long to call?

He said he wasn't going to be at work today so it's not as if he's busy.

I was starting to feel agitated and the beginnings of the familiar pull to have something to calm my nerves was taking hold. Looking at my watch once again I saw that it was now after two. Glancing around, I walked quickly down the passage and entering my room, went straight to the wardrobe where I found the bottle of gin that I had put there. The lid gave a satisfying click as I opened the bottle and I took a long heavenly mouthful. I took another smaller mouthful and breathed out with pleasure. Returning the bottle to the wardrobe once more I wiped my mouth and quickly left the room. I knew that I hadn't been away from the front desk for more than a couple of minutes so was quite pleased that I had managed to get back to my post without anyone seeing me. Feeling more relaxed, I continued with my work for the remainder of the shift although thoughts of what Michael was doing were never far from my mind.

'Michael! Whatever took you so long? I have been so worried not hearing from you.' I answered the phone in agitation as his call came through the following day. 'When am I going to see you?'

'Calm down Joan please,' he pleaded. 'I spoke to Susan yesterday and she has taken it very badly so I felt that I couldn't leave her on her own and the children were very upset. You do understand that don't you? In any case I need to organise somewhere to go to' he finished, 'just give me a bit more time.'

'Yes, but how much time Michael?'

'Well, just a couple of days I suppose. Let her get used to the idea and we can go from there. Let me know when you have time off and we can get together. But don't worry, things will work out.'

Reluctantly, with dread, I could only agree.

I spent an anxious evening unable to settle, as the conversation continued to play in my head. Surely he wasn't going to change his mind! No he would never do that and in any case I know that the moment I was in his arms once more any doubts he had would be pushed to the back of his mind. I know I can persuade him. Let's face it, he can't resist me. He is just finding it difficult at the moment. I poured myself a nice strong drink and sat back on the bed trying to relax. I will speak to him again in the morning I told myself.

Before I could phone him the following day, he walked into the hotel looking tired and unkempt with dark rings under his eyes. Looking at him I felt more irritation than sympathy to be honest. But I also knew that I could bring a smile to his face. 'Well … hello stranger,' I said with a swagger and approaching him slowly, I walked around him running my hands down his chest. 'What brings you to these here parts?' I drawled with an American twang. He gave a deep chuckle and grabbed me in a tight hug. 'You are irresistible you know,' he said smiling and kissing my face.

'I know!'

I smiled.

And so we both agreed to give him more time to sort things out at home. A couple of days grew to a couple of weeks and after only seeing him a few times since I had moved to the hotel I decided it was time to look for accommodation that was more suitable for the three of us and a bit more private for Michael's visits. I found a lovely three-bedroom cottage to rent situated just up the road from the hotel so it would be easy to walk to work at any hour. I knew that this was a good move as it felt more settled and permanent and both the children were very happy that they would now each have their own room. Rudi in particular was so excited and all he talked about was getting Happy back. I think he understood when I told him that Happy was settled with his dad but he could see him whenever he wanted. With the children being happier, it lifted my spirits and I felt that it wouldn't be long now until Michael joined us.

Moving to the cottage, it was apparent that it was going to be more difficult having to go all the way there each time I needed to have something to calm my nerves. Having a couple of sips ... ok, a couple of *mouthfuls* if you want the truth ... in the afternoon had become a regular activity. I looked forward to it after lunch every day and would visualise myself gulping down mouthfuls and feeling the warm glow take over my body. So to make it easier, I started to keep a small bottle of gin in my handbag. *Genius,* don't you think? This in itself created its own problems. The reception desk was in full view of the lounge area and the comings and goings from the kitchen, so there was always the risk of someone seeing me drinking from the bottle. So I thought I could perhaps take myself off to the ladies each time I felt the urge.

There was also the risk of someone seeing the bottle in my handbag as well. I would just have to take the chance and be extra careful.

The children continued to attend school in Margate and since our move they both walked together to school in the mornings. So I was surprised one day to get a phone call from the headmaster of the junior school to say that Rudi had not been into school all week.'The little minx,' I smiled to myself. 'Whatever has he been up to?' Once lunchtime came, my first thought was to check the dining room. And there he was, sitting and tucking into his lunch without a care in the world. He looked at me wide eyed when I asked him why he hadn't been to school.

'I don't like school,' he said with a determined lift to his chin. 'Well, unfortunately you have to go. So in future Jennifer will take you right to your classroom.' He just nodded and looking down, continued eating his lunch.

Life was a bit more pleasant living in the cottage. We still ate most of our meals at the hotel but I had taken to cooking the odd evening meal especially when I knew that Michael would be visiting. I would always go out of my way to have everything perfect although a lot of my crockery was still packed as the cottage was fully equipped. But I thought that Michael would probably not even notice even though he was used to the finer things in life.

His visits had however, become noticeably more strained for some reason. He was still voicing doubts about leaving Susan, always claiming that the time was not right. Despite this, and hoping to seduce him into choosing a future together with me, I went out of my way to ensure that I was captivating and at my most seductive in order to keep him entranced. I had the utmost confidence in my ability to charm and I used it to the full. That's what I had been taught. Right?

He arrived unexpectedly late one afternoon and I could tell just by looking at his face that things were not right.

'Go to your rooms both of you and find something busy to do,' I said quickly to Jennifer and Rudi, my heart thumping in my chest. They scampered off without protest and stubbing out my cigarette and with a radiant smile on my face, I opened the door.

'What an unexpected surprise.' I kissed his face and not having any response, I stepped back and looked at him.

'We have to talk,' he said

My heart sank and I was filled with alarm. I turned and without a word led him into the lounge where I shut the door and sat on the edge of the sofa hoping he would join me. He remained standing in the middle of the room, his hands in his trouser pockets jiggling the car keys uneasily. I could tell he was tense and it only increased my own anxiety.

'I can't do this any more, Joan. I can't cope with the hurt that I have brought on my family and ... '

'No please Michael, you can't ... '

'No, Joan. I have made up my mind. It is not going to work. I cannot live with the thought of the destruction that I have wrought on my home life.'

I jumped up and stood close to him and said softly, 'But you know how good it is between us. You don't really want to give that up? Do you?'

He didn't even hesitate. 'I have to!'

'You *don't* have to. You promised me! And I have given up *everything* for you. I won't have it!' I exclaimed my voice rising in panic'

79

'I'm sorry, Joan. It was good between us but I have made my decision.' And he just turned around and walked out. Without another word. Without looking back.

I slid slowly to the floor, the hurt closing my chest and I sobbed ... silently, my mouth wide open.

Wrenching, racking sobs.

I cried for all the broken promises, for all the disappointments, for all the shattered dreams. I cried for my broken marriage, for my reduced circumstances, for my lack of money. I cried for the child I had been, abandoned by my father and stepfather and left by my mother. I cried for myself. I felt abandoned once more, cast aside as if I was not good enough.

I felt shattered.

Into small pieces.

Eventually I got up from the floor and went to the kitchen and poured myself a neat gin. Although I had got used to drinking it neat, I did sometimes use tonic as a mix to make it go further. Not tonight. After draining the glass I poured myself another and picking up the bottle and my cigarettes, made my way back to the lounge. The familiar warmth was soon upon me and I was immersed in my foggy thoughts as I sat and drank for the rest of the night.

Needless to say, I don't remember much of the evening. Well ... I know that *was* the intention now wasn't it? I woke up the next day feeling grim and glancing at the clock through one half closed eye, I saw that it was way after eleven. Falling back onto the pillow with a groan I realised that I should have been at work hours ago. Well, they are just going to have to do without me for the day, I thought to myself. Holding my head in my hands I stumbled to the bathroom and found some painkillers in the cupboard. Going to the kitchen to fetch some water I was confronted by the mess left over from last night. I grabbed a half empty bottle of gin, swigged down the painkillers and turned and walked out.

'Mom ... *Mom*!' I opened my eyes blearily 'There's nothing to eat in the fridge' said Rudi shaking my arm and peering into my eyes

I foggily thought to myself that he must be home from school already. 'I'm not well today. Go down to the hotel and get some lunch and tell them I am sick', I said with a dry, shaky voice.

I managed to get myself to work the following day telling them that I had had a migraine. I'm not sure that they believed me though, but I was beyond caring. I had my trusted bottle with me in my handbag and because I was still feeling so hurt, so *raw*, I was using it more often and earlier in the day than usual.

I just *needed* to, you know.

The moment I felt my thoughts taking over, I would have another mouthful. The moment I thought of Michael and his undying declarations of love, of his proclaiming to need me desperately, of his *betrayal*, I would have another mouthful.

I mindlessly managed to get myself through the following days and weeks with some degree of outer normality or so I thought. Evidently the hotel management did not agree as I was called into the office early one morning unexpectedly. Clutching my handbag with its precious contents to my chest, and with a thudding heart, I waited for the axe to fall.

Fortunately for me and with great reluctance, they gave me a warning and another chance. I was to take the rest of the week off and get myself straightened out and return back to work on Monday fully sober. If I couldn't do that then I would lose my job.

Flooded with embarrassment and feeling dismayed that the staff and management had been aware of my drinking all the time, I made my way home. My first instinct when I got there was to pour myself a drink but the humiliation of the confrontation I had just endured stopped me. I mean ... I am *Joan Garden* for heavens sake! I am somebody of *importance*! I couldn't believe that I had come to this. I had to pull myself together. I *had* to.

Feeling depleted and weary but determined, I managed to cut down on my consumption quite considerably during the following days and returned to work on the Monday chastised and sober but with my head held high. I would not let them see that I felt embarrassed if it was the last thing I did.

#

Every morning a bundle of daily newspapers was delivered to the hotel for the guests to read. It arrived with a resounding thump as it was thrown down onto the verandah by Ben, the young lad who did the deliveries. I hauled the bundle to the counter and selected a number of copies to put aside for the guests to help themselves to and I took some copies into the sitting room to have available for those guests that wished to sit and read in comfort. Then I grabbed my own, lit a cigarette and sat down to have a brief read through the day's news.

Wife of well known local Doctor found dead

The headline jumped out at me. My hands flew to my face and I stifled a cry. Horrified, and with an overwhelming sense of dread, I continued reading.

Susan Johnston was found yesterday evening by the maid, unresponsive on the bathroom floor of her home in Margate. Paramedics were called but there was nothing that they were able to do and she was pronounced dead at the scene. The police were in attendance and have advised that Mrs Johnston had appeared to have taken her own life. No foul play is suspected. Susan was the wife of ...

Oh my God!

This cannot be happening!

I couldn't read any further. I put the newspaper down and took a shuddering breath. I felt *sick! Responsible!* I never expected this. I never *wanted this*!

With shaking hands, I tried to phone Michael but there was no reply from his surgery or home telephone. I have no idea what it was that I would have said to him if I had managed to get hold of him. What can you *say*?

He must be feeling absolutely devastated but I guess at the same time he wouldn't want to be talking to me. As you can imagine. Does he blame me for this? Do I blame myself?

Feeling horrified and thoroughly sick and shaken, I continued with my day as best I could, trying to pretend that there was nothing wrong. My mind was in a whirl and I was struggling to ignore the constant pull to get a drink to blot out the harrowing turmoil in my head.

Later on that evening after a stiff gin and after having had time to mull over my situation, I came to the realisation that I had to get away. I had started to feel like an outcast in my own town, repeatedly getting a cold reception and hostile looks wherever I went. I had lost my friends, or those people who I thought were my friends, and people avoided me in the town. This wouldn't have bothered me if I had Michael by my side, but coping with it alone was a humiliation and a huge burden. And now with the latest development of Susan's death, I would be more vilified than ever. Blamed even.

So I decided that I needed to have a fresh start. I would move to Pietermaritzburg where Aunt Rachel was currently living. Was I running away with my tail between my legs? Possibly! I know that the situation was of my own making and I did feel awfully responsible in a way but I didn't do it all on my own. I felt let down and abandoned.

Even though our divorce was not yet finalised, Ian was kindly paying me a monthly maintenance which I could live on whilst I looked for work. Explaining my plans to him, I told him that Granny Kid was not well and that she needed us and I would be moving to Pietermaritzburg with the children. But I asked if Rudi could stay with him for a while until I got myself settled. He seemed to agree to this quite readily. I think he was quite pleased that I was moving away from the area.

#

I found work easily at the Ansonia Hotel in Pietermaritzburg. It was a large busy hotel in the city centre and once again I was working at the front desk. This really suited me as I enjoyed the contact with the guests and it lifted my spirits and took my mind off my troubles and my gin bottle for a while. I had still been trying to cut down on how much I was drinking and so far had managed to last most of the day without a drink. Which I thought was quite good. Don't you think?

Michael was never far from my thoughts though. I tried so hard to get my mind under control but it just went round and round like a stuck record, the same thing over and over again. I wondered what he was doing now. I wondered how he was coping with the loss of Susan.

Did he blame me?

Did he blame himself?

I wished that I could speak to him, just to hear the sound of his voice and I found my hand on the phone on a number of occasions, wanting so badly to pick it up and dial his number. I wouldn't have phoned him at the surgery anyway as the thought of having to speak to Ann at reception was too mortifying for words.

What was he doing?

What was he thinking?

I should have seen our break up coming to be frank but I had chosen to ignore the signs. Even quite early on in our relationship he had broken dates or just not arrived at our prearranged meeting place leaving me up in the air and full of questions then already. But I always had an excuse for him then. Not any more. Did he not possess any backbone and spunk? I felt a mixture of anger, resentment and longing for him and on top of that pain for his loss, all at the same time and I was bewildered and confused.

But I enjoyed the fact that in the city I was incognito so there wasn't that awful fear of bumping into somebody who knew me or my past. In my head I had wiped the slate clean and reinvented myself.

There was a convent across the road from the hotel which was ideal for both children. Jennifer was twelve by this stage and in her first year at High School. Once Rudi arrived he would join the school as well and remain in class two. I had employed an Indian maid called Marie who seemed responsible enough, to see to both Jennifer and Rudi's needs during the days whilst I was working.

Unexpectedly my visit to Aunt Rachel at her care home turned out to be traumatic.

She didn't know who I was!

She just wasn't *there*!

I was told by the doctor who looked after her in the home that she had dementia. This explained to me why her letters were somewhat jumbled and also why I hadn't heard from her for some time. I felt like I had been hit in the stomach. She was my only link with my childhood self, my anchor. I felt that I had been abandoned by her too!

#

Coping with my feelings of betrayal and rejection by Michael and the loss of Aunt Rachel ... because although she was still there, she was actually lost too ... was a huge daily struggle for me. A struggle that I didn't always overcome successfully. There were times when I didn't want to get out of bed in the morning to face the day. What was the *point*? Michael and I were never going to be together! Aunt Rachel was never going to get better! Why couldn't I just close my eyes and block out the world? It all seemed too much to cope with at times but it was made easier by my faithful gin bottle that was never far from my side.

Work was very busy as the Ansonia seemed to always be short staffed and I didn't see much of the children at all during my stay there. I had been feeling very tired anyway and at the end of every shift I poured myself a strong drink and went straight to bed.

I had only been working there for about three months when I saw an advertisement in the newspaper for a receptionist position at the Savoy Hotel in Durban. The salary was far better than what I was currently earning, and I missed the seaside. So I applied and within a couple of days I received an answer to say that I had got the job. I think Rudi was very happy because he never seemed very settled at the convent somehow. Before long we had packed up our possessions and were headed off to Durban.

The Savoy was a disappointment. It was run down and tired and needed a jolly good scrub to be honest. No wonder they couldn't keep staff! Our living quarters consisted of just one room with three old beds against the far wall and only one wardrobe for all our things. It only had a small window looking out towards the back of the kitchen so the room would be very hot as well as cramped. I looked around wondering how I had come to this. Feeling overwhelmed I just closed the door and left the room.

But, never one to turn down a challenge, I picked myself up and took charge of the reception area as soon as I started work. With resolve, I completely cleared the area of all unnecessary junk and got the cleaning team in to give it a mighty good going over. With a large bunch of flowers picked from the garden and placed in a shiny recently cleaned brass vase on the counter, the area looked and smelled transformed. The wooden floors had been scrubbed and gleamed like a mirror in the sunlight and there wasn't a cobweb in sight. I then got the team working on the windows and the outside seating area, scrubbing the black and white tiled floors and washing down the rattan sofas and glass tables. It was looking better already and rather satisfying.

The children were sent off to school in Musgrove Road which was quite near the hotel and they seemed to settle in quite readily. Rudi certainly seemed a lot happier.

I had been struggling with feeling unwell for some time, even whilst still living in Pietermaritzburg I knew that I didn't feel right. But it had now got to the stage where I was feeling so sick that I didn't even feel like a drink. I had been so busy with the move to Durban and then settling into life at the Savoy that I had been ignoring how unwell and tired I was. All I wanted to do was sleep but I was kept awake half the night by an annoying persistent cough. I eventually decided to do something about it and made an appointment to see a doctor.

Dr Blankenburg ushered me into his office with a smile. 'Do take a seat Mrs Garden. I have got your X-ray results here and I have rather a lot to explain to you today'.

I sat down and looked at him with apprehension.

'I'm afraid that you have an abscess on your left lung which is now infected. This is why you have been coughing so much. We are going to have to operate to remove your lung.'

I burst into tears. Which was so unlike me but I was so *tired*. After he had explained the procedure to me and why he had to take such drastic action I calmed down somewhat, realising that I didn't have an option. 'But who will look after my children whilst I am in hospital?' I asked in a fresh flood of tears.

'Let me see what I can arrange,' he said kindly. 'In the meantime I have put together some medication for you which you must take every day for the next seven days and I will see you back here next week.'

I walked numbly out of his surgery to the bus stop and sat down, my thoughts in turmoil. The idea of the operation really scared me and I just wanted it all to go away. I had nobody to turn to. I couldn't speak to Aunt Rachel, she didn't even know who I was. So that wasn't an option. I couldn't speak to Michael as he didn't want me anymore. Any friends that I thought I had, were not my friends anymore either so they certainly wouldn't be interested in my troubles. There was nobody else.

Getting off the bus I made a detour to the bottle store and bought myself a small bottle of gin. I had had a shock so I *deserved* a little something you know. I mean … what would *you* do?

Hardly able to wait, I hurried home along the busy street as quickly as I could, thinking only about that first mouthful and the oblivion that would follow.

Thankfully the doctor had booked me off work for the next week so that I could get some rest. I got plenty of rest as I spent most of the time in bed … drinking, except when I had to get up to go to the bottle store to buy more gin of course. The days passed in a haze of alcohol until I woke up one day too tired to even get myself out of bed. I once again realised that I needed to pull myself together. I vaguely remember seeing the children on occasions during this time but other than that I hadn't given them a thought. I didn't have to worry about preparing food for them as they ate their meals in the hotel dining room and I can only presume that Jennifer helped Rudi get ready for school in the mornings.

I knew that I needed to contact Ian. He had remarried … apparently. He didn't waste time now did he? Our divorce had come through soon after my move to Durban and he had married soon after. He married a woman whom he had been seeing during our marriage. She had four children so I think he had his hands full. But I wanted to get him to look after the children while I was in hospital. I mean, he hardly saw them as it was so I felt it was time that he did his fair share. My phone call was not met with enthusiasm but he did agree to take Jennifer. But not Rudi. I had to be content with that. But the problem of where Rudi would go, remained.

The appointment with Dr Blankenburg was soon upon me and I made my way to his surgery in a sober state having managed to stay off drink for the previous two days. He showed me to his office once more, his reassuring smile calming me. He listened to my lungs and gave me further information about the procedure that he was going to perform.

'I have given some thought to the dilemma that you find yourself in with regards to your children. After chatting to my wife we have agreed that we would be happy to take in both your children for the duration of your hospital stay and convalescence.'

I looked at him dumbstruck. Was I hearing this right? Was he really offering to look after one of his patient's children?

'I don't know what to say,' I said feeling overwhelmed, then remembering, 'I have arranged for Jennifer to stay with her father for three months so it will only be Rudi. He is really easy though.' I hesitated. 'Are you certain that you want to do this?'

'We would be delighted to help. You just need to concentrate on preparing for your operation and on getting well again and back on your feet. It is going to be a long slow process and you will need all your strength.'

I left there marvelling at how there were such wonderful people in the world. Although at the back of my mind, I also wondered if he would be as gracious and helpful if he knew my past.

As my operation was scheduled for three days' time I knew that I had to speak to the children about what was going to happen. Jennifer accepted that she would have to stay with her father until I was well enough to come home again. Rudi was horrified.

'I don't know Dr Blankenburg!' he exclaimed, tears welling in his eyes. I explained to him how Dr Blankenburg kindly offered to look after him and that his own son, whose name was Richard, even went to the same school. He still wasn't happy, but there was nothing that I could do.

Wentworth Hospital was a large sprawling hospital serving the greater Durban community. It was known for its specialised services and had the best cardio thoracic unit in the province at that time. I was to be admitted the day prior to surgery to enable them to prepare me and perform certain tests that were needed so that I would be ready for surgery early the following morning. Carol Blankenburg, Dr Blankenburg's wife fetched Rudi and I from the Savoy and drove us to her home on the Berea so that she could show Rudi where he was going to be spending the next couple of months. He was wide eyed and quiet but seemed resigned to what was happening.

En route to the hospital, we stopped off at the Wentworth Hotel for lunch. It was extravagant I know, but I ordered a dozen fresh oysters. Well, why not! You never know … I might not be here tomorrow so I've got to enjoy it whilst I can!'

#

'I talk to the trees, but they don't listen to me, I talk to the stars, but they never hear me' I sang under my breath looking longingly out of the window from my hospital bed at the tops of some large trees and tall palms swaying in the wind. There was no one to talk to. So I sang to myself. I knew all the words and sang the whole song over and over, loving the end 'I tell you my dreams, and while you're listening to me I suddenly see them come true'. Wishing fervently that they would come true and longing for something elusive that I couldn't quite grasp, I sighed and closed my eyes and dozed.

The operation had gone well. I was hooked up to machines for the first four days afterwards and for the following week I floated in and out of sleep between bouts of painkillers. My chest felt as if someone was standing on it and my tongue felt so dry it was stuck to the roof of my mouth. I was grateful that I lay propped up by numerous pillows, making it easier to breath and easing the pressure on my chest. I was so *happy* that it was over and I was still in one piece. Do you know what's it's like when you hear some exceptionally good news? Or you pass a very difficult exam that you have been working towards for a long time, with brilliant marks? You feel on top of the world. Invincible. As if you are *unstoppable*. That's how I felt. A weight had been lifted off my shoulders and I felt ready to tackle anything that the world threw at me. This felt like a second chance.

Day by day I slowly progressed until I was disconnected from all the machines and tubes and encouraged to get out of bed. I threw back the sheet eagerly and swung my feet carefully over the side of the bed to touch the floor. Gingerly I stood up and walked slowly and shakily over to the window. It was west facing and I looked out onto a garden with a huge expanse of lawn and a couple of inviting benches placed periodically in the shade of the many large trees that I had seen the tops of from my window when I was lying in bed. I drank in the green. After seeing only a hospital ward for the past week it was a feast for the eyes. Tiredness overwhelmed me once more and I gratefully made my way back to the bed to lay down.

I was starting to feel a lot better and seemed to be ravenously hungry all the time. If I had to tell you that the food here wasn't all that bad, I don't suppose you would believe me. But it wasn't bad at all. In fact, there was even a menu and I could choose what I would like to eat each meal time. It was only once I was breathing normally and eating properly again that I realised how unwell I had been feeling all these months. Although my alcohol consumption probably did not help at the time let's face it! But I was starting to put some much needed weight onto my small frame and the hollows in my cheeks had started to fill out. But the best thing was that I hadn't been having any alcohol of course. And I didn't feel like having any either.

Other than Rudi, no one came to visit me throughout my stay in hospital. Well I had no one that would want to visit now did I?

After spending nearly three weeks in hospital, I was sent to a convalescent home for the next couple of months to enable me to get my strength back and fully recover. There wasn't much to do there other than read or go for quiet walks in the grounds of the home which actually suited me fine. I learnt to play cards and would sit and play rummy with the other patients in the afternoon to pass the time.

I did a lot of reading.

And as there was plenty of time ... I did a lot of thinking.

I realised that it was time that I buried Michael in the past and moved on with my life. This was my second chance after all. A new beginning.

It was beautiful and sunny to match my positive mind-set on the day I was discharged. I felt marvellous. And I knew that I looked good too. It was *always* important to me to dress well. The months of being alcohol free and eating a normal diet were reflected by a couple of much needed extra pounds on my small frame and a healthy glow to my skin and hair. I had ordered a taxi to take me to Dr Blankenburg's house where I would pick up Rudi and head off back to the Savoy where my job was waiting for me. I was humbled and so grateful to the Blankenburgs for all that they had done and felt that I would never be able to repay them. Rudi was so excited to see me and hugged me tight not wanting to let me go. He was look-ing happy and said that he had enjoyed his stay and had made friends with the Blankenburgs' two boys.

Back at the Savoy my enthusiasm dipped somewhat when I was confronted once more by the small dingy room that would be home for the three of us once more. Casting that aside, and grateful for the management at the Savoy for keeping my job open, I plunged myself back into work determined to show that I was ready and able. I can do this. I *can*!

Working in the hotel industry and particularly at the front desk had exposed me to a lot of people that I would not normally have come into contact with. And of course being utterly charming and friendly was just par for the course and I constantly picked up contacts and got to know many people in numerous industries. One of the guests was so taken with me that, after speaking to his brother who owned a hotel in East London, he offered me a job at the Windsor Hotel on East Londons shore front.

I was tempted.

But I decided to remain where I was for the time being as I thought it better for the children to remain at the same school until the end of the year at least. As it turned out my decision did not last long. I had many clashes with the hotel management team over the following months, all connected to the general day to day running of the place and we just could not find common ground. One day things came to a head and I had just had enough and I handed in my notice. Emboldened, I contacted Dave Carter from the Windsor Hotel and secured myself a new job. Then I scraped together the cost of a passage on the Pendennis Castle for the three of us, took myself off to the travel agent and booked the trip to East London. So by that evening it was all organised.

I announced to the children that we were off on an adventure to East London in a couple of days.

I felt optimistic about this move. It really felt like a new beginning for me. I hadn't had a drink since before my operation, which was five months ago now. I was feeling so *well*, so vibrant … happy?

Going on a cruise liner was a new experience for me having never been on one before. I dressed with care in a bright yellow floral dress with a square neck that showed off my shoulders and a wide full skirt. With my matching handbag and shoes, I knew I looked a pretty sight. Rudi was beside himself with excitement and to be honest, I was excited too. It was an *adventure!*

Pulling up alongside the ship in the taxi, it looked enormous. So tall. And the gangway was hanging in a rather precarious position I thought. It might be a bit difficult to walk up with my high heels but it's too bad as I am not taking them off. Rudi bounded up ahead with Jennifer and I made my way carefully up the iron gangway gripping the side for fear of falling and not daring to look down at the water far below. Thankfully I got to top without mishap and laughing with relief, I almost fell into the arms of a *very* handsome young seaman who guided me over the lip of the door into the ship.

'I'd like to introduce you to Captain Len Green,' said the young seaman standing next to a portly grey haired man dressed in ship's whites with his hat under his arm. We got chatting immediately and he invited me to dine at his table that very evening. I certainly hadn't lost my touch now, had I?

The couple of nights aboard ship were entertaining and good fun. I felt that I was leaving behind my old life and hoped that I would be able to put the hurt and betrayal of the past behind me. It was exciting to be dressing up for dinner once more and I took great care with my appearance that first evening wearing a dark blue satin evening gown that showed off my figure to perfection. All the gentlemen stood up when I came into the room and I could see the appreciation on their faces. Feeling emboldened, I accepted a glass of wine with dinner. How could I not?

Just a *tiny* one, I told myself.

I will sip it slowly and make it last all evening, I told myself.

Just one glass won't do any harm, I told myself.

Before I knew it, I had finished three. And it's not as if I don't know when to stop.

Really!

But they just kept on filling my glass. What could I *do*? Not having had a drink for at least five months the wine went straight to my head. But I was amusing and fascinating and thoroughly entertained the captain and all at his table that evening. Captain Green was so enamoured that he agreed to slow the ship down to a 'dead crawl' when we passed Margate and he would send a signal to shore to my friend Ronnie Baker who lived on the hill. This he did much to Rudi's fascination.

I managed to keep it to just three glasses, *I think,* that evening and I had a wonderful time. There were a number of hostile looks from two of the ladies who were seated at my table and I could only think that they disapproved of the attention that I was getting from their men. But we *were* having such a good time. Ok … I *was* flirting just a *teeny weeny* bit. But I didn't mean any *harm* by it. I was just back to my old self.

I didn't see the children much throughout the voyage. They seemed to be very occupied with one thing and another and had met a couple of children of a similar age and spent the time running around the deck or swimming in the pool.

We docked in East London on a grey wet morning. A bit like my mood to be honest. I had really had a ball on board and felt depressed about having to leave the ship and get back to the reality of my life. It had felt so *good* to relax and let go a bit. But with a pounding head and feeling thoroughly irritated I hailed a taxi and bundled the children and our luggage into the back and we headed off to the Windsor Hotel.

Another hotel, another room. Although this time we had two rooms, one for myself and one for the children so it was an improvement on our previous accommodation. Dave Carter was pleasant and my position as assistant manager allowed me more freedom and I could more or less run things the way I wanted.

There was an army barracks next door to the hotel and the hotel bar catered mainly for the servicemen who frequented it regularly on their days off. There was quite a strong army and police presence in town. It was 1961 and South Africa had just become a republic after being under British rule and they might have been expecting trouble of some sort. There was new currency that had been launched which we all had to get used to and had to be quite careful not to make any mistakes when totalling figures for the guests.

Both Rudi and Jennifer were sent off to the local school once more and I think they settled quite quickly although Rudi was still struggling with reading. I should have spent more time trying to help him but things always seemed to get in the way and normally I would have had a gin or two by the time he came home from school anyway so I was in no state of mind to be much help. Or that's my excuse anyway.

I had been feeling so *well* since I had recovered from my operation. So *healthy!* I had told myself that I would stay feeling that way if I could. But bit by bit, little by little, I had started drinking again. A little drink here and another small one there that might turn into two or three. It was just so *relaxing* you know. I seemed to be fine early on in the day but come the afternoons and I would really need a boost. Dave Carter I'm sure suspected that I had a little tipple in the afternoons which sometimes became a bit more than a tipple. So to save myself any embarrassment of being asked to leave, I organised another job in yet another hotel, further up the road into town.

Over the years I had remained in contact with Fritz Cohen, my old boss from my modelling days. I was delighted one day to receive a phone call from him, asking me if I would like some modelling work. I had just turned forty but could pass for much younger as I was still very attractive with a slim figure. I was ecstatic and was convinced that going back into modelling work would mean an end to all my troubles. How could it not when I loved it so and I felt so good about life when I was modelling?

The decision taken and not giving a thought to uprooting Jennifer and Rudi once more after only six months in East London, I was soon packing up our belongings and heading for the train station where we would catch the train to Johannesburg. This was really the beginning of my new life. I just knew it.

CHAPTER FIVE

Rudi

We pulled into Johannesburg station in the early hours of the morning. It was cold and dark and the fog hung thick over the city, grey and unwelcoming. The station platform was very busy as people in their coats and hats bustled about all seeming to have somewhere of importance to go. I waited on the platform with my mother and sister, shivering with cold as a porter brought our luggage on a large iron trolley and then we followed him out of the station entrance to the taxi rank.

The smell hit me first. Even though it was cold with a light mist, the air hung heavy with a promise of midday heat to come once the sun burnt through the cloud. The smell was thick and strong, a combination of vegetation, rotting meat and unwashed bodies, mixed together with the acrid odour of Boxer tobacco, the brand favoured by the Africans who used to roll their own cigarettes. I wanted to gag. I put my hand over my mouth as we made our way through the stalls set up by African vendors on the pavement outside the station entrance. It was a fascinating display of fruit and vegetables, together with traditional herbs and spices, brightly coloured fabric, cheap shoes and sandals. In the one stall there were huge piles of dried roots and leaves and what looked like skins, clumps of sticks, dried rats, seeds and powder and some gloopy looking lotion in jars. I had never seen such a mix of things in one place before. It was vibrant and very noisy as the traders shouted out their wares and tried to encourage us to buy. Mom was having none of that and herded us briskly through the throng straight to a waiting taxi and we headed off to what would be our new home for a while.

My mother had arranged for us to stay with Mary Kelly who she said, was an old friend of hers that she used to work with in Johannesburg many moons ago. She used to be the housekeeper at the Rand Club where my mother also worked, long before I was even born.

Mary had a large house in an area called Turffontein. It was near the Turffontein race course and if I stood on a chair at the window in the dining room, I could see the horses running around the track on a Wednesday and Saturday afternoon when there were race meetings. It was exciting to see them galloping past the window, the sound of their thundering hooves getting nearer and nearer and then fading into the distance once more as they went past. Sometimes I got up really early and I would be able to see the horses doing their early morning training runs in the half light and if I opened the window I could hear them snorting as they ran past.

Mary told me that you could put some money on a horse and if it ran first then you could get lots back. I wasn't entirely sure how the money stayed on the horse all the way to the finish of the race but I thought, when I have some money, I will ask Mary and she can show me how it is done.

Once again I was sent off to school. Another school. Another daily mission to be endured. The school was about a five mile bus ride each morning and I would catch it by myself, just around the corner from where we were staying. I was nine now after all. The bus was a big red double decker and I loved the curved staircase that used to go up to the top floor. I always used to try and get the seat right in the front at the top so that I had the best view. It was the only part of my school day that I enjoyed.

My mother had gone away modelling somewhere. She had a mobile modelling job where she travelled from town to town with five other ladies in a small bus, together with all their dresses and garments, make up artists and photographers. She was gone throughout the week and only came home at the weekends. Sometimes she was gone for two weeks at a time. It seemed awfully long when she was away, but when she was back home I didn't see much of her either.

Mary and her husband Jack, or Aunt Mary and Uncle Jack, as we were told to call them, used to look after us. Most mornings Aunt Mary would hand me a bag which contained two empty milk bottles and send me off to the dairy to get some milk. If I was early enough I would get to see the horses running past so I always tried to time it so. The dairy wasn't far from the house and once there, they would fill up the empty bottles with milk and put a new silver cap on to seal them. Then I would hurry back home looking forward to opening the milk and scooping out the white ring found inside the silver cap. If I collected twelve of these rings I could take them to the local café and they would swop them for a toy animal. For *free*! So I started a collection of toy animals: Lions, elephants, wildebeest and baboons. My favourite were the giraffes. I lined them all up on the windowsill and played with them every day when I came home from school.

Life with Aunt Mary and Uncle Jack was pleasant. They had a fox terrier called Trixie that reminded me a bit of Happy but he wasn't such a friendly dog. One day I pulled his tail whilst he was eating, which was a stupid thing to do I know and I should have known better, and he turned around and bit me in the face. I should have called him Jaws after that quite frankly! So off we went to the doctor, blood everywhere. She gave me three stitches in my face and an injection in my bum which was humiliating. I mean I had to show my bum to a lady, even though she was a doctor. Eeeuw!

Uncle Jack had promised me that when he was at home during the weekend he would teach me how to shoot a gun. A real gun! It was a rifle with a long barrel. A point two two. We headed off one afternoon towards the old deserted mine dumps that were scattered around the countryside quite near to where we were living. These were like big hills that were made up of rock and sand that had been discarded when they were mining for gold years ago. We set up some targets about twenty yards away up against the dump and Uncle Jack fired the first shot. He was quite good of course. I was very excited but when the gun went off for the first time it gave me such a kick it nearly knocked me off my feet. But Uncle Jack showed me how to hold it correctly and also how to stand solidly so that I won't fall over. I thoroughly enjoyed myself and was sorry when it was time to go home.

It was winter in Johannesburg and much colder than what I had known before, having mostly lived at the coast. All the leaves had finished falling off the trees and I helped Uncle Jack to rake them into a huge pile in the centre of the big front lawn. I wanted to jump in the middle of the pile just for the fun of it but thought I better not, especially after all our hard work. Uncle Jack might not be too pleased. Once all the leaves were piled high, Uncle Jack allowed me to use a match to set it alight. It made an awesome big fire with lots of smoke. Fortunately it was not a windy day and the smoke just went straight up in the air. Uncle Jack told me that he does this every year when it's nearly winter. I thought it would be nice to live in Johannesburg forever where I would get to do that every year too.

#

'Rudi, your mom has been in an accident. She is fine but I am going to fetch her and thought you would like to come with', Uncle Jack said cautiously one day. I jumped up, my heart pounding, grabbed my jumper and was in the car before he had moved.

'I take that as a yes then,' he smiled at me when he got into the car. I smiled back and gave a small giggle which made me feel better and eased the fluttering in my tummy.

We drove quite a way out of town through the far neighbouring suburbs until we came to the road that went through an African settlement area. Darkness comes suddenly in Africa and as we had left any street lights far behind us, we were crawling along, keeping a careful look out for any stray goats or cows that tend to wander onto the road as if it belonged to them. It wasn't long until we came across a couple of police vans parked at the side of the road as well as the convoy of buses that Fritz used for his assignments, all parked along the opposite bank except for one which was in the middle of the road. Fritz was standing talking to a couple of policemen making rigorous gestures with his arms, the sound of his voice urgent and angry.

'Stay here Rudi, please and I will go and fetch your mother', said Uncle Jack. I watched anxiously as he climbed out of the car and went across to where all the buses were parked and where a group of people were standing to one side. A couple of minutes later he came walking back, his arm around my mother who appeared to be rather upset. I jumped out of the car and ran over to her and gave her a hug. She stopped walking and hugged me right back saying over and over 'My boy! My boy!' She kissed the top of my head and still holding onto me, climbed into the car and sat down with a sigh.

Fritz had apparently knocked over somebody with the bus. I think he had killed him but I wasn't sure as my mom and Uncle Jack didn't speak about it on the journey back home. All I knew was that my mother was upset.

My mother was really shaken by this incident and went to lie down as soon as we got home. As it was a Friday evening she was expected home for the weekend anyway. Throughout the weekend she was very subdued, but it was nice to have her at home for a change. On Monday morning she didn't go to work. She didn't go to work on Tuesday or Wednesday either. She said she needed a break.

Every day when I came home from school, the first thing I did was look for her to make sure that she was still there. And she was. Sometimes I found her sitting at the kitchen table, with pink cheeks and sparkling eyes, glass in hand, chatting to Aunty Mary and Uncle Jack. Sometimes she was in bed sleeping and I would tiptoe into the room and look down at her, just to make sure, and tiptoe out again and close the door quietly behind me. And sometimes when I came home she would be sitting in the lounge and staring out of the window.

I would go and sit next to her ... softly.

So I didn't disturb her.

And I would put my hand on hers just so that she knew I was there.

In case ...

Just in case she needed me.

A week later my mother announced to my sister and I that we would be going to live in Rhodesia. Her stepfather had invited her to go and live on the farm which was near a town called Hartley (Chegutu) about forty five miles from the city of Salisbury. My stomach did a flip! I had started to feel settled staying with Aunty Mary and Uncle Jack and I really enjoyed it when Uncle Jack did things with me like shooting and stuff. I didn't want to leave them but the thought of staying on a farm excited me and eased the feeling of impending loss.

Before long we had packed our belongings once more and after an emotional goodbye to Aunty Mary and Uncle Jack, we headed to Johannesburg station and were soon boarding the train bound for Salisbury. Mom was really cheerful on the trip which lifted my own spirits and I began to feel some excitement about this latest move. After spending two nights on the train, a very similar journey to our trip from East London, we arrived at Salisbury station where we caught the connection to Hartley.

#

The hot sun beat down on my bare head as we stood on the gravel road outside the small station building waiting

106

for our lift to the farm. Across the road a lone donkey stood with head hanging, flies noisily buzzing around his ears, flicking his tail periodically as he waited for the *umfaan* to finish hitching him to a derelict wooden cart. There was no breeze and the air was dry and dusty.

Hot and thirsty, Jennifer and I went and sat in the shade of a nearby tree hoping for some relief from the heat. It wasn't long before we heard the sound of a motor and saw the dust rising along the road in the distance. We jumped to our feet and walked over to where my mother was standing beside our rather battered suitcases. The car came into view and stopped where we were waiting, covering us all in a cloud of thick brown dust.

'Wow!' I couldn't help myself. 'What a cool car!'

'It's a Cadillac.' The man climbed out, looking at me from beneath thick white brows. 'You must be Rudi. I'm pleased to make your acquaintance,' he said in a very posh voice holding out his hand for me to shake. I felt rather grown up as I shook his hand in turn, giving him a quick smile. This must be Mr Shepherd-Cross that mom has been speaking about I thought to myself. He was her stepfather I was told. Which means that he was not her *real* father. I was told to call him Uncle Arthur.

'Well, come on then. In you all get'

We jumped into the car, mom in the front and Jennifer and I at the back, the smell of the warm leather seats, clean and familiar somehow.

It wasn't long before we turned off the road onto a smaller track that took us past some African houses scattered underneath tall eucalyptus trees that ran almost the length of the road. Eventually we drove through two large ornate gates and wove through the trees up a sweeping drive coming to a stop outside a large two storey house surrounded by lush grass and well tended flower beds. There was a flag flying gently in the breeze from a pole fixed to the low roof on the one side of the house. Mom said it was a Union Jack. I liked that as then thought of it as Uncle Jack's flag. The house itself was painted white and looked very grand with a large covered wraparound verandah on which were an assortment of easy chairs and sofas where you could sit in the shade and enjoy the view of the garden.

Two large brown dogs that had been lying asleep in the shade of the covered verandah, bounded out, tails wagging furiously and barking a noisy greeting in unison.

'Come and meet Brutus and Caesar. They are Rhodesian Ridgebacks and are the best watchdogs in the world.'

I jumped out of the car eagerly and both the dogs romped over to me boisterously and started licking my face. They were huge and I could stand and put my arm around them both without bending over. From the moment that I felt their warm tongues on my face and hands, I knew that I had made two friends.

The front door opened and two maids came out dressed in black dresses with white frilly aprons, and collected our suitcases and took them to our rooms. Inside the hallway it was immediately cooler and we were shown through to a lovely sitting room with huge glass doors leading out onto another section of verandah not visible from the driveway. Jennifer and I were handed a glass of orange juice and a biscuit each and were told to take it out onto the verandah. Only too pleased to be able to be with the dogs once more I made my way outside with Jennifer whilst the adults remained in the sitting room to *discuss the situation!*

After sitting down carefully on the top step trying not to spill my orange juice, I nibbled at my biscuit and looked around. The air was heavy with heat and it was very quiet except for the occasional sound of a bird. Dark green grass rolled away from the bottom step of the verandah almost as far as the eye could see, with a scattering of bushes and tall palm trees swaying gently in the warm breeze. Like a big park. There were large flower beds that were a riot of colour and I could smell roses. I knew it was roses because my mother always had roses in a vase on the dining room table at home in Ramsgate and it was the same smell. I breathed in deeply and decided that I liked it here.

'Rudi, let's go upstairs and I will show you to your room,' Mom was at the glass door beckoning me with a smile. I jumped up and followed her back through to the hallway, the black and white tiles gleaming in the sunlight. We went up a grand wooden staircase with a green carpet running down the middle of the steps exposing the polished wooden steps on either side. Going up the stairs, I noticed pictures on the walls in heavy gilt frames, all of various hunting scenes. Mom said that they were paintings, originals by a famous artist. I thought it all looked rather dark.

I followed mom into a big airy room with two single beds that were covered in bright checked quilts with a cheerful rug on the floor to match. My clothes were already unpacked into the chest of drawers and I scrambled to find where the suitcases had been stored.

'What are you wanting the suitcases for Rud?'

'My animals!' I said in panic 'Where are they' I opened the familiar old brown case and thankfully there they were. I retrieved them with relief and placed them care-fully one by one on the windowsill so that they could look out. Feeling comforted I jumped onto the nearest bed and gazed out of the window. It was so nice not to have to look out onto a street or even worse, a wall for a change. The vast garden below with its neat bright green lawn filled me with longing and with a sudden pang, images of Jabulani flooded my head. The grass flowed down as far as the tree line and beyond that the blue hills shim-mered in a haze of heat. I decided that I was *definitely* going to like it here.

Dinner that evening was very grand. I was told to have a bath and change my clothes before I could go down to the dining room. Wearing a chequered blue shirt with buttons down the front that Aunt Mary had given me and plastering my hair down with some water to stop the curls from standing up all over the place, I was ready.

The dining room was a huge room with a long wood-en table in the centre surrounded by ten ornately carved chairs with high backs. There were five places set for din-ner and so many knives and forks set out at each place that I didn't know where to start. At each place setting there were two wine glasses and Uncle Arthur told me that they had their own wine cellar where every day he would choose a bottle of wine that would be served with that evening's meal. Each dinner was a three course meal served by two male African servants wearing the traditional tunic of long white top with red trim and white trousers to match.

There was a lady at the table who I hadn't seen be-fore. She was German and she said that her name was Ida Shepherd-Cross. She said that we had to say grace before each meal. I had only done that with the nuns at the convent in Pietermaritzburg so it was strange to be doing it again. But I did it to please her.

#

I had got myself into a little daily routine. It gave me a feeling of belonging I think. First thing in the mornings, sometimes just as the sun was peeking over the distant hills, I would get dressed and make my way downstairs to where the dogs were lying on the open verandah. After they had given me their normal wet greeting we would wander off together down the driveway and out onto the road towards the milking shed. The air was fresh and cool early in the day and there were normally a couple of had-edas on the front lawn, plunging their long curved beaks into the soft soil, searching for worms. The dogs would sometimes bark and chase them off and they would rise up into the air with their raucous cry and settle down again on the grass a few yards further away.

The milking shed was a long, low, corrugated iron building with a green roof and a large barn to the side which housed all the tractors and farm implements. There were also a couple of huge sheds with rows and rows of racks which I was told was for drying the tobacco leaves after they had been cut.

It was always a hive of activity in the milking shed as the cows were brought in to be milked. It was noisy and warm with a strong smell of cow dung hanging in the air. I would sit up on the wooden partition and watch, waiting for the first small bucketful to be ready so that I could take it back to the house for breakfast. But not before I had taken a couple of warm frothy mouthfuls.

Breakfasts were a huge spread. It was like being at a hotel. There was always porridge of course. Then there were kippers, bacon and eggs, sausages and fried tomatoes, as well as kedgeree and brown or white toast. And big bowls of fruit salad. All laid out on the sideboard ready for me to help myself.

After breakfast with the day stretching before me, I had taken to exploring the farm. There had been no mention of school which suited me down to the ground given that it was a test of endurance for me. So I thought it best to make myself scarce and stay out of sight in the hope that things would stay that way and nobody would remember that I should be at school.

With a spring in my step I would wander over to the cluster of barns, sometimes helping the African farm workers clean out the cow sheds, using a large pitchfork to shovel straw into a big pile. Then I would grab a broom and sweep the concrete floor as it was hosed down. The farm workers used to call me Wadudu, (which means insect in Swahili, the local African dialect), I think because I was everywhere and always busy doing stuff.

But a lot of the time was spent with my new found friend. I had been sitting on the step outside the kitchen one morning when I noticed a young African boy standing under the large tree which provided much needed shade for the cluster of outbuildings which housed the farm offices. This was unusual as the only Africans allowed near the house were the domestic workers and cooks. He looked younger than me and had a wide pleasant face with a white toothy smile which he used often. A well worn football was at his feet and he glanced towards me and studied me with interest. I got to my feet and ventured over to him.

'Hello. I'm Rudi.'

'I'm Lexington, like the cigarette' He gave me his hundred watt smile.

He gestured to his football, kicked it a couple of yards away and we both ran after it. And so we bonded just like that. Although he was African he spoke perfect English so it was easy to communicate. Together with Brutus and Caesar we spent many happy hours together roaming around the farm and exploring the outbuildings and barns. One day Lexington took me to an old swimming pool which was quite a long way from the house. It was half filled with dirty green water and covered in leaves. There was a small building to one side that looked like old changing rooms but it was also half falling down in places. We decided to build a raft that we could put in the water and paddle across. Lexington had a panga and we cut down some bamboo and bound it together by using long pieces of grass like ropes, the way the Africans do. We felt very proud when we put it in the water and it floated. The dogs weren't happy and for as long as we were on the raft in the water, they would run around the pool barking.

One day not long after we had finished making our raft and whilst we were busy launching it for another session on the water, I heard Brutus barking excitedly. Getting off the raft I walked over to the old change rooms and there lying on the warm top step I saw a large grey snake.

'Lexington, come look here quick!' I said urgently.

'Ai that's a black mamba,' he said with big eyes, backing away. I ran quickly to the farm office to call Uncle Arthur and he grabbed his shotgun and followed me back to the pool. Lexington, meanwhile had been attempting to keep the dogs away from the snake and at the same time trying to make sure that he didn't lose sight of it. The snake had moved off into the bamboo that grew thickly at the side of the swimming pool, but he was still visible from where we were standing. Uncle Arthur took aim and with one shot of the shotgun, the snake was dead. Brutus tried to grab the head but as the snake was still moving, its fang penetrated his paw. Brutus yelped and ran off into the undergrowth.

'Brutus' I called chasing him frantically.

'Brutus! Bruutuuus ... ' I called over and over.

After searching for a while we still couldn't find him so we made our way back to the house. I spotted him lying on the grass and ran over.

'No! Brutus! Nooo!' I cried. His dull eyes looked through me and I knew he was dead. The black mamba is Southern Africa's most poisonous snake and the venom is fast acting particularly on something as small as a dog. Brutus had no chance. I was inconsolable and for days afterwards I would cry myself to sleep.

South Africa did not have television, so it was most exciting to discover that Uncle Arthur had a television set. Although it was only black and white I thought that this was the most fun thing ever. The programs only started at about five in the afternoon and ran for a couple of hours each day. My favourite program was *Bonanza* which was all about cowboys and it used to be the first thing that was shown every day. I tried to make sure that I was back indoors in time for the programs to start in the afternoon. Even although I was nine already I still hadn't learned how to tell the time so periodically throughout the afternoon I would go to Uncle Arthur's farm office and ask him if it was time yet for the television to start. He was the only one that was allowed to switch it on. I think I made rather a nuisance of myself especially one day when I think I had asked him three times already and he said, 'My boy, it's not yet time! I will call you! In the meantime go and do something busy'

I rolled my eyes. Where have I heard *that* before? Adults can be so *tiresome* at times!

#

As I had always kept myself busy with matters of importance around the farm, I hadn't seen much of my mother at all since we had been there. A lot of the time she wasn't at the breakfast table when I was there tucking into my bacon and eggs. I just presumed that she ate her breakfast later. Most days she joined us for lunch but seemed to only pick at her food and often sat smoking one cigarette after the other, the blue smoke hanging in the room.

Dinner times were different. The adults would always meet for drinks on the verandah before dinner, around about the time when I was watching *Bonanza* which suited me fine then I knew I wouldn't be disturbed. They would all have a G and T or two, which I had discovered was exactly the same as Jim's drink. I knew that mom loved Jim's drink but I also knew that it made her sleep so that was possibly why she was never at breakfast. Sometimes visitors would arrive from the neighbouring farms and join them all for 'cocktail hour' as I heard them call it. Dinner would then be late, but I didn't mind as I would just carry on watching the television for longer.

After having their G and T's or two, the adults would then make their way to the dining room for dinner. Mom was usually on top form. As if she had come out of her shell. Dressed in one or other of her cocktail dresses she would be entertaining and funny and laugh raucously at her own jokes. She would down her wine in a couple of gulps and hold out her glass for a refill, all the while recounting some entertaining escapade of which she was a part. And another thing that I noticed she liked to do, was drink wine from someone else's glass when they weren't looking or when they went out of the room for whatever reason. She could be captivating. But possibly not after a number of G and T's and an equal amount of wine. I did notice Uncle Arthur looking rather disapproving sometimes and it made me feel uncomfortable and I wanted to ask her to stop. But I wasn't sure how, so I never did.

Between mealtimes I hardly saw her as I was too busy outside. Although I do know that she drove into Hartley a couple of times with Ida and Jennifer to do some shopping. She always liked shopping. I couldn't see the attraction myself to be honest as I found it rather boring.

One day we were all gathered in the dining room having lunch. Mom was a lot perkier than usual for this time of the day and I noticed and she ate her food with relish.

'The Youngs have invited the children and I over for cocktails this evening and I was thinking it might be nice to go,' mom said to Uncle Arthur. Mr and Mrs Young lived on the neighbouring farm about a fifteen minute drive away.

'That's a splendid idea,' said Uncle Arthur putting down his fork and dabbing his mouth with his napkin. 'I would join you however I have things to see to on the farm this afternoon. Why don't you take the car? I won't be needing it anymore today.'

Mom beamed at him.

Mid afternoon the three of us piled into the front bench seat of Uncle Arthur's Cadillac and made our way down the drive and out onto the gravel road. This was the first time that I had left the farm since arriving here nearly two months ago. It felt strange.

Mom was chirpy and singing one of her favourite songs as we drove along and it reminded me of the day we went together to buy my school uniform. She was singing then too. That was when I was small. But I somehow felt reluctant to join in with her singing this time so I just smiled at her.

I don't think that she was used to driving on gravel roads much because we were weaving from side to side quite a lot. We were coming around quite a sharp bend when she skidded suddenly and drove off the road straight into a tobacco field. We stopped with a shudder.

'Ow!' I rubbed my elbow where it had hit the dashboard with a thump. Mom laughed out loud and started the engine once more and tried to reverse out of the field. But the more she tried the deeper the car sank in the soft ground. Exasperated, she got out of the car to survey the damage and decided that Jennifer and I must walk the rest of the way to the Youngs' farm to get help.

We set off down the road together walking quickly as best we could on the uneven gravel surface. The last of the sun's rays were glinting off the tops of the tobacco leaves in the fields on either side of the road for as far as the eye could see. Daylight was starting to fade and I was beginning to feel a bit nervous as Lexington always told me not to be out after dark because that was when the leopards hunt. Looking apprehensively over my shoulder and flinching at the slightest movement in the big tobacco leaves on either side of the road, I was hoping that it wasn't much further. Towards the end of the long straight road there was a turnoff to the left and it was with relief to see the sign for the Youngs' farm entrance.

Mr Young was very helpful and bundled us into his truck and drove back to where mom was still sitting in the car. After trying for nearly two hours to pull the car out with a rope attached to his truck, Mr Young went back to the farm to fetch the tractor. In no time at all the car was back on the road. Damaged, but not drivable. So we were driven back home by a very kind Mr Young to deliver the news to Uncle Arthur.

He was *not* happy!

It was about a week later that mom told me that we would be leaving the farm and going to live in Salisbury. My heart sank. I felt sick. I *loved* it here! *Loved* it! Yes I know that I wasn't going to school at the time which was partly why I loved it so. But … what about my friend Lexington? What about Caesar? Now I won't get to see the new ridgeback puppy that Uncle Arthur had promised to get!

As always, I had no control over events so it was with a heavy heart that I said goodbye to Lexington and giving Caesar one last big hug, I got into the car. I had said goodbye to Uncle Arthur the night before and he had shaken my hand and reminded me to be good. I felt that I would miss him because he had always been kind to me and he loved to hear stories of what I had been up to on the farm. The drive to Salisbury was very quiet and I got the feeling that Aunt Ida did not want to be Mom's friend because she didn't talk to her at all.

#

Back to the city. Back to all living in one room.

Mom had rented a bachelor flat in the centre of Salisbury across the road from a big park. It was in a block of about eight flats and it had two floors. We were on the ground floor right at the end. The neighbours on the one side of us were quite nice. They were an old couple ... well, I think they were old because they both had grey hair ... and they used to invite me into their flat when I came home from school and they knew that mom was not home yet. I was always starving by that time of the day and they sometimes gave me juice and a couple of chocolate biscuits which I loved.

Our flat was just one room ... well that's what a bachelor flat is, isn't it! ... with a bathroom to one side and a small kitchenette along one wall with a hot plate, small fridge and a place for washing dishes. There was a green Formica table, where I placed my row of precious animals, and two chairs against the opposite wall where we could sit. Apart from three single beds there was also quite a large chest of drawers where all our things would have to be kept and on the top of that there was a television set. Immediately my spirits lifted. Now I could still watch *Bonanza* every afternoon!

Mom had lost herself again. Gone was the dressing up and gaiety. Gone were the pranks and the mischief making. Gone were the smiles. I tried my best to not be a nuisance and stay out of the way but it made my stomach feel fluttery when she was like that and I just wanted my old mom back.

It wasn't long before I was sent to school once again. At this stage I hadn't been to school for about three months so it was a bit of a shock to the system to have to go back. I was sent to Blackiston Primary School which was a mile or two away from the flat. There was a young African lad who worked in the block of flats where we lived and mom arranged for him to take me to school on his bicycle. I would have to sit sideways on the crossbar whilst he sat in the saddle and pedalled. I was so *embarrassed*! Each day I got him to drop me off long before we came to the school so that I could walk the rest of the way. Jennifer went to the high school. I think she was in about standard seven or year nine.

Mom had got herself a job as a receptionist at a doctor's surgery in town. She must have worked all day because she was never at home when I got back from school. There often wasn't anything to eat either other than dry bread. Sometimes Jennifer had money and she would go to the shop and get something to cook before mom came home from work. Mom always brought a bottle of wine home after work and would finish it before supper which often consisted of stew out of a tin with bread. It wasn't very nice.

I had been at school for about a month when mom started to stay at home all day. I was happy because then she would be at home when I got back after school. But she wasn't very talkative and didn't want to do anything with me and kept on telling me to *do something busy*. It made me want to roll my eyes, which I *did*, but I made sure that I turned around first so that she didn't see.

One day I came home from school as usual and climbed the stairs to the flat. The door was half open. I pushed it wide and there were people who I didn't know in the flat. All the furniture was gone. I gasped. There was a man walking off with our TV set. I was just about to run after him when a lady approached me and said,'Hello, you must be Rudi. I'm Jane from the Child Welfare. Your mom is not well so we are taking you to another home where they will look after you while she recovers. Your sister will join you later.'

'But ... but when will she be better?' I stammered my lip trembling

'She needs a long rest. But in the meantime you get to remain at the same school and Mr and Mrs van der Walt will very kindly care for you.'

I was plunged into depression. My world was falling apart once again. I slid down the wall and sat on the floor. I didn't *want* to go to the van der Walts! I didn't *know* them! I put my head on my knees and sobbed and thinking why on earth we couldn't have just stayed on the farm!

I was driven through one of Salisbury's outlying leafy suburbs where all the streets were lined with trees and the wide grass verges were green and well kept. The van der Walts lived in a large four bedroom house in one of the tree lined streets. We were met at the door by a short plump lady with curly brown hair and spectacles, wearing a blue apron that seemed to be covered in flour. There was a big mole on her chin which had a couple of hairs growing out of it and I couldn't stop looking at it.

'Hello Rudi,' she said with a smile, her eyes disappearing behind her chubby cheeks. I looked at her in surprise.

She knew my name! 'I'm Mrs van der Walt but you can call me Aunty Sonja. Come in to your new home.' She led me through to the kitchen where she sat me down at the table and poured a glass of juice from a carton out of the fridge and handed it to me. 'Get that down into you,' she said 'When you are finished I will take you to your room and leave you to unpack your things whilst I chat to Jane.'

'Thank you,' I said not knowing what else to say. After finishing my juice I was taken upstairs to a large airy bedroom with two beds. A battered suitcase was on top of one of the beds together with my school satchel. Once I was left alone I opened the suitcase and started putting the clothes haphazardly onto the shelves in the wardrobe. Jennifer's clothes were all mixed up with mine but I really didn't care. I just couldn't be bothered to sort them. Once the suitcase was empty I closed the lid and clicked the latches down into their holes and put the suitcase under the bed. Sitting on the bed I suddenly remembered my animals. Frantically I ruffled through the clothes on the shelves and took another look inside the suitcase. I realised that they weren't there. They must have been left behind at the flat. I sobbed for my loss. They were the only toys I had.

Aunty Sonja had two children, a boy who was a teenager about Jennifer's age and a girl a couple of years older than me. The girl whose name was Lizette went to the same school as I did although I didn't know her. It wasn't long before Jennifer arrived and I felt a little better. She didn't know anymore than what I did about where our mother was.

Our lives settled into a routine of sorts living with the van der Walts. Aunty Sonja dropped all four of us off at school in the mornings and brought us back home again in the afternoon. She would sit us down at the table in the kitchen and we were given lunch. We were often given toast and tinned spaghetti which I hated, but because I was hungry, I ate it even though I wanted to puke! It put me off spaghetti for life! Well, the tinned kind anyway.

I didn't get on very well with Lizette. She was a pain in the neck and used to tease me *relentlessly!* She would sidle into my bedroom, prod me in the chest and say,

'You are just a skinny orphan'

Not knowing what to say to her as I *was* skinny, I knew that, and I wasn't too sure about the orphan bit, but I just looked at her.

'And you've got curly hair like a girl. Girl's hair. Girl's hair' she would chant loudly in my face when she didn't get a response.

'Go away and leave me alone.' I turned away and went and sat on the bed. Sometimes she had had enough and she left me alone … until the next time. Then she would come up with something else.

I decided to get my revenge. I unscrewed the light bulb from the bedside lamp that was on the table between the two beds and put it to one side. When she came into the room in the afternoon, as she always did, I called her over.

'Put your finger in this hole' I said to her showing her the place where I had unscrewed the bulb from.

'No!'

'Look, I can put my fingers in this hole and nothing happens. Why don't you try it?'

As she put her finger in the hole, I put my hand underneath the table and I switched the lamp on. She screamed loudly with pain as she felt an electric shock shoot through her hand. Aunty Sonja came rushing into the room and I got into big trouble for doing that. I didn't care though. I was secretly *so* pleased with myself because I had taught her a lesson. It didn't worry me that I had hurt her. It wasn't as if I had *scarred* her or anything. I just wished that her hair had gone curly as well! And … she never teased me again. *Result*!

Every so often I would ask about my mother always to be told that she was still not well and I would get to see her at a later stage. One day Aunty Sonja sat me down and told me that they had made arrangements for both Jennifer and I to go back to Margate to live with my father. This really lifted my spirits as I had happy memories about life in Margate. I could maybe see Happy again? And what about my friend Freddy? I could play with him again. Maybe my life was going to be a bit more settled from now on.

CHAPTER SIX

Joan

I had forgotten how busy and crowded Johannesburg was. Exiting Johannesburg railway station after our journey from East London, I was greeted by a mass of bodies lining the pavements around the building. Vendors and informal traders of all descriptions were trying to display their wares, shouting over one another to be heard above the din. The smell was strong and I saw Rudi put his hand over his mouth as we walked along. I hurried them through the throng to the taxi rank where we clambered into the car with relief.

I had made arrangements to stay with Mary Kelly, who had been quite a close friend when I worked at the Rand Club. Not having any children of her own, she readily agreed to look after Jennifer and Rudi during the week whilst I was away working on assignments. This would leave me free to concentrate on my work. I was hugely excited about going back modelling and felt that this was a turning point in my fortunes.

When Fritz had contacted me to offer me a position he had mentioned that it was a mobile modelling job. This meant that I would be out on the road working from Monday to Friday at different locations and then have a break at home over the weekends. The week's assignments and venues were planned and booked well in advance. We would be visiting a different town each day for the five days that we were on the road. Mondays were always the busiest and longest of the week. We would need to leave very early in the morning and drive to the first town on our list so that there was plenty of time to set ourselves up for that day's assignments which were usually scheduled to start at twelve midday. Then after we had finished, which was normally after two in the afternoon, everything would be packed up again and we would head off to the next town on our schedule where we would spend the night. The following days were more leisurely and there was more time to organise ourselves.

But modelling life on the road was tough. Conditions weren't ideal to say the least. The facilities varied from town to town depending on the venue. Our shows were often in large halls or sometimes in hotels, so there would normally be a couple of rooms that we could use to work from, some for our changing area and others for all our equipment and props. The crew would set up a number of large mirrors with surrounding lights, against a wall and folding tables would be placed in front of them so we could sit and have our makeup and hair done. Our garments were hung from racks that were wheeled in and placed in the order in which we would need them. It could be a scramble and quite a challenge to juggle the space sometimes if all five of us models needed to change at the same time. Tempers flared often and there was much backbiting and prima donna moments of which I am not innocent. But everyone knew the part they had to play and it did seem to go quite smoothly in the main.

Travelling on the bus to the next town after a day's work and relaxing with a much needed cigarette between my fingers, I always felt a sense of achievement, and anticipation for the evening ahead. We would arrive at our next destination en masse and all pile out of the vehicles and head into the hotel that we were booked into for the evening. There were fourteen of us in total: Five models, of which I was one, of course. Then there was Fritz who was in charge of everything including the garments. They were his creations after all. There was Jonny and Mick who were the technicians. They sorted out the lights and did most of the heavy work, Dave who was just a dogsbody really, Austin and young Craig who were the photographers, Marco who was in charge of our hair, Charmaine who did our make up and Anna who was in charge of all the clothing accessories and was also the seamstress. She was invaluable let me tell you. What that girl couldn't sew. She was a marvel!

Once I arrived in my room which I normally had to share with one of the other girls, I headed straight to the bathroom and had a long divine drink from the bottle in my bag. Feeling fortified, I checked my appearance in the mirror, touched up my lipstick, then headed down to the hotel lounge where, after freshening up, we would all meet for the evening.

Our first drink ordered, we would then settle in and begin a post mortem of the day's activities. These were usually quite productive gatherings and gave us the opportunity to iron out any problems that we were experiencing and fine tune the following day's run. Sometimes these sessions could be rather lively and would carry on until the early hours on the odd occasion after a gramophone and some records was produced and it turned into a good old bash. It didn't happen all that often though as Fritz could be a bit inflexible when it came to down time telling us that in order to perform well we needed our beauty sleep. He was right of course. It didn't stop me from sometimes drinking late into the night with whoever was willing to keep me company. I'm *sure* he didn't notice. Did he?

I was having fun. I *knew* I would love it. On the whole, although quite trying at times, life on the road was *fun*. Putting behind me all that had happened in the past, I was able to live in the moment, enjoying playful pranks and having a captive audience. I felt young again, valued and important, and I loved being the centre of attention. We seemed to bond very well as a group and there was always much witty banter thrown about amongst us all. I enjoyed the dressing up too of course. Who wouldn't? Fritz's designs were clean and chic and had proven very popular wherever we went. I was the oldest of the models by far, but you would never have guessed as my slim figure and unlined skin belied my age and I knew I looked great.

Yes ok, before you ask! ... I was relying on having the odd mouthful of gin here and there. Well not *relying* exactly. Just one or two sips in the morning to ease me into the day and then perhaps another after lunch. Just a *teeny weeny* bit. It wasn't doing any *harm*. I mean, I was on top form! And I was coping absolutely *fine* with the work and nobody noticed a thing.

One Friday after a long week on the road we headed off for home after a late start to our return journey. It was raining and getting dark and the mood in the coach was buoyant as we all looked forward to our weekend break. All of a sudden I heard a shout from Fritz as he veered to one side to avoid a pedestrian who had staggered drunkenly into the middle of the road. Unfortunately he wasn't quick enough and there was an awful dull thud as the man somersaulted over the bonnet and hit the windscreen in front of me before sliding down the bonnet onto the road. I screamed in fright as the coach came to a shuddering halt. Fritz got out and ran over to the man lying in the middle of the road. But there was nothing that we could have done. I climbed out shakily not really wanting to look to be honest and stood at the side of the road where a crowd had started to gather. We waited about twenty minutes for the police to arrive and Fritz suggested I phone Jack to come and fetch me as he thought that the formalities could take a while. As it turned out, the man had died at the roadside and Fritz had to go to the police station later on that night to fill in some papers.

I walked up the road with a couple of our crew and phoned Jack from a call box to explain what happened. He said he would leave right away but it would take at least three quarters of an hour for him to reach me. Stepping up into the coach to wait, I lit a cigarette with a trembling hand and sank back onto my seat closing my eyes with a sigh. What an end to the week! I fumbled in my handbag for my bottle then remembered that I had finished the last inch this morning. I felt quite weepy. *Honestly*? If only I could have a quick drink. Shaking my head in irritation as the tears ran unbidden down my cheeks all I could think about was to hope that Mary had something to drink when I got home.

It didn't seem long at all when Jack arrived. He walked me to the car and Rudi jumped out and ran and grabbed me around the legs in a tight hug. 'My boy, my boy!' I said stopping to hug him back and kissing the top of his head the tears still coursing down my face and trembling on my jaw as we walked over to the parked car. I will not cry! I will *not*! If I start to cry I might not be able to stop. I swiped at the tears with determined irritation and climbed into the front of the car.

Back at home after a stiff drink ... ok, more than one ... thank goodness, thank *goodness* Mary had some gin, I felt really tired and went to have a lie down. I think it must be the shock. I just felt so shaky and weepy. I'm sure I will feel better in the morning.

I slept really well considering and as it was the weekend I was able to have a little lie in which I felt that I needed. Feeling a lot better I rose and dressed with care as was my habit and decided that I would head to the shops. I needed to get some gin.

Just after I got home from shopping I had a telephone call.

'Fritz! How are you?'

'I'm ok but rather feeling rather shaken still. But I just wanted to tell you that I have decided that the time is right to stop mobile modelling. I am going to concentrate more on design in the future. I have been phoning everyone this morning so I wanted to let you know before you heard it from someone else.'

'What! No, Fritz! You can't be serious!' I exclaimed horrified, sitting down abruptly. 'Why? When things were going so well!'

'I have been thinking about it for some time actually. The schedule is punishing and I just feel it's time for a change. After last night I just don't have the heart to carry on anyway. So the decision was made for me'

'Yes but Fritz, why don't you give it some time? Surely you will feel better after a break perhaps?'

'I had thought of that but like Austin pointed out, he can't hang around waiting for me to make up my mind as he needs the work. So both him and Craig are looking for work elsewhere and I suggest that you do the same. I'm sorry for this Joan.'

'But what am I going to *do*?' I found myself pleading! No! No! *No*! I was flabbergasted!

And furious!

Just when I thought I had found my niche, now *this* happens! Overnight I had lost my job, my income, *myself*!

I replaced the receiver and sat back, thoughts racing in my head. Throughout the weekend I couldn't think straight, I couldn't concentrate, I couldn't focus. My emotions were in a turmoil and I reeled from anger, to despair, to pity and back again. I didn't want to see anybody and I didn't want to talk to anyone. Monday morning came and I didn't even get out of bed. The same on Tuesday and Wednesday until Mary bustled into the room midday Wednesday and handed me a strong cup of tea and insisted that I get dressed and come to the kitchen for something to eat. Which I did. After splashing my face with water and pulling on on an old frock … how I looked at the moment was the least of my worries … made my way to the kitchen.

She was right. After a hearty plate of scrambled eggs and two slices of toast with loads of melted butter, I felt a lot better and my mind wasn't so foggy. I pushed away my plate with a satisfied sigh and lit a cigarette.

'This came for you yesterday,' said Mary handing me a letter. 'I hope it will cheer you up.'

I knew who it was from before I had even opened it as I recognised the writing on the envelope: My stepfather Arthur Shepherd-Cross. At Aunt Rachel's insistence, all those years ago to write to my stepfather, I had built up a reasonable relationship with him over the years even though our correspondence was sporadic. I hadn't seen him since Ian and I had made the trip to Rhodesia early in 1947. I read his letter with interest, a plan starting to form in my mind. Well ... why *not*? I thought. It will be another adventure and I have nothing to lose. I wrote back to him immediately explaining my circumstances and asking if the children and I could come and stay on the farm for a while. I knew that there was plenty of space there as it was a huge house and they had plenty of money too, which helps. With a bit of a spring in my step I went out and posted the reply straight away then sat back to wait.

Although it was only ten days later that the reply arrived, it felt like a long time as my rollercoaster emotions continued to plague me. But I needn't have worried. The expected letter with Arthur's distinctive handwriting landed on the mat one windy morning. I ripped it open with anticipation and let out a satisfied sigh when I read that he was happy to have us stay. Just as well because I was running out of money. Gin was *expensive*!

Once Ian's maintenance arrived I was able to buy train tickets for the three of us. Don't ask me what had happened to all the money that I had earned from modelling! I just don't know what I had spent it on! Admittedly I spent a bit every night at the various hotels that we had stayed at. But surely not *that* much! Oh well it didn't really matter now as I had the tickets and we were off once more.

The train journey was pleasant and uneventful and as before I was able to leave the past in the past and enjoy the present. Well, for the moment anyway. I felt quite buoyant actually and was rather looking forward to relaxing on the farm for a while and enjoying the luxury provided and lavish entertainment that Arthur indulged in. I mean, who wouldn't? It would be nice to be able to sit back and have others run around me for a change.

Rudi was quite perky on the journey. He could be a funny little thing at times. Maybe he was just following my mood, but whatever the reason, we were a cheerful bunch when we arrived at Hartley station after nearly three days travelling.

The heat! I had forgotten about the heat! We emerged from the station building into the stifling midday sun bearing down on our bare heads, the heat shimmering and rising in waves off the iron roof of the trading store on the opposite side of the road. We stood alongside the building on the gravel road that stretched far into the distance and waited for our lift. I lit a cigarette and blew the smoke out into air that was already thick and dust heavy. There was a limp flag hanging forlornly from the railway station roof, not a breath of wind disturbing its folds.

It wasn't long before Arthur arrived in his pride and joy ... .his light blue Cadillac. He had aged over the last thirteen or so years. He was a large man but still tall and thickset, his hairy muscular arms brown from constant exposure to the African sun. His hair was now almost white, his bushy eyebrows matching in colour and he still had a commanding air about him. He got out of the car and in two strides was kissing me on both cheeks and telling me how marvellous I was looking ... he knows how to flatter! He opened the car door for me and I climbed in ready for the next stage of our journey to the farm. The journey took about an hour travelling on gravel roads all the way. I thought that surely a Cadillac was not really suitable for driving on these roads. I never said anything to him of course. We bumped along slowly leaving a trail of dust behind us as far as the eye could see.

'It's really good to see you again Joan,' said Arthur slowing down briefly to offer to light my cigarette. 'I'm sorry it never worked out with Ian, but I'm sure a young lady as attractive as you will soon find someone else.'

I had never told Arthur the real reason why my marriage had broken down and about my affair with Michael, *obviously*! He still believed that Ian had been having the affair. I had told him that I left Margate and had gone to live in Durban and then Johannesburg. I had also led him to believe that my modelling job was based in Johannesburg city centre and was much more glamorous than it actually was. I'm not sure *why*!

'Why, thank you, Arthur. Do you have any neighbours who could fit the bill?' I asked cheekily thinking that I could only ask!

'There are one or two, but they are otherwise occupied and very attached,' he responded with a twinkle.

We soon arrived at the well remembered farmhouse, sitting large in its surrounding lush gardens and trees. Little had changed. A wave of nostalgia brought me up short and I closed my eyes briefly before getting out of the car. Arthur handed over our luggage to two maids who had emerged from the house and heralded us into the cool hallway. The same black and white tiles of my childhood, were still as shiny as ever. It all looked exactly as I remembered and I felt an unaccustomed sense of ... comfort?

Ida was Arthur's wife. She was of German descent but spoke beautiful English. She said she was educated at Cambridge and originally came to Rhodesia when she was involved with malaria research some years ago now. We sat in the lounge with its vast folding doors open onto the verandah with the lovely garden beyond.

'I understand that you have just lost your modelling work, but have you any idea what it is you are going to be doing next?' asked Arthur handing me a cup of tea which I accepted gratefully with a slightly trembling hand. I hadn't had the opportunity to dig into my suitcase for the bottle that I stashed there last night and I was starting to feel a bit shaky.

'I'm really not too sure,' I said slowly trying to sound as if I had given it much consideration. Because I *wasn't* sure. Actually I had not even *thought* about it. I hadn't thought beyond coming to stay on the farm. 'I was just hoping to have a bit of a break for a while really,' I added.

'Well, you take as long as you need. In the meantime make yourself at home. Your bags will be up in your rooms now and I'm sure you and the children will want to freshen up. We normally gather on the verandah at five for drinks before supper so we will see you then.'

Pleased with his response and realising happily that I was not under any pressure to find work, I called the children and we headed up the familiar stairs leading to the bedrooms. Our clothes were already unpacked. I didn't have to do a *thing*. It was like having my own personal maid. I threw myself across the bed and stretched luxuriously. Mmmmm ... I could get used to this!

I sat up suddenly having a brief moment of panic. What had happened to my bottle, or bottles should I say, as I had more than one. A *reserve* stock, so to speak. Just so that I had enough to last me, you understand. *Yes!* There they were! My eyes lit up as I spotted the bottles placed neatly next to a cut glass decanter of whiskey and a pair of glasses grouped together on a tray on top of the chest of drawers. Smiling with relief I had a quick sip sighing contentedly.

Drinks in the evenings was a posh affair, for which we were expected to dress in evening attire, followed by an equally elegant meal in the large dining room. I ran a bath, indulging in the perfumed bubbly water for half an hour and stepping out pink and glowing. The green cocktail dress that I chose to wear was one of my old favourites from Margate days. I hadn't really had the opportunity to wear it much since. Knee length and full skirted showing off my shapely calves and a neckline that draped off my shoulders to perfection. I looked at myself in the mirror and knew that I looked ravishing. With a string of pearls around my neck and earrings to match, I slipped my feet into elegant sandals with diamanté straps and was ready. After a languid mouthful of gin and touching up my lipstick, I made my way downstairs in a flutter of anticipation.

Rudi and Jennifer had discovered the television. They were both in the lounge, Rudi sitting on the floor cross legged in a blue checked shirt that I didn't recognise. Where did he get *that* from I wondered. Studying him a bit closer I noticed that his hair was wetly brushed down to one side, one or two curls escaping untidily around his ears. I felt a pang of guilt. I realised that he had made the effort to bathe and dress as he had been told by Arthur, with no help from me. But I *had* been quite busy getting ready myself. Hadn't I?

Suppressing my guilt, I wandered through the lounge and out through the large open double doors to where I could hear voices coming from the wide wraparound verandah. This side of the house was shaded from the setting sun and it felt pleasantly cool against my exposed skin. There were a number of deep armchairs placed in a semi-circle to one side, their blue and white floral cushions soft and inviting. A tall elderly black man, whose name was Kachin, dressed in a smart white tunic and holding a tray of dripping glasses approached me and with a slight bow offered me a drink. I eagerly accepted and made my way over to where Arthur was standing.

My eye was immediately drawn to his companion, a dark rugged looking man standing with a drink in hand talking to Arthur.

'Joan, don't you look a picture?' Arthur's eyes lit up in appreciation. 'Let me introduce you to our nearest neighbour Charlie Young.'

'Lovely to meet you Charlie.' I looked at him appreciatively. 'Did you have far to come?'

'It's a good fifteen minutes' drive from our place.' I could see him assessing me. 'Arthur mentioned that you are here for a little while. We have the occasional get together over at the farm so we must organise something during your visit.'

My interest was piqued although I wasn't sure who the 'we' was. Was he married? Probably. There was no Mrs Young here that I could see. 'I'd like that' then wanting to find out more about him I said, 'So what exactly do you farm?'

Charlie was the only guest that first evening which I didn't mind as I had him all to myself. He was interesting and entertaining and so *charmingly* funny. I don't think that I have laughed so much in ages. It felt good

and seemed to bring out my playful side and so naturally, I flirted outrageously. Well it was such *fun*!

After moving through into the dining room, a large
light room with a spectacular wooden table running the
length of the room, we were served a first class three-
course meal by two African waiters. The accompanying
wine was ice cold and poured into the very best crystal
glasses. Arthur was a superb host and went out of his way
to make me feel at ease and was able to steer the conversation away from boring subjects like the pros and cons
of stud farming or the best available price for maize, to
around topics that he thought I would find interest in.
The wine flowed freely and by the end of the evening I
was not too sure how much I had consumed. But I think I
managed to behave with reasonable decorum as was expected of me. Except possibly when I was saying goodnight to Charlie and went to kiss him seductively on the
cheek and I stumbled into him. Not on *purpose*. Really!

Each day took on a rhythm of its own, often gov-
erned by my level of consumption the night before. I
would normally rise rather late in the mornings having
overindulged most evenings and I would need the time
to set myself up for the day. Although to be fair, the first
couple of evenings that I was on the farm I was reasonably restrained.

One lunchtime Ida mentioned that she had a doctor's
appointment in Hartley the following day and she wondered if I would like to go with her and have a wander
around the town. I was really pleased as I had run out
of gin and I also needed to buy some personal items. I
didn't have much money left but I was confident that it
would stretch to a couple of bottles of gin. I think it was

the first day since I had been on the farm that I had got out of bed before eleven in the morning.

Ida had her own car ... a small truck. It was a much more suitable vehicle for the rough roads and served as a farm vehicle as well. The journey was pretty bumpy and dusty and as there was no air conditioning in the truck, a hot one as well. Ida parked outside the doctor's surgery and we agreed to meet back there in an hour. I wandered off in search of a bottle store and pharmacy which I found easily enough. Hartley wasn't such a big town in those days. The first thing I bought were two small bottles of gin.

Because they were important.

Actually, I wanted to buy three bottles but I didn't *quite* have enough. I was just a *bit* worried that two wouldn't last me until I could next make it back into town, but in thinking about it, I realised that I wouldn't have any more money until Ian's payment arrived in my account anyway. Nevertheless, I went looking for some nail varnish remover and deodorant which I needed. Walking past a clothing shop next door to the pharmacy, I spotted the most divine dress in the window. It was exquisite! A plum coloured lace creation with thin satin straps and short skirt.

It stopped me in my tracks.

I really needed to try it on.

The bell over the door tinkled as I entered and a dark haired lady looked up from the counter and smiled. 'Can I help you?'

'Yes, please. I am Joan Garden,' I said because I was somebody important even though she didn't know it. 'I would love to try on that dress that is in the window. Would it be my size?'

She walked over to the window 'What size are you, dear?'

'A thirty four.'

'Well, aren't you in luck? This is just the right size for you. Why don't you take it to the alcove over there and try it on?' she said pointing in the direction of a curtained-off area and handing me the dress.

I thanked her, fingering the heavy fabric and walked across to the alcove and drew the curtain closed behind me. Slipping the dress on over my head it fell effortlessly in luxurious folds to my knees. Turning to look at myself in the long mirror I was thrilled with how the dress clung to my figure and seemed to bring out my colouring. It looked absolutely stunning on me and I felt like a million dollars.

My heart sank when I saw the price.

It was expensive!

I didn't have enough money. *Really*! Where does it all *go*!

I sat down heavily on the stool provided in the alcove and turned my bag upside down searching for any loose coins that could have possibly fallen to the bottom. To no avail.

I had to have this dress.

I *had* to!

Taking a deep breath I opened the curtain and knowing that I looked stunning, I walked out into the centre of the shop as if I was modelling.

'Oh my,' said the shop assistant, 'that does look fabulous on you'

'It does, doesn't it? and it's for a very special occasion but,' I let out a long sigh. 'It's *such* a pity. I really don't know what to do. I have just over half of what you need at the moment until I get my cheque next week.' Well, she didn't know that it was actually the week *after* next. I wasn't going to tell her that. She might be put off. 'I am staying with Arthur Shepherd-Cross for a while. I'm sure you know him. I am his stepdaughter,' I said charmingly with a sweet smile.

Her eyes lit up. 'Oh are you Arthur's stepdaughter? Well I think that puts a different light on things. Arthur is very well known around here. I'm sure I can make an arrangement for you to come back next week to pay the balance. That shouldn't be a problem at all.'

Thrilled with myself for being so clever, I paid her all the money that I had in my purse, which was far less than I said I had, but there was nothing I could do about that, and I left the shop with the promise of returning next week to pay what I owed. I walked triumphantly back to the car with my precious purchase hardly able to wait for cocktail hour that evening when I could show off my new dress.

#

Life at the farm was slow and luxurious. I rose late in the morning, although more often than not I barely made it to lunch let alone breakfast. Well, first of all, I needed my beauty sleep. And secondly, I needed time to make myself *presentable*. My standard of perfection can only be reached by putting in the time and here at the farm I had plenty of that.

The sun would already be high in the sky and beating down with intensity when I surfaced. I would wander over to the bottles on top of the chest of drawers and pour myself a small gin and take it to the bathroom. Self indulgence was one of my top priorities. Always at the forefront of my mind. I loved nothing better than a long pampering bath where I would lay back and soak for ages until the water was long cold. Sometimes I woke up with a bit of a throbbing head which was an irritation so I would have another top up ... just to relieve the symptoms really. Climbing out of the bath, I lathered myself all over with perfumed body lotion to keep my skin from becoming dry. Then browsing through the wardrobe I would carefully choose my outfit for the day. You never knew who you might meet and you always need to be prepared. After performing my daily routine of skin care and applying my make up to perfection, I would attend to my hair, check myself in the full length mirror and then make my way downstairs.

On the mornings that I managed to make it to lunch, I would see Rudi and Jennifer at the table for the first time that day. I was often not at my *best* at this time of day you understand, and sometimes the chatter at the table would get to me. Often I would sit and pick at my food not feeling very hungry at all, and answer in monosyllables when spoken to. To be honest lunchtime and dinnertime were the only times that I spent any time in Rudi or Jennifer's company. Admittedly I was not very approachable or enthusiastic at lunch sometimes. Well I was still trying to clear my groggy head a lot of the time and I *know* that I should have been more pleasant as I didn't even see them during the day. I have no idea what either of them did with themselves although I knew that Rudi was out and about on the farm a lot. So I thought they were both obviously busy which was fine by me. At least they were out of my hair!

The afternoons were often spent lazing about, sitting on the verandah reading a magazine with a cigarette in hand, or taking a stroll in the garden in the late afternoon in the long cool shadows cast by the low sun behind the eucalyptus trees. There was a grand piano in the corner of the lounge that Ida loved to play, which she did regularly. I would lay back in one of the hammocks that Kachin had erected and swing from side to side humming along to the sounds of the notes drifting out into the garden. I could hear the gorgeous melodies of *Oklahoma* and *the King and I* and sometimes, a bit of Sinatra thrown in too. It was quite nostalgic.

I could be sitting anywhere in or around the house and I would always be approached by a regal Kachin asking if 'madam would like something to drink'.

I couldn't say no now could I?

I was waited on hand and foot and didn't have to lift a finger.

My stock of two bottles of gin had not lasted very long at all. I could never *understand* how it could be finished so *quickly*! I used to have a couple of drinks when Kachin served me in the afternoons but I knew that I had to be a bit careful. By a bit of luck one day, I came across a cabinet in the dining room with the door standing open displaying bottles of different alcoholic drinks, including gin. So *this* was where the drinks were kept. Now, I mean ... I wasn't thinking of *doing* anything that I shouldn't. It was just that I suddenly saw all these bottles on the shelves and thought that they are not going to miss *one*, now were they? Realising that this was an ideal opportunity as there was no one about, I grabbed a full bottle of gin off the shelf and made my way with hurried steps back to my room, glancing around to make sure I wasn't seen. I have no idea what I would have said if I was discovered!

Giggling to myself with relief, my heart pounding in my chest, I topped up the remaining small gin bottle on the tray and hid what was left in the bottom of my wardrobe.

I had found a source of top up.

A local supplier so to speak.

Ingenious!

Feeling enormously pleased with myself and to celebrate being so creative, I poured myself a sneaky half tumbler of neat gin and brazenly took it out onto the verandah where I sat, a picture of innocence. Just by looking, nobody could tell that I was drinking gin at all. They would think it was a tumbler of water.

It was now over eight weeks since we had packed our bags and left Johannesburg. It seemed like a lifetime ago. Feeling very relaxed and welcomed on the farm I had over time, allowed myself to become rather reckless. What with a couple of glasses of gin before breakfast and another one or two in the afternoons before cocktail hour, I was consuming rather a lot and becoming careless. Twice more over the last ten days I had managed to replenish my own stock of gin by taking a bottle from the cabinet in the dining room. I had noticed lately, that in the afternoons when I was sitting on the verandah, I no longer saw Kachin at all.

There were occasions when both Arthur and Ida were not too pleased with my behaviour, especially when they had guests. But surely they could see that it was just high spirits! Wasn't it? I couldn't help it that I had knocked over a full glass of red wine at the dinner table onto the lap of the wife of the police commissioner. *That* was an accident. The glass just got in the way of my hand when I was talking. And it *was* funny! Although ... come to think of it now ... I think I might have been the only one to laugh at the time. And also, that time when I kept on drinking Bruce Fortescue's wine instead of, ok, as *well* as, my own, and he would look at his glass with such *puzzlement* that I couldn't keep a straight face and laughed so much I couldn't stop! I don't think that was appreciated either. Okay, and I did tell lots of stories and get rather loud at times. But I always thought that I was charming and entertaining.

Arthur clearly did not realise that I had been drinking from before lunchtime most days because he quite happily offered to lend me his car to drive over to the Youngs for cocktails one evening. The Youngs had been fairly regular visitors since my first encounter with Charlie all those weeks ago. I had met his wife who seemed a bit reserved but nice, but it didn't put me off behaving as if she wasn't there and continuing with my crusade to seduce Charlie.

Why you might ask?

I don't know why!

When I have already burnt my fingers in the past!

You would think that I had learned my lesson!

Well, I enjoyed seeing the appreciation light up in his eyes when he greeted me and I just continued to flirt openly with him whenever we met.

It was just something I *did!*

Because I enjoyed it.

I *knew* it was wrong but I did it anyway.

So I was rather surprised to receive the invitation to Charlie's farm for cocktails. But in typical fashion, not wasting too much time on trying to work out the reason why, I rounded up the children instructing them to wash and dress and headed for my room to do the same. Dressing with my usual care in a short light blue dress with cap sleeves, I poured myself a quick inch of gin and swallowed appreciatively, wiping my mouth carefully with a tissue and reapplying my lipstick. Jennifer and Rudi were waiting for me downstairs and we headed off to the car.

It had been a while … many months, possibly a year … .since I had last driven a car. It took some getting used to, especially since this was an automatic and the dust roads were very rough. The front seat was like a long bench and all three of us were sitting in a row. I was in a singing mood. Rudi wasn't singing but just smiling. The sun was shining, I was all dressed up, on my way to a cocktail party, driving a nice car. Life was great!

Coming around a bend, the road just seemed to end suddenly and I drove straight over the edge of the gravel and into a tobacco field. The car came to a shuddering stop. Surrounded by tobacco. I burst out laughing and couldn't stop. I just thought it was so funny. Thrusting the car into reverse, I wound down the window and tried to reverse back out of the field. The car went back about a foot then seemed to sink into the soil. The back wheels just spun around, sand spewing out from under the tyres until eventually I knew that I was thoroughly stuck. I didn't feel like laughing anymore. Climbing out of the car to take a look, my high heels sinking into the sand, I struggled to keep my balance as I hobbled over to the rear. The white wheels were deep in the sand and the sides of the car were on the ground. Exasperated, I told Jennifer and Rudi to walk the rest of the way and ask Mr Young for help. Well … I couldn't possibly walk all the way in these heels now could I?

Clicking my tongue with irritation, I sat back in the driver's seat leaving the door open and lit a cigarette, breathing out a long plume of smoke into the still air. I needed a drink!

It was about half an hour later when I heard the sound of a car coming down the road from the direction of Charlie's farm. Climbing out the car and smoothing my dress down I walked over to the side of the road to meet the car.

'Joan! What has happened here?'

Laughing gaily and scratching my head, I said. 'It must be these gravel roads. I just seemed to lose control somehow. I'm sure you will be able to get her out and back onto the road in no time,' I said flatteringly.

Charlie jumped in behind the wheel and went forwards and backwards for couple of feet for a while but it was apparent that the car was well and truly stuck.

'I'm going to have to go back to the farm and get the tractor,' said Charlie jumping back into his car and heading back up the road.

It was getting dark but felt a lot cooler thank goodness. Both the children were subdued. I was more irritated than anything because it looked as if I was going to miss cocktails this evening.

It wasn't long before Charlie arrived with the tractor: A huge big green John Deere with yellow wheels that were taller than I was. He hooked a chain up underneath the car somewhere and with no effort at all the car was back on the road.

'Oops!' Looking at the side of the car I giggled and hiccuped putting my hand to my mouth. The passenger side was scratched from bonnet to tail and the one side of the car was dragging on the ground.

It was not drivable.

Charlie suggested that he take the three of us back to Arthur's farm and said that he would come back and get the car onto a trailer and discuss with Arthur what to do. I lurched over to Charlie's car and fell heavily into the seat, wondering vaguely what I was going to tell Arthur. But I consoled myself with the knowledge that Arthur would know it was an accident. I must have dozed off because the next minute we were pulling up at the farm. Charlie came inside with us to discuss the damage with Arthur, for which I was grateful as I couldn't seem to remember very *clearly* what had happened. I plonked myself down on the nearest chair and seemed to have difficulty following the conversation somehow. I needed a drink. As soon as I could escape, I went upstairs to my room, walked straight over to the drinks tray, grabbed the recently topped up bottle of gin and drank a couple of mouthfuls straight out of the bottle. I knew that I was delaying the inevitable confrontation with Arthur but my immediate need was more important. Wiping my mouth with the back of my hand with a sigh, I sloshed some gin into a tumbler and taking it across the room, I collapsed into an armchair and drank.

I didn't see Arthur until before dinner the following day. I slept too late to go down to breakfast ... as usual ... and I avoided lunchtime but of course couldn't resist the five o'clock cocktail hour. I was rather hungry to be honest as I hadn't eaten since yesterday. I dressed with my usual care as it did make me feel good and made my way downstairs fortified by a number of my own pre-dinner drinks.

'Ah, there you are,' said Arthur with a slight smile as I walked out onto the verandah. 'I think you and I need to have a talk. Let's go into my study so that we aren't disturbed.' He ushered me through to his office and closed the door firmly behind him, showing me to a seat. He remained standing with his hands behind his back and looked sternly at me. I smiled uncertainly at him.

'This is not easy for me to say, but it needs to be said. You have betrayed my trust Joan and my generosity. And quite frankly I am appalled at your behaviour on three counts. Firstly, there have been a number of bottles of gin that have mysteriously disappeared from the drinks cabinet in the dining room. I wouldn't have given it a thought but the maid stumbled upon some empty bottles under your bed and thought it strange so she reported it to me. Secondly,' holding up a finger to silence me as I was about to interrupt, 'Secondly, I offered the loan of my car to you on trust. You knew that you had been drinking but you were still happy to drive even though you could be putting your children's lives in danger never mind your own!'

'But Arthur, I was feeling absolutely fine to drive'.

'Do you take me for a fool?' He was shouting now. 'You could barely stand when you got home last night let alone drive a car! Charlie had to hold you up and help you walk to the house when he dropped you off yesterday.'

Had he? I don't remember that. I didn't look at him.

149

'And thirdly, there is a certain lady in a dress shop in town who is *still* waiting to be paid for a dress that she allowed you to take home. Again *on trust*.'

Oh yes. I had forgotten about that hadn't I?

'It's time that you started looking for work and it's time those children returned to school. You have been here for almost three months and you have made no attempt to sort yourself out. Well that stops here and now!' He thumped his fist on the desk. Lighting up a cigarette, without offering me one, he continued. 'Now this is what you are going to do. Every day you will look in the newspaper for work as well as a place to stay for the three of you in Salisbury. Once you have found something Ida will happily drive you and the children there.'

I didn't know what to say. He did look rather cross although I couldn't quite see what all the fuss was about! I hadn't been drinking all that *much*! And the damage to the car was not *that* bad. So I thought that maybe in a day or two, Arthur would calm down and this will all blow over. If I really *really* try from *right now*, to cut down on my drinking, I'm sure it will all be okay.

So I just nodded mutely at Arthur. I thought that if I let him see that I was sorry and that I am going to reform, then he will soften.

But things hadn't blown over at all. I had been very, *very* good about cutting down on my consumption and had managed to reduce it to just one (large) gin in the evenings and a glass of wine at the dinner table which was strictly controlled by Arthur anyway. I made sure that there was no supply in my bedroom to tempt me at any time and I think that Kachin must have been told not to serve me alcohol as he always offered me orange or apple juice instead. I had started eating better too and really, I did *feel* better. Healthier.

Two weeks had gone by and unfortunately Arthur did not budge. All my efforts were in vain. I mean, couldn't he *see* that I was trying hard to get myself straightened out? Couldn't he *see* that I was religiously looking every day in the papers like he said I must? Couldn't he see that I was trying to be positive and upbeat and ... and *charming*. Okay, so I was charming mainly in the hope that he would start to waver and perhaps feel that he had been too harsh on me then he would back down and tell me that I was welcome to stay as long as I liked. But all my skilful manipulation came to nothing. Was I losing my *touch*?

I had eventually been able to find a flat in central Salisbury and with Arthur's recommendation, I secured a position as receptionist at a doctor's surgery not too far from the flat. The children were registered at their respective schools, with their uniforms all purchased and labelled. Once again, thanks to Arthur's kind help. I began to feel that he would be happy to be rid of me!

And then we were ready to move off once again.

The journey into Salisbury with Ida in the recently fixed Cadillac was quiet and tense. I even attempted a little light conversation but was met with a rather icy glare. *Honestly*! Anybody would think that I've committed a major crime or something! Like *murder*! It's just *ridiculous*!

Ida hadn't been the ally that I thought she would be during my little crises. She was scathing in her criticism of my behaviour and made no attempt to hide her disdain and contempt, treating me with cold disparagement. I had gone on the charm offensive with her at the outset, thinking that if I could get her on my side then Arthur would surely follow. I had the utmost confidence in my abilities to persuade anyone over to my way of thinking. But it hadn't worked now had it? It had become so bad that when she walked into a room and I was there, she just turned around and walked out again. Stupid bitch! Who did she think she was anyway? She was not my goddam *mother*?

We were dropped off rather unceremoniously, at the side of the road in front of a small block of eight flats in the centre of Salisbury, Ida making a hasty retreat back to the farm without so much as a wave goodbye. Our bachelor flat was on the ground floor of the block but was unfortunately not furnished. Knowing that I needed to organise some furniture rather urgently, I unlocked the door with the key that had been sent to me on the farm two days earlier and we dumped our cases on the floor and headed out to the nearest furniture store.

I managed to get loads of things. Three beds, a table and chairs, a chest of drawers, a hot plate for cooking and a small fridge. Also a couple of plates, cups and bowls and a pot and pan and some utensils. All bought on hire purchase. *So* clever! All I needed to do was to pay a little bit each month and I still had my allowance from Ian in my pocket. Then I had a brainwave. I could *hire* a television. And that's what I did. Feeling awfully pleased with myself, I really felt the need for a drink.

Just in celebration you understand.

But no. *No!*

I must be strong.

I am strong.

I am *strong*! So I resisted the temptation to go out and buy a bottle of wine. I was starting my new job the following day at the doctor's surgery and I wanted to be at my best.

It was nice to start afresh. I sent Rudi to a school which was about one and a half miles up the road and he seemed to settle in well enough. There was a young African boy who was employed as a cleaner at the block of flats where we lived and I persuaded him, for a fee mind, to give Rudi a lift to and from school every day on his bicycle. Rudi looked so comical perched on the crossbar that I couldn't help laughing. I don't think that Rudi was impressed.

The neighbours were nice. There was a retired couple who lived next door who seemed very friendly and helpful and after a time, seemed to have become quite fond of Rudi. They would wave him off to school in the mornings and sometimes invite him to their flat in the afternoons when he got home from school.

Work was quite different to what I was used to in the hotel industry and the surgery was very busy from the moment the doors opened. But I used my charm as always and managed to get through the first couple of days without too much of a hitch. But it *was* stressful.

After my first week at work I thought that I really *deserved* to have a little drink just as a *reward* for my hard work. I hadn't bought any alcohol since we had moved to Salisbury so I had been *really* good.

I would just have the one glass.

No more than one!

I would be strong!

And that would relax me and then I would be able to have another glass tomorrow.

Situated just around the corner from the doctor's surgery there was a large well stocked bottle store. How convenient is *that*! At the end of my first week at work I popped in on my way home and bought a bottle of wine. Gin was expensive but wine was just as good. As I didn't have to use cash to buy my furniture, I still had quite a lot of my allowance left. So feeling in a celebratory mood, I went to the butcher and bought three fillet steaks. Yes I know it was extravagant but it was just for a treat you understand. I mean I'd *earned* it hadn't I? And in any case, fillet steak would go *so* well with the wine.

I hurried home with my purchases in a fever of anticipation hardly able to wait until I was in the door before the lid was off the bottle and I had poured my first glass.

Bliss!

Ok … so I was halfway through my *second* glass before I knew it. I couldn't *understand* how I had finished the first one so quickly. But never mind. Deciding that I needed to slow down a bit, I cooked our meal whilst sipping the rest of the glass.

Fortunately, the following day was a Saturday and I didn't have to go to work. With a pounding head I told Jennifer to take Rudi out to the park across the road and I spent the rest of the morning in bed surfacing some time around midday. Searching for something to drink I discovered the empty wine bottle on the floor in the kitchen area. Had I really finished the whole bottle? *Blast*! I don't remember drinking more than two glasses. Exasperated, I glugged down a couple of glasses of water and decided that as it was the weekend, I would buy myself another bottle. But this one I would take more slowly and *definitely* make it last until well into next week. Realising that I had to hurry as the bottle stores closed on Saturdays at one for the rest of the weekend, I got myself dressed and out the door in record time.

Deciding that I was going to buy some more fillet steak again for our meal that evening, I headed off to the butcher. Well, I might as *well* as we had all *enjoyed* it so much and we had to eat *something.* Making my way home through the park I spotted Rudi on the swings and I joined Jennifer who was sitting on a bench nearby in the shade of a large flowering tree. She was fifteen going on sixteen and becoming a pretty young lady. She seemed to have grown up overnight. I realised that I hadn't spent much time with her at all over the last year or more really. She was a bit sullen and not wanting to talk so after a while I left and went back to the flat.

This time I was a bit more restrained. Actually I felt rather *proud* of myself. I only opened the bottle of wine at five o'clock and poured myself a generous tumbler full. I didn't have any wine glasses so a tumbler was just as good. And I made it last until dinnertime when we sat down to eat our gorgeous steak and I had a *teeny weeny* top up. I successfully managed to control myself that evening and there was more than half left in the bottle for Sunday.

It became a bit of a pattern really. Every day after work I would go to the bottle store and buy a bottle of wine.

Simply because I wanted to and I *could* control it.

I had proved it!

Hadn't I?

Sometimes I downed a glass or two first and then made us all something to eat and sat back and enjoyed the rest of the bottle before bed. Sometimes, or perhaps if I'm honest, most times, I had finished the bottle even before I had cooked dinner. Then I would ask Jennifer to open a tin of something for the two of them. I wasn't hungry by that stage.

I can't remember *when* I decided that I might as well buy a small bottle of gin to keep in my bag so that I could have a top up at work. Just to maintain the glow you understand. But that is what I did. And it worked really well. For a while. It took the edge off things and I glided through my work days so easily. Although sometimes I was a little clumsy and seemed to bump into things and drop the odd file here and there. But I always covered up pretty well I thought. And sometimes I found it difficult to get my words out correctly even after trying several times. I thought it was rather funny.

Although I didn't think it was very funny on the day that I arrived at work and I was called into the office and told that I had lost my job! My heart sank! I thought I had been crafty in covering my activities! Making my way home after I left work for the final time, I called in at the bottle store once more for supplies. As it was only midday, I went and sat on a bench in the park away from the main walkway and away from passers by and I drank from the bottle that I had just bought. The surrounding beauty of the lush gardens was lost on me. With my mind once more finding solace in a fog of drink I began to feel better. It was a lousy job anyway, I thought belligerently, wiping my mouth with the back of my hand. They had it in for me from the start. I'll easily get another job!

Making my way home sometime later I stumbled up the couple of steps to the flat almost knocking into the dear couple that lived next door. I greeted them and laughed gaily whilst I fiddled with the front door trying to get the key in the lock. After dropping the keys, twice actually, and almost falling on my face whilst trying to pick them up, which I thought was *hilarious*, I eventually managed to get the door open. I almost lost my footing as the door swung open into the flat, dragging me with it. I went straight and lay down on the bed and passed out.

The following day as consciousness gradually returned, my first thought was that I needed something to drink. I sat up shakily and looked around. There was no sign of either Jennifer or Rudi and I wondered what the time was. Then I realised that I wouldn't be going to work now would I? Searching in the kitchen area I came across a small amount of leftover gin in a bottle on the drainer. Slugging it back in one gulp I lit a cigarette and mulled over my options. I just felt too *tired* to do anything about finding another job today. It was just so much *effort*! I really need a drink just to perk me up. Then I will start looking properly tomorrow. *Honestly*!

With this thought in mind, I got dressed and headed out to the bottle store. This time I came straight home and sat and drank steadily for most of the day until the bottle was empty. I did this every day for the following week or two I think. I don't remember seeing the children much at all actually. I think I might have been sleeping by the time they came home. I do remember going to the supermarket once and buying some food. It's all a bit hazy somehow.

There was also a time when there was a lady in the flat and she was talking to me but I couldn't make sense of what she was saying. What was she *doing* in my flat anyway! I wish that these people would just leave me alone. I want to sleep.

CHAPTER SEVEN

Rudi

It was the first time that I had been so close to an aeroplane. Any plane. Let alone a huge Viscount. It was a silver monstrosity of a thing with two huge propellers on each side and quite a pointy nose. The tension in my tummy eased a bit as I stared at it in awe and I couldn't imagine that this huge piece of metal could lift itself into the air. I scrambled up the steps, Jennifer behind me, and stepping into the aircraft I was shown to my seat by a lovely lady in a bright red suit and pillar box hat, smelling of lilies. She gave me a kind smile.

'You must be Rudi and Jennifer. I'm Mandy,' she said, 'I'm here to look after you during your flight'

With Mandy's help I buckled myself into my seat and settled in whilst the aeroplane taxied noisily onto the runway ready for takeoff. I took a deep breath and sighed.

I would *not* think of my mother.

I would *not* think of the horrible few weeks that I had spent with Aunt Sonja and that horrid brat Lizette.

And I would *not* think of that stupid school that I was made to go to *or* that stupid bicycle ride every day.

My eyes filled with tears and I turned to look out of the window. As the plane left the ground, I felt a small flutter of excitement as the runway and airport buildings became smaller and smaller like toys and in no time at all we were in the air and flying away over the city. I breathed in again and watched how the glass in the window misted up with my warm exhale. It reminded me of the mist at the farm in the early mornings when I went to watch the cows being milked. I was filled with a sudden longing to be back there and I rested my head back wearily on the seat and squeezed my eyes shut.

I must have dozed off. Mandy was standing over me with a tray in the one hand and a bottle of orange juice in the other. I accepted the tray with anticipation, running my tongue over my lips and realising suddenly how hungry I was. I hadn't eaten much of the porridge oats that Aunt Sonja had given me this morning. My tummy had felt funny. But I tucked in now with gusto.

I was told by Jane, who had arrived at Aunt Sonja's house this morning to pick me up, that I would not be going to live with my father after all. Instead I would be going to stay with Uncle Ronnie and Aunty Pat who had been friends of both of my parents for a number of years. I didn't really know them well but I quite liked Uncle Ronnie. He had always been kind to me. I do remember he came to visit when we lived in East London and he gave me some pocket money.

I was kind of looking forward to going to live with Uncle Ronnie actually. Just a little bit. I hoped that I would enjoy it there and I also hoped that I would be able to stay a while like the Child Welfare lady said.

'Now then young man,' said Jane. 'We are going to send you to stay with your Uncle Ronnie and Aunty Pat in Margate for a while so that your mom has time to get better. You will go to school there and I'm sure that you will settle in just fine'

I wasn't entirely sure that I could believe her.

#

We were met by my father at Durban airport and he drove us down to Margate. His car was familiar. I think it was the same Opel Kapitan that he used to drive when we lived in the Ramsgate house. Jennifer was going to stay with him at the hotel he was managing in Margate and I would be collected by Uncle Ronnie from there when we arrived. My dad was the same as I remembered him and although I did a lot of the talking in the car, well I was a *bit* unsettled, the two-hour journey seemed to fly by. Once we arrived in Margate I jumped out of the car and said eagerly,

'Please can I go say hello to Freddy and to see Happy before Uncle Ronnie arrives'. Happy and my friend Freddy lived a couple of houses up from where my dad's hotel was. Having being given 'the nod' I set off running excitedly down the road to Freddy's house. I arrived at the house out of breath but feeling comforted with the familiar surroundings, and knocked on the door.

'Rudi! Where did you come from?' A surprised Freddy opened the door and let me in.

'I've come back to stay with my Uncle Ronnie and I'm also going to go back to Margate school. Where's Happy?' all in one breath.

'Hello, young Rudi. My how you have grown! I believe that we need to welcome you back to Margate. I know Freddy is going to be very happy as he has missed you so.'

Freddy's mother, who I knew as Aunty Blanche, walked into the hallway and herded us into the kitchen where she poured some juice into two small glasses and gestured for me to sit down.

'Mom! Did you know that Rudi was coming back?'

'We kept it a secret from you Freddy so that it would be a surprise,' she said with a twinkle. Freddy gave a loud whoop and chanted 'Rudi's back, Rudi's back' and started prancing around the kitchen and punching the air with excitement.

It made me feel special.

As if I *mattered*.

And my eyes welled up.

Trying to cover up my emotions I jumped up and whooped around the kitchen after Freddy. Then I remembered about Happy.

'Where's Happy?'

Freddy came to a standstill and looked at me.

I looked from Freddy to his mother, heart hammering. Both were looking at me.

'Oh Rudi, I'm afraid that Happy ran into the road and was hit by a passing truck six months ago. He was so badly injured that the vet said it was best to put him to sleep.' Freddy's mom came over to me. Shaking my head, I backed away and looked at her not believing what I was hearing. I put my hands over my ears as if that would blot out what I had heard. 'Freddy was with him and stroked his ears in the way he enjoyed. I am so sorry to have to tell you this as I know how much you loved him,' she said putting her arm around me whilst I cried for my furry friend, with Freddy not knowing what to do, but looking on awkwardly. After being comforted for a while by Aunty Blanche I knew it was time that I went back to my dad to wait for my lift. Promising to see Freddy at school, I said my goodbyes and walked back up the road to the hotel. Fresh tears blurred the way.

\#

Uncle Ronnie and Aunty Pat had already arrived and were standing waiting to collect me outside my Dad's hotel. I was still upset about Happy that I had forgotten to feel apprehensive but all the same my tummy did do one or two cartwheels. But I needn't have worried. After settling me in the car they drove the short distance to their big house on the hill, Aunty Pat chatting to me all the time and asking me questions about the things that I did and didn't like and what I enjoyed doing.

'Well, I don't like greens,' I said at once just so that they knew and there wouldn't be any confusion later on.

Aunty Pat chuckled and her chins wobbled which made me laugh too. I felt lighter somehow.

Uncle Ronnie and Aunty Pat lived in a large rambling house, up on the hill on the outskirts of Margate. Uncle Ronnie ran a large successful construction company and I think Aunty Pat used to help him in the office a couple of days a week. They had two teenage daughters Sheila and Lorraine.

Their home was a reflection of their success. With four large bedrooms, two airy reception rooms and a study leading onto an open plan kitchen and diner, it was spacious and welcoming. There was a shiny polished passage that ran through the middle of the house and you could stand at the front door and see right down to the back door and all the rooms fed off from the passage like branches of a tree. I would spend many an hour in the future sliding up and down that passage in my socks.

The house was set in a large piece of ground that was grassed and surrounded by many trees and enclosed by a green diamond mesh fence which kept the dogs from running out into the street. The road leading up to the gate was gravel and it was maintained by the local council who would send out their big yellow grader every so often to smooth out the ridges and ditches that formed as a result of the run off from the heavy rain that was common in the area. On the one side of the large property Uncle Ronnie had built about ten huge aviaries which were his pride and joy and housed all sorts of exotic birds.

Pulling up outside the house, I saw a tall girl with long brown hair come running out to the car.

'You must be Rudi. I'm Sheila. And this is Peanut and that one is Max.' As a small fox terrier and a large brown dog noisily clustered around, tails wagging furiously. 'Come, let me show you to your bedroom', she said grabbing my suitcase and pushing the two noisy dogs out of her way.

My sadness momentarily forgotten, my eyes lit up. I would have some doggy friends here too. Giving them each a pat I followed Sheila into the house.

I had a bedroom all to myself. This just gets better and better. As with all the rooms in Uncle Ronnie's house, my bedroom was large and airy with the same shiny wooden floor as the passageway. There were two beds, one against each wall and they had matching bedspreads with animals on. I thought they were the nicest that I had ever seen. There was a small desk in between the beds which served as a table and I even had my own bedside lamp which I had to switch on just to make sure that it worked, thoughts of horrid Lizette popping unbidden into my head. It made me smile. On the one bed was a small package with my name on. Sitting down carefully I reached for it and turned it over, looking at it puzzled.

'Go on! Open it! That's for you,' said Sheila leaning against the doorframe looking on.

'But it's not my birthday!'

'I know silly! But it's for you anyway.'

I pulled off the wrapping eagerly and uncovered a treasure trove. On the top was a book. My worst nightmare. My anxiety went up a notch. As I didn't want to seem ungrateful, I opened it and glanced at the first couple of pages then put it carefully to one side. Then there was a colouring in book and a box of crayons which I thought would be fun. There was a new pair of pyjamas, with stripes and buttons down the front which I liked and also a new hairbrush, a toothbrush, and a sponge. But best of all there was a small dinky car. I think it was called a VW.

'Are these all for me?' I asked incredulously. I had never had so many things given to me before and I looked at them in wonder.

'Yes they are all yours'

'Forever?'

'Yes, forever,' Sheila finished with a laugh.

I put the reading book and colouring book and crayons carefully on the table together with the car and sat back. It gave me a thrill just to look at these treasures. But I had other things on my mind. 'Can I go and play with the dogs?' I asked Sheila.

'Of course you can. Just be careful of Max as he can be boisterous and you don't want him to knock you over,' she responded.

'I had two ridgebacks on the farm and the one was killed by a black mamba' I told her suddenly feeling tearful with thoughts of Happy flooding my mind.

'Oh that is so sad.' Sheila came and sat on the bed and pulled me to her as the tears poured down my face, giving me a squeeze. 'Let's go and get some juice and then we will go and find the dogs'.

After drinking some orange juice, I spent the rest of my first day in my new home, exploring every inch with the two dogs. Peanut was so inquisitive and busy and used to love me to throw his ball for him while Max just ambled along, tongue hanging out sniffing here and there. I liked to run in the front door, down the passage out the back door and back around the house to the front door and try and hide from them. They were always too fast of course but we did have fun. The dogs were filling a hollow.

Dinner was a noisy family affair eaten at the large oak table in the dining room which I would come to look forward to every day. The family sat and chatted about all sorts of things and there was an easy and comfortable atmosphere. There was always lots of banter and joking between Sheila and Lorraine and Aunty Pat joined in sometimes too. I was starting to feel a bit more relaxed in my new surroundings and although I did have a little cry that night in bed, it was mainly because I was sad about Happy.

#

Life with Uncle Ronnie and Aunty Pat soon settled into a pattern of sorts. The routine of everyday life was settling and made me feel secure. I really felt part of the family. It was a nice feeling. To belong.

I was sent back to Margate school. The dreaded word 'school' felt like a *swear* word! *Truly*! I had already missed a total of six months of schooling by then, so I *was* finding it very hard to catch up, especially English and arithmetic. Uncle Ronnie very kindly organised for me to take some extra lessons after school. I didn't think that they made much difference. What I *did* enjoy was the woodwork lessons and art classes where we made things out of papier mache. I loved working with the tools. But that's partly because I didn't have to read.

After school every day I walked home alone along the back road. There was always fresh bread and a coke waiting for me in the kitchen. I would eagerly take my sandwich and coke and go out and sit in one of the aviaries and just watch and listen to the birds whilst eating. I would give them some crumbs and eventually some of them became so tame that they would sit on my head and hand and wait for the crumbs. I used to love it. I was supposed to do my homework in the afternoons too but most of the time I didn't. When Aunty Pat asked me, I told a white lie and said I had done it. Well … it was *easier* to tell a lie than to do the work. It was only a *white* lie in any case.

The teachers at Margate school had decided to raise money to build a swimming pool in the school grounds. At the moment, if we wanted to swim we had to go down to the tidal pool on the beach which wasn't always practical apparently. You can imagine hundreds of kids running amok on the beach and some of them not knowing how to swim. It would be a shambles. We were asked to collect as many bricks as we could and place them outside our classrooms. Whichever class had collected the most bricks would get a packet of sweets and chocolates to share. My eyes lit up. Uncle Ronnie was a builder so I'm sure that he must have lots of bricks lying around I thought. So over the weekends, Freddy and another boy called Butch who I had become friends with since my return to school, borrowed two wheelbarrows and set off for Uncle Ronnie's builders yard. There we loaded each wheelbarrow with about ten bricks as they were *heavy* and wheeled them the mile to the school. Once there, we stacked them in a pile outside our classroom. We did this for three weekends in a row until there was no more room to stack the bricks. And of course our class won mostly because of Uncle Ronnie's bricks. It was the first time that I had ever won anything. Even although it wasn't actually for me but for the whole class, it felt really good.

Sometimes over the weekends, Uncle Ronnie would ask me to go with him into the bush to collect food for his birds in the aviaries. He gave me my very own penknife with a red handle which I could use to cut long grass for the birds. He said that penknives were only for special boys. I felt enormously important. We drove out in the truck to some bushveld not too far from the house. Parking on the side of the gravel road, we got out of the truck and I followed Uncle Ronnie across the brown grass. He said that we were looking for big dry mounds of red earth, which were ant nests. When we came across one Uncle Ronnie would cut out a large piece, all the ants scrambling around the honeycomb inside, and carry it to the truck placing it in the open back. We normally collected two lots of ant nests as well as an assortment of different grasses which I cut very carefully with my penknife. Once all was loaded into the back of the truck we would head off home. Back at the aviaries, Uncle Ronnie said that I was in charge of giving the birds the different grasses whilst he placed the ant nests in the bottom of the cages. The birds would flock there to feed. They loved it.

I felt very proud to be Uncle Ronnie's' helper although I did start to feel a *little* bit bad about the white lie that I told Aunty Pat about my homework.

Sheila and Lorraine had become my two mini mothers. Sheila especially was the bossy one, but I think she just pretended to be fierce because she always had a smile on her face. She would often grab me and plonk me in the bath at night, saying sternly,

'Come along ragamuffin, in you get! Scrub those beastly little fingers and toes. I don't want to see any black fingernails otherwise there will be no stories for you tonight.' She made sure that there was plenty of Shipmate poured into the running water so that huge clouds of soapy bubbles billowed out, almost as high as the bath.

'And if you don't clean behind your ears every day then potatoes will grow there and then we will never be able to get rid of them.' She continued with a gleam in her eye. I pulled a face because I was sure she was bluffing.

'Don't pull your face like that!' She gasped, 'if the wind changes it will stay like that forever!'

I snorted. But I stopped pulling a face. Just in case.

After bath time I would go to Sheila's room and climb onto her bed and she would always read me stories. Then because she had a radio in her bedroom, at 7.15 every night on the dot, the three of us would sit on Sheila's bed and listen to a radio programme called *Mark Saxon*. It was a series and Sheila said that it often ended each day on a *cliffhanger*. Which I thought was funny as there were no cliffs in the story. But she explained that it meant *a scary ending that left you guessing* and not somebody hanging from a cliff. That was a relief! It became my favourite program.

One night I woke up with a fright, my heart hammering in my chest, a scream on my lips. I had been dreaming about monsters chasing me and I felt scared. Glancing quickly at the dark corners of my bedroom to make sure that there were no monsters lurking there, I leapt out of bed, grabbed my pillow and ran as fast as I could, down the dark passage to Sheila's room. I tiptoed over to her bed, lifted the covers and crept into bed behind her and snuggled down feeling a bit safer.

'What are you doing here ragamuffin?' Sheila's voice greeted me the following morning, 'Have you had another bad dream? I think it's watching too much *Mark Saxon*' And she would try to tickle me and chase me back to my room as I protested loudly.

Freddy and I once more spent a lot of time together especially over the weekends. Freddy's dad used to operate the projector at the drive-in. A projector, I was told was a machine that was used to show movies and a drive-in was a place where you went to see the movie. But the best bit was that everybody watched the movie whilst sitting in their cars. You drive your car and park in rows in front of a big white screen that was erected at one end of a large tarred area. Each car would have its own speaker which was attached to a pole in the ground and the speaker would hook onto the car window and once it was switched on then you could hear the movie. It was so exciting as I had never been to a drive-in before. Whilst his dad operated the projector, Freddy and I would settle into the back of the car with some sweets and packets of chips and have a ball.

I had been living with Uncle Ronnie and Aunty Pat for almost six months. It was December and the school year was at an end with six weeks of holiday stretching out before me. Thank *goodness*! Playing with the dogs one day in the back garden beside the wooden gate that lead to the lane, I heard Uncle Ronnie calling me. I ran over to him and saw that he had a piece of paper in his hand. It was my school report.

'I've got your report here from your teachers and you have come thirty out of thirty!' Uncle Ronnie said

'Have I? That's quite good then isn't it?'

'Well not exactly. Your teacher has said that it is best for you if you repeat standard two again next year'.

'Oh! But what about Freddy then? Can he still be my friend? And Butch?' My chin was starting to wobble

'Of course he can. You will just be in a different class to Freddy and Butch but you can still see them at break time and after school.'

I was temporarily mollified, taking comfort from what he said. So I would have to repeat year four of school! It didn't worry me particularly. I just hoped that the work became easier to manage.

#

My first Christmas with the Bakers was the best time that I had had in my life. They were a large family with Auntys, Uncles and cousins making the journey down to Natal from the Transvaal to spend Christmas with Uncle Ronnie. There was a *huge* Christmas tree in the lounge that reached all the way to the ceiling and the pine leaves gave off such a lovely smell. I'd never had a Christmas tree before so this felt like … well, *Christmas!* I excitedly helped Sheila and Lorraine decorate the tree with bright baubles, tinsel and lights. It was *dripping* with tinsel. And when it got dark and we switched the lights on, I couldn't stop looking at it.

I had been given ten cents a week as pocket money since I had been staying with Uncle Ronnie which I mostly used to buy sweets. But I had managed to save some and with two weeks to go until Christmas that would give me an extra twenty cents. I planned to use this money to buy the family some small gifts to put under the tree. I went into town to the chemist which was not too far to walk and very safe those days. I was almost ten now anyway. There were lots of fancy perfumes and soaps and things on display and I took a long time to select what I wanted to buy. So in the end I bought a bar of Lifebuoy soap for Uncle Ronnie and bath oil for Aunty Pat and the girls. Taking my precious purchases home I got some paper from Sheila and wrapped everything up and put them carefully under the tree.

On Christmas Eve I struggled to get to sleep and lay awake for ages and ages, hugging myself with excitement, not being able to stop thinking about what lay under the tree and picturing everyone's faces the next day when they opened their gifts.

I was woken up by Sheila shaking me. 'Come on sleepyhead! Don't you want your presents?' Leaping out of bed and realising that I must have fallen asleep eventually, I ran bare foot to the lounge and was greeted by cries of 'Happy Christmas, Rudi' from everyone in the room. I couldn't believe that I was the last one to get up! I dived under the tree retrieving the presents that I had wrapped the previous day, proudly read the name and handed them out, watching with pleasure as they were unwrapped and admired. Then I was handed a long package with a bulge at one end all wrapped up in bright red and green paper. I put it on the floor and pulled the paper off to reveal a fishing rod and reel.

I wanted to cry.

And laugh.

I couldn't believe that this was for me. But it was. I threw my arms around Aunty Pat and Uncle Ronnie in a big hug. This was my best Christmas *ever*!

Amidst all this excitement I didn't once think of my mother. The time spent with the Baker family was so enormously different to what I had been used to at home in the past. There was always something going on, rowdy squabbles between Sheila and Lorraine, noisy family chatter in the evenings when we used to play board games or cards, the radio always blaring with the latest songs. I felt as if they cared about me. As if I belonged. These new experiences filled my head and there was just no *space* left for thoughts of her to enter. I was able to block her out. It made me feel unhappy to think of her anyway. I had asked Aunty Pat about my mother once a couple of weeks after I started living with them and she said that mom was still not well.

My dad came to visit me once. He was married to another lady who had children too and when he came to visit he brought his two stepsons with him. They were both older than me and I didn't like them so I spent the afternoon in my bedroom and only came out once they had gone. I also was a bit frightened that he had come to take me away from Uncle Ronnie. My dad came into my room and spoke to me for a while and said that he was now running the Palm Beach Hotel in Margate and that my sister went to boarding school and was home at the weekends.

The next time I saw my dad was the following year 1963 after I had started back at school in year four or standard two. I was ten years old by his stage. Uncle Ronnie was building the border post at Sani Pass between Lesotho and South Africa and he asked me if I would like to go with him when he went out there to check on the builders. I jumped at the chance and excitedly packed a small bag for an overnight stay. My dad was now the manager at the Sani Pass Hotel which was situated at the bottom of the pass. The plan was to spend the evening at the hotel and then make our way up Sani Pass to the border post the following day. Uncle Ronnie, my dad and I all had supper together that evening and although I chatted quite a bit about school and my fishing rod and Freddy, I felt that my dad was a stranger to me.

After spending the night at the hotel, we headed out early the next morning. We had to drive a 4x4 up the steep winding gravel road that led to the top of the pass. The road was very narrow in places with steep drops to the one side and when I looked back down, I could see the road winding back on itself, snakelike, down to the bottom. Scattered in the valley down below were the remains of a couple of car skeletons which had obviously gone over the edge of the road sometime back. We had to drive very slowly and carefully so that we didn't go the same way. It was awesome.

The view from the top of the pass over Natal was beautiful. We were so high that it seemed that we were in the clouds. Well we could have been except the sun was shining that day. There was a large wooden building which was a small pub and it had a bar and a big lounge with a huge fireplace for much needed warmth in the winter. The builders all slept in caravans and the lady who ran the pub cooked their meals every day. It could get very cold with lots of snow and normally the pass was closed during the winter months as it became too dangerous to use.

After spending some time exploring the area Uncle Ronnie called me over and asked me if I would like to stay and he would come back in a week to fetch me. I was delighted. The lady whose name was Sue, said she would see that I was looked after. I shared a caravan with one of the builders whose name was Billy. He snored rather loudly at night and kept me awake a bit but I didn't tell him. But he did teach me how to fish in the small dam that I found not far from the building site. It was so quiet there. It reminded me of the farm. He also showed me how to use a pellet gun and how to chop wood. I thought I was very grown up. So I spent my time either fishing, shooting, chopping wood or just exploring. I felt literally on top of the world. The week sped by and it seemed no time at all when Uncle Ronnie was back to fetch me.

By this time I had been living with Uncle Ronnie and Aunty Pat for over a year. I was very settled in my life and felt valued and happy. School was always an issue but I decided that I couldn't fight it so I just did what I could manage.

'Rudi, I have some news of your mom,' Uncle Ronnie said sitting down next to me one day. 'She is now feeling much better and living in Durban and she would like you to go and stay with her for the weekend. How do you feel about that?'

I looked at him trying to find the right words. I wasn't sure how I felt although it did unsettle me.

'You don't have to go if you don't want to,' he said interrupting my thoughts.

'No, it's fine. I will go and see her,' I agreed hesitantly, because I *did* want to see her but I was afraid at the same time. I didn't want anything interfering with my new life with Uncle Ronnie. But I hadn't seen or heard from her for over a year. She was apparently working in a hotel in Durban and Uncle Ronnie would drive me there on the Friday and collect me again on the Monday which was a public holiday.

Uncle Ronnie fetched me from school on the Friday afternoon and we drove straight through to Durban to the hotel where my mother was working. It was with some trepidation that I climbed out of the car and turned towards Uncle Ronnie to say my goodbyes.

'Here is some pocket money for you to spend on whatever you like whilst you are here and this' handing me a piece of paper 'is my telephone number just in case you need me. Keep it in a safe place.' I nodded, gave him a hug and went to greet my mother.

She was looking well and happy and greeted me with a big smile. I gave her a big hug. I used to love it when she was happy as it made me happy too. But she seemed a bit like a stranger to me now and I felt a bit uncomfortable. Her room in the hotel had two beds and I was to share it with her. It brought back some unwelcome memories of other hotel rooms from the past but I just pushed them to one side. She smoked a lot which was irritating and it made me cough. She also worked a lot and I didn't see much of her at all. She had a friend called Dot who also worked in the hotel and she had a room next door to ours. After work on the Saturday mom said she was going to see Dot next door. Sitting on my bed wondering what I could do with myself I heard my mom's voice and my name mentioned. Getting up from my bed, I walked towards the half open door and listened.

'Well Dot, it's the only thing I can do. If I run away with him to East London then all my problems will be solved. They wouldn't know where I am!'

I froze. My mind was in a whirl. I don't want to go to East London! Then remembering the telephone number in my pocket, I bolted downstairs to the call box and dialled the number on the piece of paper.

'Uncle Ronnie, Uncle Ronnie, I overheard mom tell Dot that she is going to run away with me to East London. I'm scared and I don't want to go.' It all came out in a rush when he answered the phone.

'Rudi, try not to worry. I will come tomorrow and pick you up'

'Are you sure?'

'I'm absolutely sure. You sit tight and I will see you tomorrow.'

I went back to the room feeling a lot better. When my mother returned I didn't tell her that I had overheard her conversation and I also didn't tell her that I was being picked up the following day either. I did tell her that I wanted to go back home. It was so nice to call Uncle Ronnie's house, *home*. So I repeated it softly to myself.

The following day mom wanted to take me to the funfair but I said that I didn't want to go. I was afraid that Uncle Ronnie would arrive whilst I was gone, although she did not know that. But it wasn't long and I heard his voice downstairs and I grabbed my bag and ran down with relief to meet him. He wrapped me in a big hug

'You are safe with me Rudi,' he said. I nodded feeling a bit like a traitor when I saw my mom walking into the room. We said a very awkward goodbye.

It was about four or five months later when Uncle Ronnie spoke of my mother again.

'Your mom has moved from Durban to Paddock which is a town about half an hour's drive from Margate. She is managing a guest farm there and would like you to spend the weekend with her.'

I felt a bit uneasy but thinking quickly I asked, 'Can I bring a friend?' Maybe if I took a friend, she wouldn't be able to run away with me.

'I am sure she will be happy with that,' said Uncle Ronnie. 'I know she really wants to see you'

So it was arranged with my friend Butch Webster's parents that he could come with me to Paddock for the weekend. Uncle Ronnie drove us up to Paddock and turned into a long gravel drive that led to the old farmhouse which served as the main building for the Guest Farm. It looked very pretty nestled in the hills and was surrounded by lots of pine trees. There were a couple of tennis courts, bowling greens and a large swimming pool which seemed to be home to a pair of geese. The long low buildings were covered in bright red bougainvillea that spilled over onto the ground. The double glass doors opened and my mother came out onto the drive to meet us.

She was really looking well and greeted us with a welcoming smile and happily showed us around. Mom cooked us a meal that evening and we played cards together afterwards which was such fun. She was in a really good mood. Almost like she used to be.

Butch and I shared a room that night and stayed awake giggling into the early hours. The following day we were up early and went to have a game of tennis. Neither of us knew how to play but we managed to get the ball over the net and back again to one another which was the main thing. Mom called to us asking if we would like to go with her to Port Shepstone as she had some errands to run. We were happy to do that as hopefully we could go to the café and spend our pocket money on some sweets. All three of us sat in the front of the car on the long bench seat. On the way there, mom swerved suddenly for some reason and drove off the road in a huge cloud of dust and came to a stop in some bushes. Both Butch and I were thrown up against the dashboard and the seats came loose in the car. Mom said it was a cow that she swerved to avoid, but I'm sure I didn't see one! A passing farmer picked us up and took us to Port Shepstone Hospital where we were all examined and the cuts and bruises patched up by the nurse on duty. The nurse got in contact with Uncle Ronnie and he arrived not long afterwards to take Butch and I back home to Margate. My mother was taken back to the guest house and I'm not sure what happened to the car. It brought back memories of the accident we had when we lived on the farm in Rhodesia. Only this wasn't to- bacco fields. It was like being back there. I really didn't want to *think* about that. I don't think that Butch was allowed to spend the night with me again.

Despite the unsettling visits to see my mother, life with Uncle Ronnie and Aunty Pat continued to be full and busy. After the last disappointing visit, I settled back into my routine without giving any further thought to seeing her again. I just got on with my life. I was enrolled in the local cub pack and loved all the things that we were taught, especially making fires. Aunty Pat would sew all the badges that I had earned onto the shirt sleeve of my uniform and I would walk around feeling very proud of myself. I also had a friend who liked boxing and together we made a big punch bag out of sacking, filled it with sand and hung it from a tree in the garden. Then I could practise boxing every day. Although the dust used to puff out of the bag each time I hit it, I pretended that I was on my way to stardom. Well, you had to start *somewhere*! I had made lots of school friends and many afternoons after school and most weekends we were off to one another's houses. We took the dogs out for long walks in the fields, we went camping in the garden and fishing for sardines during the annual sardine run. Life for me was brimming with busy days and loads of fun. The best time ever. Except for the one day when Aunty Pat tried to convince me that what I was eating was chicken when I knew very well that it was *pheasant!*

But a lot of the time I felt I could *burst* with happiness.

My second Christmas with Uncle Ronnie was just as special as the first. It wasn't long after Christmas, just as I had finished helping to pack away all the Christmas baubles and tinsel into big boxes ready for next year, when the subject of my mother came up again. She had apparently moved back to Margate and was staying with friends and once again she wanted to see me. I agreed reluctantly to see her, feeling confused by my conflicting emotions. Half of me wanted to see her but the other half didn't want her to disrupt my life. I felt I was betraying her by not wanting to see her and I always left confused and unsettled after my visits with her.

I thought if I crossed my fingers behind my back for luck as often as I could when I was with her, then the visit should go ok.

Mom was still looking very well and happy. She told me that she wanted me to come and live with her. She was going to buy a house in Margate for us both and I would even get to have my own room. And we could get a dog. And that she was going to buy a car. And ... to top it off she had already opened up a clothes shop in Margate which would bring in an income.

So crossing my fingers didn't really work.

Well ... it only worked up to a *point*!

She was trying to entice me back by promising me all these things.

I didn't know what to think.

I didn't know what to do.

I loved my life with Uncle Ronnie and I also loved my mom.

I didn't want to have to choose!

CHAPTER EIGHT

Joan

They told me that I was an alcoholic which is the biggest load of rubbish I have ever heard!

I let out a snort.

I let out a loud, disbelieving snort.

I mean I don't even *look* like an alcoholic. Alcoholics are scruffy and dirty, have lank unwashed hair and black underneath their fingernails and they wear the same clothes every day. And they smell. And they hang around the streets with other alcoholics. Okay so I have never seen a fat alcoholic. They are all skin and bone. Which is fine. I am just *naturally slim*. I dress with care every day. I am *clean*! I am *nothing like them!* And in any case, just because I have a couple of drinks doesn't make me an alcoholic! *Ridiculous*!

#

I opened my eyes, consciousness gradually returning, and looked up at a ceiling I did not recognise. I turned my head to look around the room puzzlement crowding my thoughts. The room was bright with cheerful blue and yellow curtains fluttering in the slight breeze which was cooling on my face. There was a comfortable looking easy chair in the far corner and a chest of drawers with a row of books on the top against the opposite wall. Well, it's definitely not a hospital ward! I pushed myself up onto my elbows just as a young girl in a white coat walked into the room.

'Joan, how nice to have you with us a last. How are you feeling?' She stood beside me and held my wrist lightly between her fingers looking at her watch.

'I think I'm fine. Where am I? Why am I here?'

'Your very kind neighbours were concerned about you and called us in to help. You are in a small rehabilitation centre on the outskirts of Salisbury. Do you remember what happened? Anything at all?'

'Not really. It's all a bit fuzzy actually.'

'Well never mind. We are here to help you get better. In the meantime, just to let you know that the Child Welfare have taken over the care of your two children, Jennifer and Rudi.'

I swallowed. 'Wh ... where are they?' the realisation dawning on me.

'They have both been sent to a foster home in Salisbury where they are reasonably settled for the moment. They still go to the same schools as before so at least there is that continuity for them.'

I lay back on the bed suddenly feeling dizzy. Why can't I remember anything? 'How long have I been here' I eventually asked.

'A little over two weeks. We had to keep you sedated as you were very agitated. But it looks like you have turned a corner now so as soon as you feel up to it, get yourself up and out of bed and get those juices flowing,' she added with a smile. 'In the meantime I will bring you a nice cup of tea. Oh, and the bathroom is through that door on the left. You might want to have a good old soak after your tea. Once you've done that then we can have a chat.' She bustled out the room to get my tea.

I'd much rather have a big glass of gin to be honest.

Feeling irritated, I glanced down at myself looking at the unfamiliar clothes that I had on. What on earth was I *wearing*? Some old flannel nightshirt from the nineteen hundreds! I swung my legs out of bed, noticing that the nail varnish on my toenails *definitely* needed attention, and made my way to the bathroom. Glancing in the mirror, I was shocked at how drawn I looked. Splashing my face with warm water and patting it dry with a soft towel I felt marginally better. I walked unsteadily back to my room and found that my tea had arrived in my absence together with a couple of biscuits. I sat in the chair and wolfed the biscuits down and sipped my tea more slowly whilst I tried to come to terms with where I had found myself and to make some sense of my befuddled thoughts.

Okay. In the first place, if it wasn't for getting fired from my job at the doctor's surgery, all this wouldn't have happened now would it? I *needed* to have a drink after that. I mean I really didn't expect to lose my *job*. Yes, and I know that I'd had been having more than a couple of drinks and *possibly* at work as well. But I *deserved* them. What with having to leave the farm under a cloud and the way Ida treated me. As if I was a *criminal*. And don't forget that job was *stressful*! Anybody would need a bit of relaxation now wouldn't they?

And in any case I knew *exactly* what I was doing so they can't tell me *anything*.

I had everything under control.

And how *dare* they think that they can just cart my children off without my permission.

Who do they think they *are*!

By this stage I had worked myself into a state and I decided that I needed to sort this out. But where were my clothes? If I could get dressed then I would feel much better. I pulled open the door of the wardrobe that I had noticed in the corner of the room and found a couple of my dresses hanging there. Grabbing the nearest one I pulled it over my head, ran my fingers through my hair and stormed out of the room. Marching angrily down the corridor I came to what looked like a reception desk with a dark haired young lady sitting behind it talking on the telephone. I waited impatiently for her to finish her conversation drumming my fingers on the counter top in irritation.

'Right!' I said the moment she had replaced the receiver. 'I demand to know who gave you the right to take away my children without my permission. You can't just do that you know. And what has happened to my things, my furniture. So just tell me where everything is? I must get out of here. Call a taxi for me then I can be on my way.' I knew I was rambling on but I needed to do something. I felt a hand on my arm and turned.

'Joan … *Joan!* Just take a deep breath and let's go back to your room and we can chat about what options are available to you.' It was the same young lady that I had spoken to when I woke up. Looking at her name badge I said,

'But Lucy, they can't do this to me. How *dare* they! It's not right! I just had a couple of drinks! There's nothing *wrong* with having a couple of drinks surely!' We were walking back to my room, Lucy's warm hand guiding me along.

'Now you sit in that comfy chair whilst I grab your file and a fresh pot of tea for us both. I won't be long.' She went out and closed the door behind her.

I sighed. I knew what was coming for heaven's sake! Yes, I was angry.

Angry that the Child Welfare had interfered in the first place.

Angry that I had lost my job.

Angry that I now found myself having to answer to people. I just wish they would mind their own business!

I mean, everything was under control.

It *was*!

Well ... maybe I *had* allowed things to slip a *little*. But why do I have to be punished?

Lucy bustled back into the room interrupting my thoughts, carrying a tray and a thick green file under her arm. After handing me a cup of hot strong tea she sat back and opened the file.

'Now,' she said with a smile, 'I know that you are not happy about where you find yourself at the moment and I also understand that you are anxious about your children. So let me put your mind at rest. Your neighbours realised that there was something amiss when Jennifer knocked on their door and asked to borrow some money so that she could buy some bread. They took it upon themselves to make sure that both Jennifer and Rudi had a cooked meal in the evenings and they also tried to encourage you to eat. But it was evident that you needed more help than what they were able to give, so they called in the Welfare.'

Not wanting to meet her eye, I looked down at my hands suddenly flooded with shame at the reality of my behaviour. Had I really been so unaware of what was going on around me?

'What is going to happen now is this. In order for you to have your children returned to you, you are going to need to do two things. The first is to complete the compulsory rehabilitation program here with us which is a minimum of six weeks long. This is the easy part. Secondly you are going to have to prove that you can hold down a job and remain alcohol free for a minimum of a year.'

I sighed. I know I can do it as I had done it before anyway. By myself!

But *six weeks*!

Six weeks!

It's just that when I have all these problems then I *need* to have a drink. It's just not *fair*! And another thing. ... I don't want my children looked after by strangers.

'Can arrangements be made to send the children to their father in South Africa?' I asked Lucy. Surely this would be better. Then when I got out of here I could go back there and find work.

'I'm sure we could make some enquiries for you. Leave it with me and I will let you know. In the meantime your rehab program starts from tomorrow. Here are a couple of booklets for you to read to get yourself started.'

I took the booklets from her letting them fall into my lap, tiredness sweeping over me.

'This is a lot for you to take in I can see. Go and have a nice relaxing bath before lunch at one o'clock. The dining room is just down the corridor. I will see you later.'

Lucy bustled out closing the door quietly behind her and leaving me with the turmoil of my thoughts.

#

The program was tough.

I'm not going to deny it. I always believed that I could do this by myself. Previously I had managed by sheer *will power* to cut down and in some instances to stop drinking altogether. Look what happened at the Regent Hotel. I just stopped like *that*! And what about before I went in for my operation with Dr Blankenburg. I hadn't had a drink for a while then either. So I *can* do it alone.

I don't know why I have to go through this every day and talk about myself and listen to other people's stories. I'm not *interested*! I'm not like these other people. I just want this to be over so that I can get out of here.

Realising that I needed to pull my weight to some degree otherwise I was jeopardising myself, I eventually knuckled down and got with the program. Literally! To be perfectly honest I *was* feeling a lot better in myself both physically and mentally which I know was a combination of rest, three square meals a day and no alcohol. And it did make it easier to cope with life when I was feeling well I have to admit.

The six-week period came and went and I was eventually given the green light after a stay of two months. Thank *goodness*! The plus side of being there for that length of time was that I had maintenance money building up in my bank account which would be an enormous help to me starting afresh. A room in a boarding house in the centre of Salisbury was arranged for me to live in until I had organised myself. I was still being monitored by the Welfare so I knew that I had to behave myself. Although I had no desire to have a drink actually I felt so well and strong.

It was nice to be free again. My room was very basic but that didn't bother me much. Whilst I was in rehab, the children had been flown back to South Africa. Ian had agreed to look after Jennifer but Rudi was sent to stay with Ronnie and Pat Baker. I was a bit annoyed about Rudi staying with the Bakers actually. They were more friends of Ian's than mine, particularly Ronnie of course. His wife Pat was always outspoken and although she had supported some of my fund raising functions over the years she never became a friend of mine. Why did they have to become involved in my business anyway?

The children were both at school in Margate and had settled in well, I was told. Despite feeling rankled that the Bakers were now embroiled in my private life, I was more comfortable knowing that both children were well looked after. I could now concentrate on deciding what I was going to do with my future.

Taking myself out for a walk in Salisbury city centre soon after I was dropped off at my new lodgings, I saw a familiar figure walking ahead of me.

'Charlie? What are you doing in the big city? He swung round.

'Joan! How have you been? Looking as good as ever I see.' He placed a hand on each arm and kissed one cheek then the other.

'I can't complain Charlie,' I said deliberately vague 'The children are back in South Africa with their dad at the moment so I am footloose and fancy free.' I said enticingly. I know ... I just can't resist it! 'How long are you in town for?'

'As long as I like,' he said giving me an appraising look. 'Would you like to go and have a coffee?'

I nodded.

Knowing that look.

Enjoying that look.

Well, why not?

Coffee led to a long lunch. I managed to avoid having any alcohol. I also managed to avoid mentioning that I had a problem with alcohol. And of course I didn't mention anything about being in rehab. Why *would* I?

Charlie had some business that he needed to attend to that afternoon but we agreed to meet up again later on that evening. As he kissed me goodbye outside the restaurant, I felt on top of the world. I hadn't felt like this for *ages*. What had I been *missing*? I must go and buy myself a new outfit for this evening and perhaps have my hair done as well. I excitedly made my way to a large department store that I knew in the area to look for something that took my fancy. A bright red dress caught my eye and I knew it was the one I had to have. It fitted like a glove and as red was my favourite colour, I knew I was meant to have it. It was a *bit* expensive really but then I hadn't bought any clothes for *ages* and I had done so well in rehab that I was *due* a little something. After spending some time at the hairdresser I made my way back to my room looking forward to a long soak in the bath then getting myself ready for the evening ahead.

The restaurant that Charlie chose was down a small lane off the main street and served mainly Italian food. We were shown to a small table at the back which was laid beautifully with a white tablecloth and shiny silverware. There was a single red rose in a vase and a small candle in the centre of the table giving out a soft light. The ambiance was gracious and intimate, enhanced by the soft background music and flickering candlelight.

I basked under Charlie's appreciative gaze as he pulled my chair out for me to sit, his hand briefly touching my back. I knew I looked attractive. I had taken extra care in getting ready for this evening making sure that my finger and toenails were perfect, that my makeup was perfect and my hair was perfect. I had put on my very best lacy underwear as well. Just to make myself feel alluring you understand. And it had worked.

The evening was fun and I found myself relaxing and laughing heartily at some of the things that Charlie said. He was so *funny*!

'You are so entertaining Charlie. I haven't laughed like this in ages,' I said looking at him directly across the table from me. 'And we haven't even ordered our food yet!' Charlie had the wine list in front of him and I knew that I needed to be straight with him. 'I'm not drinking alcohol at the moment Charlie.' Well, I *wasn't* was I! 'You go ahead and order wine for yourself.' I felt quite pleased with myself for being strong actually.

'Well, I'm impressed with the choice you've made Joan. I think that shows how strong and tenacious you are. I always knew you had it in you.' He finished taking my hand in both of his and giving it a squeeze.

There. He thinks that the decision to cut down on my drinking was my own. Well, why wouldn't he. Let him carry on thinking that. I knew I was being deceptive but I wasn't ready to talk about my time in rehab and the events leading up to going there.

Knowing that Charlie accepted my explanation for not wanting to drink, the rest of the evening passed very pleasantly with much laughter amid a growing intimacy between us. At the end of the evening when he invited me back to his hotel, I didn't hesitate. Why would I?

After that, Charlie returned to Salisbury regularly to see me. Sometimes it was just for the day and we would have lunch together and walk in the park holding hands and kissing occasionally. Other times he would book into a hotel and we would spend a blissful night together which I wished would never end. He had given me back my confidence. I felt *wonderful*.

I never asked about his wife and he never mentioned her either.

It was better that way.

I had been staying in the boarding house for a month when I it was time to go to the prearranged appointment with Lucy to discuss my progress.

'You seem to be doing really well and I think you should feel proud of yourself Joan. Have you come to any decision about what you are going to be doing in the future?' said Lucy.

'Well I think that I would like to return to South Africa so that I can find a job and work towards getting Rudi back.' I hadn't really given this much thought but the moment the words were out of my mouth, I realised that this *was* what I had to do. And yes! I did feel rather proud of myself actually!

Telling Charlie of my decision to leave Salisbury was the hardest part. We had previously discussed the possibility of me returning to South Africa sometime in the future and he had hinted that he might consider joining me. I realised that he wasn't aware about my time in rehab or about the fact that my children were taken into care by the welfare because of my drinking. But he didn't *have* to know that now, did he?

We were due to meet the following day and he had arranged to spend the night which I was looking forward to. Anxious to get it off my chest I broached the subject almost as soon as he had arrived.

'I have had to make a difficult decision Charlie and one which I hope you are going to be happy with,' I said, stroking his hand that was on my thigh. 'You know that we have been saying that it would be nice for us to go to South Africa and start a new life together? Well I have decided that I need to do that. My children are happily at school there and my place is there with them.' I turned towards him. 'But I would like you to join me.' I'm not sure whether I *loved* him exactly but it was nice to have all the attention from him and I *really* wanted him to join me!

Charlie looked at me blankly for a moment then seemed to collect himself. 'Joan, I don't want to lose you. This has meant a lot to me and I can't bear the thought of being apart from you. When were you thinking of leaving?'

'Possibly as soon as next week actually. Oh do say that you will join me, Charlie!'

'Of course I will! Did you think I wouldn't? I won't be able to leave next week with you though as I need to make arrangements for the farm. But possibly the week after would be good.' He gave me a big smile and drew me towards him, holding me close, burying his face in my hair.

I was satisfied with that.

The days flew by and I was soon at the train station saying an emotional farewell to Charlie with the promise that he would write and see me in a couple of weeks. I had, with Lucy's help during the last week, managed to secure work at the Tudor House Hotel in Durban as a receptionist. Lucy had also given me a letter with instructions to hand it to the Durban Child Welfare so that they can continue to monitor my progress with the aim of getting Rudi back in the future. Jennifer was settled with Ian and it was better for her to remain there with him.

I was feeling upbeat and positive. I hadn't had a drink now for over four months. I had been especially good, I thought, particularly when I was with Charlie because he still drank wine and I had stayed strong. I couldn't *wait* for him to join me in Durban. It was going to be a whole new life for us both. Although I did have a little *flutter* of apprehension when I realised that I didn't know how I was going to explain to him that the children were not living with me! But, you know what? I will cross that bridge when I come to it.

The Tudor House Hotel was built in the old English Tudor style and was quite a quaint looking black and white building. The décor was a little tired and dark but the staff were cheerful enough and I settled into my new surroundings relatively quickly. I had a room with twin beds and a bathroom en-suite which was a bonus.

The first thing I did after settling in was to write to Charlie to let him know that I had arrived safe and sound and to say that I would start looking for a place for us to stay as soon as he lets me know when he is arriving. A couple of days later I had my first interview scheduled with Durban Child Welfare. The social worker who was handling my case was a woman about my age by the name of Marlize. She was very Afrikaans and spoke English with a broad accent. She sat quietly reading my file whilst I waited, feeling slightly uncomfortable. Finally she looked up at me and said with a smile 'This all looks in order. It seems that you are coming along very well. What we need to be doing going forward, is to meet up every second week just to monitor your progress.'

'Yes but when will I get Rudi back?' I asked anxiously

'Well, first of all we need to take things slowly and one step at a time. We will monitor your progress as I said ...'

'Yes, but for how long?' I interrupted

'For as long as it takes, Joan. Let's see how you go over the following four months and then we can talk about maybe arranging a visit. Would you like that?'

'Four *months*! I can't wait that long.'

'I'm sure that you are going to cope just fine. Look at what you have achieved already' said Marlize trying to sound encouraging. I tutted. Don't they *understand* that I have been *so* well behaved. I left the welfare offices feeling enormously frustrated. Surely they can see that I have been trying! For Pete's sake! Isn't it good enough?

Four *months*!

I walked crossly back to the hotel to begin my shift. My heart skipped a beat when I saw a letter with a Rhodesia stamp waiting for me. Eagerly I slit it open with shaky hands and I excitedly devoured Charlie's letter. Once I had finished reading it I held it to my chest beneath my open palm and closed my eyes. I suddenly realised that he had made no mention of when he was arriving in Durban. Snapping open my eyes, I read it through again more slowly this time, and … *no*, there was no mention of him coming out here at all, let alone a date when he's expecting to arrive. My heart quickened. No. Surely I'm just being over imaginative. Just because he hasn't mentioned it, doesn't have to mean that he is not coming. Does it?

I wrote straight back to him that night as soon as I had finished my shift. Actually, I had started it whilst I was still at work as I couldn't concentrate anyway and my thoughts were going round and round in my head and I *had* to get them on paper. I ran out when it was still dark and put the letter in the post box on the corner. There! All done! I should get an answer in less than a week if not earlier. I had given Charlie the telephone number of the hotel and asked him to phone me. Just to clear up any possible misunderstandings you understand. Because I needed to know. I had asked him to be straight with me. Although I don't know how I will *bear* it if he has decided to stay in Rhodesia.

And so I waited for a reply or better still, a phone call.

And I waited.

And *waited!!*

A week went by. Then two. Becoming increasingly depressed I had to acknowledge to myself eventually that Charlie was not going to get in touch now was he?

He never intended to come to South Africa!

Surely I should have known!

It was just a repeat wasn't it?

How could I have been so *stupid?*

Of *course* he was never going to bloody leave his wife!

I blundered through the following couple of weeks with the familiar rollercoaster emotions impacting on my ability to function. Through all of this turmoil however, I had managed to remain strong, well *reasonably* strong really. I must confess that I did buy one or two small bottles of gin. Just small bottles. The smallest I could find. And I was very good because I managed to drink only when I had finished work for the day and each bottle lasted me a couple of days.

So that shows how *strong* I was.

And nobody knew!

And that first mouthful!

Oh … .my … .*days!*

Heaven!

My second visit to the Child Welfare came and went and then there were only three months left before they would assess my case. Then there were two months left. Then one.

After all these months I still hadn't heard a word from Charlie and had eventually accepted that I never would. I was still feeling very angry with him for leading me on and angry with myself for being taken in by it all. Again! But it was fun whilst it lasted I guess.

Although I had drunk a couple of bottles of gin during my *emergency* I didn't consider it to be wrong. It hadn't affected my work, now had it? And nobody needed to know anyway. I was feeling confident that a visit from Rudi would be arranged any day now. Sitting down in front of Marlize in the familiar office with the dull painted walls I waited with anticipation whilst she finished her conversation on the phone. Replacing the receiver she turned to me. 'Well Joan, I must say that you have been doing really well and I am very happy with your progress. It is now eight months that you have been under the guidance of the Welfare. We should be able to arrange a visit for Rudi to stay with you over the long weekend at the end of this week. Would you like that?'

'I would love that,' I said smiling with satisfaction.

'Good. Then after his visit, we will see how you get on over the next three months or so and we can then decide how we are going to go forward.'

'I don't understand. I thought that after Rudi's visit then you would start the ball rolling to get him returned to me!' The satisfied smile was slipping from my face.

'Joan, in order for Rudi to be returned to live with you permanently you have to be able to provide him with a home. Yes, you are employed at the moment and bringing in an income which is great. But a room in a hotel is not considered a home unfortunately.'

I looked at her aghast! She hadn't mentioned this to me before. Or had she? Shaking my head to get rid of my muddled thoughts, I jumped up and started pacing the room.

'But working in a hotel is what I know,' I said pleadingly.

'Perhaps you might consider moving back down to the South Coast where it is a bit more rural and affordable. You could rent something for you both to live in. Don't despair. I'm sure we will work out a solution for you,' said Marlize coming around her desk and patting me on the arm.

Despair! *Don't despair!*

When my life is being ordered around by bureaucrats! I mustn't *despair!*

Feeling thoroughly let down, I took my leave and made my way back to the Tudor House. I mustn't despair! *Really?* But actually … .on reflection, I do seem to remember Marlize mentioning something about a stable home environment for Rudi some time ago. I guess at the time, I only heard what I wanted to hear which was when he would be allowed to visit. I now realised that getting Rudi back wasn't going to be as straightforward as I originally thought.

But nevertheless, I felt bitter and indignant that other people were in control of my life and could dictate to me when I could see my own child. Needless to say I didn't sleep well that night or the following couple of nights. It was just not *fair!* I've a good mind to just run away with him. That will solve my problem.

Two days before Rudi was due for his visit, a telegram arrived on my desk. I felt the blood drain from my face. Who would be sending me a telegram? Telegrams are not usually good news. My mouth dry with dread, I ripped open the covering envelope. And sat down suddenly, all my problems fading into the background. I caught a sob in my throat. Aunt Rachel had died yesterday. I felt as if I had been punched in the stomach. Poor Aunt Rachel. She had always been so kind to me and had put my needs before her own. Although I had lost her years ago because of her dementia, this felt like losing her all over again. Images of my innocent early life with her flashed through my mind. That was a lifetime ago! What had happened to that sweet naïve Joan?

I telephoned the care home as soon as I felt able and they gave me contact details of a reputable funeral home so that I could arrange a cremation for her. After completing all of the necessary arrangements with the funeral home I then phoned Aunt Rachel's lawyer to let him know that she had died. As she never had any other relatives there was nothing left for me to organise other than to be there for her cremation which would take place the following week. Feeling totally wrung out, I left work early and went straight to bed.

Friday finally arrived and despite still feeling low about Aunt Rachel's death it was with a fever of anticipation that I waited in the reception area for Rudi to arrive. Arrangements had been made for Ronnie to drop Rudi off with me and collect him again on Monday afternoon.

When at last I spotted Ronnie and Rudi walking towards the hotel entrance I couldn't believe how tall he had grown. His hair was still blond and curly but he was now ten years old and he seemed to be growing up so fast. I rushed towards him with a big smile and he gave me a hug. I chatted to him about school and asked how he enjoyed living with Uncle Ronnie and he seemed happy enough although somewhat subdued. We spent a pleasant evening together and we had a bit of fun after dinner when I taught him to play cards. The little minx beat me at my own game. 'When did you get to be so clever?' I asked him laughing. 'I'm just a natural,' he replied nonchalantly with a cheeky smile.

Oh how I've missed that smile! My heart hurt.

The following day was Saturday and I had Rudi help me separate the cream from the milk which was a task I did every morning. The milk for the hotel would be delivered early every morning in large glass bottles with blue foil caps. The top two inches in the bottles was thick yellow cream which I used to skim off carefully and place in a glass bowl in the fridge. This would be whipped up later and used in any puddings or cakes that the chef had planned to make. Then he helped me set up some rat traps in the pantry which I think he quite enjoyed. I became busy at the reception desk after that so Rudi occupied himself for a couple of hours.

Later after my shift I went upstairs to check on Rudi and found him sitting on the bed with a pack of cards in his hand. 'I am just popping next door to see my friend Dot' I told him.

I knocked on Dot's door, opened it and walked straight in.

'Oh Dot, I don't know what to do,' I said getting straight to the point. 'The Welfare are taking so long to return Rudi to me. I have decided that I can't wait for them and I am going to run away with him'

'Goodness! Where would you go?' said Dot with a frown

'East London. I've lived there before and it's a nice city. Smaller than Durban. I could catch the train tomorrow or Monday morning. All my problems will be solved. Nobody would know where I am.'

'Maybe give it a bit more thought Joan. It's a big thing that you want to do you know. Have you considered how another move would affect Rudi?'

'Rudi will be fine,' I said impatiently. Why isn't Dot agreeing with me? Surely she can see that this is a good solution! The *only* solution! Not finding the support that I expected from Dot, I took my leave and went back to my room. I lit a cigarette and taking a deep pull I sat back on my bed, plans developing in my mind for my journey to freedom.

'I want to go back home to Uncle Ronnie.' Rudi's small voice penetrated my thoughts. Blinking, I turned and looked at him. 'I want to go back home,' he said again, almost to himself without looking at me.

I didn't say anything to him. I couldn't. I was overwhelmed with despair. Could I still run away with him if he didn't want to go?

Sleep didn't come easily that night either.

The following morning I had managed to arrange for another staff member to do my Sunday shift. I was no nearer to deciding what to do after a night of tossing and turning. But I opted in the meantime to take Rudi to the funfair.

He didn't want to go!

I couldn't understand why he wouldn't want to go and have some fun!

Then Ronnie arrived and it all fell into place. I could tell straight away by his face that I was in trouble. Telling Rudi to wait by the front doors of the hotel, he led me through into the lounge area.

'What on earth were you thinking Joan?' Ronnie said sternly. 'Rudi overheard your conversation about wanting to run away with him to East London. The poor child was beside himself. You do realise that I have to let the Welfare know what you had planned. They are not going to be happy. You are just jeopardising your chances of getting Rudi back?'

I looked at him in misery. 'I guess I wasn't thinking' I admitted reluctantly. I hadn't given any thought to Aunt Rachel's funeral either which was the following week which I wouldn't be able to attend if I was in East London.' Oh! It was just too much! Ronnie looked at me with disapproval and I was suddenly overwhelmed by outrage at his judgement. How dare he come here and tell me what to do?

'But I had actually changed my mind anyway. So you needn't have worried,' I retorted indignantly and spun around and left the room to say goodbye to Rudi. He stood stiffly as I hugged him long and hard before he left, not wanting to let him go but knowing that I had to.

Resenting that I had to.

Angry that I had to.

I felt wretched and crushed with despair. Full of despair mostly because Rudi clearly didn't want to be with me! Yes I know that you are thinking that all this is my own fault. I *know* it is. But that doesn't make it any easier now does it?

The rest of the day yawned long and lonely in front of me and filled with anger and bitterness, I only had one solution that I could think of. Or maybe it was because I *wasn't* thinking that the solution came to mind. However it was Sunday and the bottle stores were closed. But this was a hotel and there was a fully stocked bar available although it would only open at twelve for serving drinks with the midday meal. I would have to get hold of the keys somehow. Or I could wait until it opened at midday then possibly sneak behind the counter and lift a bottle. There was just a greater possibility of being caught that way because there would be more people about.

Tossing the options over in my mind I made my way to the office at the side of the foyer to see if the keys were in their place. There was nobody about so I opened the door quietly and stepped inside spotting the keys immediately hanging from a row of brass hooks. Each bunch of keys was labelled clearly. I grabbed the bunch labelled 'Bar', slipped them into my pocket and left as quietly as I had arrived, glancing around as I pulled the office door closed behind me to make sure that I wasn't spotted. Heart thudding, I walked in the direction of the bar keeping an eye out for anybody who might be in the vicinity. All was quiet. Reaching the door I took a big breath and having a last look around I dug into my pocket and pulled out the bunch of keys. There were five of which two were Yales. Glancing at the lock I realised it was a Yale so it was one of two keys, thank goodness. Inserting one of the keys into the lock and turning it with trembling hands, it was with enormous relief when the door opened silently inwards. Holding my breath I walked quickly over to the shelf where I knew the gin bottles were kept and grabbed the first one. Realising then that I hadn't really thought this through, as I had nowhere to hide the bottle whilst I carried it back through the hotel to return the keys to the office, I had to think quickly of what to do next. Locking the bar door behind me once more I nipped into the ladies powder room and managed to conceal the bottle temporarily in a cupboard under the basin.

Now just one more hurdle remained. Taking a couple of deep breaths I returned to the office and with ease I must say, returned the keys to the brass hook. Whew! That was Sneaky! But I did it.! With growing elation I returned to my room, grabbed a shopping bag and went straight back to the powder room and collected my booty.

It was a large bottle.

That didn't stop me.

I drank steadily for the rest of the day and into the evening until the bottle was empty.

I wanted to blot out the anger.

I wanted to blot out the bitterness and resentment.

I wanted to block out the loss of Aunt Rachel.

I wanted to blot out Charlie and Michael and the upset with Arthur.

I wanted to blot out Rudi and his obvious happiness when Ronnie arrived to collect him. I am his *mother* for God's sake!

So I drank.

The following day was a public holiday and I was not working. It was just as well because I did feel rather off colour. To put it mildly! But it gave me the chance to sleep it off. Through the fog of my thoughts I had reached a cloudy decision during the night to leave Durban and move to the south coast. Not Margate, but somewhere else where I could work and maybe rent something to live in. I would be nearer to Rudi there too.

Once I had made up my mind to move, I felt so much stronger somehow. More in control of my life. With a clearer head, I got out of bed around midday, had a bath and after dressing made my way to reception where the daily newspapers were kept. Making myself a cup of coffee in the kitchen, I returned to my room with the newspaper and spent the rest of the afternoon going through the advertisements for positions in the hotel industry in the south coast area. I eventually narrowed it down to two. Realising that there was no time like the present, I went to a public phone box outside in the street and phoned each in turn. With positive results.

The busy Easter weekend was in two weeks' time and the Cutty Sark Hotel in Scottburgh were desperate for a manager it seemed and were happy to take me on straight away with references to follow. First thing on Tuesday morning I handed in my one week's notice feeling rather empowered and in charge in a positive way for a change. I worked the balance of the week as required except for the Friday when I headed up to Pietermaritzburg to say a final goodbye to Aunt Rachel. The funeral was a sad dismal affair with only three people attending. Myself and two care home staff members. I felt wretched to be honest and couldn't wait for it to be over.

Then at last I found myself on a train bound for Scottburgh. The train journey took about three hours and I had plenty of time to think. I realised that I should have contacted Marlize but I would just have to write to her once I was in Scottburgh.

Nobody knew about my bout with the bottle. And it *had* spurred me on to make a decision hadn't it? Although I must admit that I was quite glad to have left the Tudor House when I did. I did hear via the grapevine that there was a bit of a ruckus when it was discovered that there was a bottle of gin missing from the bar. Poor Rick really got it in the neck as he was the only one with access to the keys. I had got away with it. The only *slight* downside of it all was, that I think that I left the empty bottle in my room.

#

I wasn't happy at the Cutty Sark. Although I was in charge, which in itself was nice, the whole place was neglected and shabby and there were areas in the building that were badly in need of repair. There clearly wasn't any money available to spruce the place up and I could just tell that it was on a downward spiral. I left there after a month and found a caretaking job straight away at a guest farm in Paddock. I had in the interim written to Marlize to tell her that I was moving to the coast, making no mention of Rudi's disastrous visit of course, and she had put me in contact with the Welfare office in Port Shepstone. As it turned out ... different office, same rules. Darn it was irritating!

Despite my frustration, I settled down readily in Paddock. The guest farm was out in the countryside, surrounded by tall pines and nestled into the hills and was picturesque in an old fashioned kind of way. It wasn't very busy which suited me fine. I had my own room with a kitchenette and small lounge area where I could relax at the end of the day. There were a couple of gardeners who kept the area around the buildings looking pretty and well kept and they also took charge of a couple of chickens that supplied the kitchen with eggs. The maids took care of the general cleaning and laundry and there was a chef who cooked simple wholesome meals and doubled up as a handyman when needed. My job was to make sure that everything ran smoothly. I enjoyed it because I was left mostly on my own.

Soon after I arrived in Paddock an official looking letter with a Port Shepstone post mark and addressed to me, was delivered to the door. Intrigued I slit open the envelope and out slid a wad of paper. Opening it out I could see that it was a copy of Aunt Rachel's will as well as a letter from a local solicitor. The letter requested me to telephone them at my convenience and after glancing through the will I realised that Aunt Rachel had left everything that she owned to me. I didn't think that she owned that much anyway but thought I would phone the solicitor right away just to clear things up.

'Mr Parks? It's Joan Garden speaking. I have had a letter from you in connection with Rachel Kidd's will.'

'Yes indeed, Mrs Garden. As you can see, you are the sole beneficiary and as the estate is quite considerable we need you to call into our offices to sign some documents. We have had a bit of difficulty in getting hold of you. It seems you were in Scottburgh and in Durban before that. But things have been proceeding quickly now as most of Rachel Kidd's assets are liquid. We are just waiting for the sale proceeds of her house in Durban to come through.'

I felt a bit bombarded. 'What do you mean by considerable?'

'The total estate is worth in excess of nineteen thousand rand (approx., GBP 100,000 in today's money),' said Mr Parks.

'Oh my word!' I sat down heavily 'Are you sure?' Silly question I know but I was dumbstruck.

'Completely sure,' chuckled Mr Parks.

Dazed, I made arrangements with Mr Parks to meet in his offices in Port Shepstone the following week to sign whatever papers were needed for him to continue. I replaced the handset and sat back, my mind a whirl. Who would have thought?

I needed a drink to *celebrate*!

And this was a *big* reason to celebrate.

And then I would stop.

Because with this money all my troubles would be over!

So I would definitely stop.

Definitely!

Over the past couple of weeks I hadn't been able to *resist* the occasional bottle. Just here and there you know. Well, maybe just a bit more than *occasional* if I must be truthful. But, I was handling it. That was the main thing. There was no one to see me either, so much the better. Okay ... so there were guests every now and then but I had things taped and to be honest, I thought I managed it pretty well as I knew that I was able to maintain a certain level of intoxication without seeming drunk. Two or three days before any scheduled meetings with the

Welfare, I would just make sure that I did not drink ... much! So you see, I *was* in control!

I had monthly visits to the Welfare offices in Port Shepstone to check on my progress and no mention was ever made of my plan to run away with Rudi. Perhaps Ronnie hadn't reported it, I thought hopefully to myself! After I had been in Paddock for nearly four months, I was told by the Welfare that I was allowed another visit from Rudi. I was super excited and vowed that this visit would go better than the first. The weekend that he was scheduled to arrive, the farm had no guests which suited me fine as we would have the place to ourselves.

Ronnie once again dropped Rudi and his friend Butch off after school on a late Friday afternoon. It was *so* good to see him again. He was looking more relaxed than our last visit and chatted happily about what he had been doing and said he was excited to see where I worked. I gladly showed the boys around the farm. They were both fascinated by the pair of Egyptian geese who had laid claim to the swimming pool and surrounding area where every year they returned to nest and brought up their young. We wandered down to a small stream that ran between two fields and the boys poked about in the cool shallow water for a while.

I cooked my favourite fillet steak for the three of us for dinner and then we all played cards for the rest of the evening. Rudi was very entertaining. He had obviously discovered the 'knock, knock, who's there' jokes and throughout the evening he would come up with different ones, each one more outlandish than the one before. Then both boys would hoot with laughter as if this was the funniest thing in the world. Actually it *was* funny to watch them and it really made me smile. I heard them giggling together long after they had gone to bed. It was a lovely sound.

Having seen the boys off to bed for the night, I settled down on the verandah with a large drink and a cigarette. I wasn't going to have a drink this weekend at all actually but the afternoon with Rudi had gone so *well* that I felt like celebrating. I stayed there lost in my thoughts until well after midnight when I realised that the bottle of gin was almost empty. Oh well! I will drive to Port Shepstone tomorrow with the boys and buy some gin at the same time. Although I knew that I shouldn't be doing that! Because I said I wouldn't! But this would *absolutely* be the last bottle that I would buy. With this thought I made my way to my room and collapsed onto the bed.

Butch and Rudi were playing tennis early on Saturday morning. I could hear their voices drifting across from the courts in the quiet morning air, shrill and happy. It lifted my heart. With a thick head I emerged from my room and downed the inch of gin that was left in the bottle. I busied myself in the kitchen preparing breakfast for the three of us then took my tea and a cigarette onto the verandah to wait for the boys.

After we had eaten breakfast we all piled into the car and I headed off down the gravel road to Port Shepstone. It was a gorgeous sunny day with not a breath of wind and I was in a singing mood. Maybe it was because I wasn't concentrating, or maybe the sun was in my eyes, or maybe I had just taken my eyes off the road for a *teeny weeny* second, but one minute I was driving on the road quite happily and the next minute I was coming to a skidding halt in a cloud of dust, straight through some bushes into a ditch. We were all thrown against the dashboard and I hit my head on the windscreen. Feeling a bit dazed and shaky I sat back in the seat and closed my eyes briefly.

We hadn't been there for five minutes when a local farmer pulled up and offered to help us. He very kindly drove us all to Port Shepstone Hospital where we were given the once over and put back together again with a couple of plasters. The nurse phoned Ronnie to collect the boys and I waited anxiously for him to arrive knowing that he wouldn't be pleased. But I couldn't help it if I had to swerve to avoid a cow! Now could I?

The farmer who kindly drove us to Port Shepstone continued the favour and drove me back to Paddock. He also helped with the recovery arrangements for the car for which I was so grateful. Although I did let out a huge sigh of relief once he had dropped me off at home and he went on his way. It all felt a bit too *much*! I needed a drink to calm my nerves. But even as I was looking, I knew that there wasn't any alcohol anywhere. That was the point of my visit to Port Shepstone in the first place. I angrily grabbed my cigarettes and making a cup of coffee went and sat outside. I didn't think that the owners of the guest farm were going to be too pleased about their car either. Well, it was an *accident!*

The car wasn't a write-off. Thank God! I did apologise most profusely to Andy Moorcroft, the farm owner. I think he was okay with my explanation and the car was covered by insurance anyway, although he clearly wasn't happy. I must admit that I did feel a *bit* shaken by the incident. And to make matters worse it did cut short Rudi's visit and we were having such a fun time together. Remembering Ronnie's displeasure when he arrived at the hospital to collect Rudi did fill me with anxiety though. I mean I can't *help* having an accident. But thank *goodness* that he hadn't any idea that I had been drinking. Although I hadn't had *much* to drink as you know. Not in the morning anyway.

The following day, time hung heavily on my hands and my thoughts returned to Aunt Rachel and my unexpected windfall. This was my chance to get myself on my feet and I made a promise to myself that I would be really strong from now on and I reasoned that if there wasn't any alcohol in the house, then I couldn't drink now could I? Which was logical.

Without a car, I was very cut off and it brought home to me how isolated the guest farm really was and I decided that it wasn't for me. Once again I turned to the local newspaper of which I had a number of copies and scoured the positions vacant columns. I struck gold once again and after a telephone conversation with the existing manager, I found a position to run The White Horse Hotel in Port Shepstone.

Port Shepstone is about half an hour's drive along the coast from Margate and is a larger town, not so much a holiday town but more industrial with a sugar mill, lime works and marble quarry all situated on the banks of the Umzimkhulu River that runs past the town and into the sea. There were many shops which catered for every need, a couple of banks and building societies, schools, churches and a hospital.

I arrived at The White Horse two days later with all my tea chests and suitcases in tow. It definitely felt much better here. More *me*! There was a lot more going on and the town had a busy and lively feel about it. I could just walk everywhere and didn't need a car. Really much more convenient.

I quickly established a daily routine at The White Horse. The hotel hadn't been badly run in the past at all, I just changed things to suit the way I liked to work. Having had a number of months to digest my imminent windfall, I came to the realisation that I would really like to get out of the hotel industry altogether. But what I wanted to do instead I really didn't know.

During my time at The White Horse, I became acquainted with two elderly sisters Dorothy and Bertha Roberts, who were staying in the hotel for a couple of months whilst their flat in Margate was being refurbished. They were both grey haired spinsters and probably in their sixties and were always dressed smartly with matching hats, bags and gloves. Bertha had a plump rosy face with twinkling eyes and wore rings on just about every finger. Dorothy was the taller of the two and according to her she was the older. She was the more outspoken of the two. Bertha would just agree with whatever she said. 'To avoid friction, dear.' She would say to me with a wink. They waved me over to their table one morning.

'You always look so busy, dearie,' said Dorothy 'Why don't you pull up a chair and join us for a cup of tea?' I hesitated, then thought, why not?

'I would love to join you. Let me grab a waiter and ask him to bring out a pot of tea and some of our cheese scones fresh from the oven.' I ordered our tea and scones and pulled out a chair and sank gratefully into it stretching out my legs. It was good to get off my feet, particularly when wearing my high heels. 'I'm Joan by the way,' I said.

'Yes, we know, dearie,' said Dorothy. 'We have noticed how you are always up and down, working so hard. You don't seem to take a breather.' Bertha smiled and nodded in agreement.

I laughed. 'I like things to work properly and to a certain standard. I don't mind the running around though. It keeps me young.'

Dorothy nodded, 'I know exactly what you mean. Bertha and I have run a successful shop in Margate for the past twenty years and what you put in, is what you will get out, I have always said.'

'Oh what shop is that then?' my mind going into overdrive as I didn't recognise them from when I lived in Margate.

'Roberts Toys and Souvenirs in Marine Drive, dear. Our flat is right next door to the Kingsview.'

The penny dropped. Of course! 'I know both the toy shop and the Kingsview.' I said wanting to be honest. 'I used to run the Kingsview with my then husband Ian Garden'

'Ah we thought so, didn't we, Bertha?' I said to Bertha that I was sure that you were that lovely young lady that we used to see at the Kingsview. 'You have a very distinctive face you see.'

We sat and chatted for about half an hour and I found them both interesting to talk to. It was incredible to think that together they had run a shop successfully for over twenty years. I made a point of having morning tea with the two sisters every day from then on and on occasions when I wasn't busy elsewhere in the hotel, we had our evening meal together as well. We became firm friends.

I eventually told them a little about my past but leaving out any mention of the affairs. I didn't want to shock them into having a heart attack now did I? They were spinsters after all! And I also made no mention of my time in rehab in Salisbury. They didn't have to know that either. I did say that I didn't drink alcohol as it did not agree with me. Well it didn't as you know! What I *did* tell them was that I was inheriting some money and that I would like to invest it in a business of some sort. But I wasn't sure what?

'Why don't you open a shop?' suggested Bertha who was normally the quiet one. 'We have loved our shop and wouldn't have wanted to do anything else.'

'Yes, I agree. What about a clothes shop for children. It could start from toddlers right up until teenager years and so cater for most ages. Margate doesn't have anything like that and in actual fact, Margate doesn't have any clothes shops at all' said Dorothy warming to her theme.

This sounded like a good idea and after mulling it over for a number of weeks I decided that it was exactly what I would do. Dorothy and Bertha both agreed to help me with the initial setting up of the business when I was ready to do so. They also very generously offered me a place to stay if I needed a roof over my head.

Every month I had dutifully attended my appointments with social welfare in Port Shepstone. It was so much easier than before as I just had to walk into town. I hadn't had a drink since the accident in Paddock, which was going on for three months now. Once again I felt proud of myself for being able to remain sober. I *knew* I could do it! With the plans to open my own business coming along nicely and knowing that once I had found a permanent place to stay after I left the White Horse, then it shouldn't be too much longer before Rudi was allowed to return.

The sisters eventually left the White Horse to return to their refurbished flat with promises to phone me immediately they had found suitable premises for my shop. They had numerous contacts and said that they knew of the perfect place for a dress shop but they just had to make some enquiries. I was quite happy to leave it to them as I think that they enjoyed being involved and seemed to have taken me under their wing. I was grateful for their input and knowledge because, let's face it, I didn't have a clue. I was feeling a bit *daunted* by it all. It wasn't a week later that Dorothy phoned to say she had found the perfect shop and it just needed a deposit from me to secure it.

The money from Aunt Rachel's estate was taking longer to come through than I had initially anticipated. I phoned Mr Parks and explained my dilemma and asked if I could have an advance or loan in the meantime to cover the cost of the shop rental. I also needed money to pay for refurbishing the premises and to buy some stock. He said that he would set it up and the money should be available in a couple of days. True to his word the money was in my bank account two days later and I wrote out a cheque with glee and posted it to Dorothy.

The shop was in a building that I was familiar with from my time living in Margate. But I still couldn't wait to go and have a look at it so that I knew the extent of any work that needed doing before I got in any stock. Dorothy fetched me from Port Shepstone on my day off and drove me to the agent to collect the keys. With huge excitement, I unlocked the heavy front door and walked into the shop looking around eagerly. With a measuring tape and pen and paper in hand I made a list of all that I wanted to be done, measuring the walls with the idea of installing some shelves down the one side. There was a large front window where I could have a display and there was space to put a small counter of sorts where I could place the till. I would definitely have to repaint the walls to get rid of the existing ghastly brown.

Armed with all my ideas for redecoration, I left the shop feeling enthused and spent the following couple of weeks getting the space ready.

I had handed in my notice at the White Horse as soon as I had found premises for my shop and I was now living with Dorothy and Bertha in their flat in Margate. It was not the *best* arrangement but it suited me for a time and at least they never had any alcohol in the home which kept temptation out of the way. And of course they had been so terribly helpful too.

Although I had mixed feelings about returning to Margate after leaving under a cloud almost three years ago, I thought that I must just hold my head up high and concentrate on getting my business off the ground. And if I am really honest, I did wonder if Michael was still the local doctor in the area and if he was, the chance of bumping into him whilst living there was quite high. I wasn't too sure how I felt about that although when I thought about it, my stomach did a little flutter.

After a couple of weeks of hard work the shop was ready to open. I had decided to call it 'Totts to Teens' and it would stock a range of exclusive children's clothes from about age two to sixteen. The walls were painted a light blue and I had shone the wooden floor so that it gleamed. The large front window frame I painted white, together with the heavy entrance door and the brass handle was shone to perfection. On the one wall the new white shelves stacked with brightly coloured garments looked inviting and towards the back I had installed a glass counter which housed the till and also gave me space to display some trinkets. After all the hard work I was very happy with the way it had all come together and was keen to open up so that I could start making an income.

Another visit with Rudi was arranged by the Welfare. I had updated them on my current situation and they seemed positive about the shop and indicated that once I had a more permanent place to live then they would consider allowing Rudi to return to me. Knowing that Rudi's previous two visits had not gone very well, I realised that I was going to have to entice him to want to come back to live with me. A day visit was planned for a Sunday whilst I was still living with Dorothy and Bertha. We took a walk together so that I could show him the shop.

'Wow!' he said excitedly, running up to a large wooden work bench which was in a room at the back of the shop. 'A drilling machine *and* an electrical saw! I saw one of these at Uncle Ronnie's once. That's awesome! I love using tools'

The room off the main shop had obviously been a workshop before. Apart from the work bench there were a couple of cupboards, a sink and a table where I had put a kettle so that I would be able to make a cup of tea during the day. I was encouraged by Rudi's excitement about the workbench.

'Do you think you would be able to make me some coat hangers if I give you some wood?' I asked him.

'I'm sure I could do that' Rudi said nodding enthusiastically. 'I could come after school tomorrow'

'I would love that.' I said. Then taking advantage of his enthusiasm I said casually,

'I would really love it if you would come back and live with me again. I have inherited a lot of money from Granny Kidd which has allowed me to buy this shop and I also want to buy a house for us both to live in. You would even have your own room again. How would you like that?' Rudi just looked at me and silently nodded. I could see that he was not sure.

'I am also going to get a car and do you know *what*? We can even get a dog! I promise!'

That should do it!

CHAPTER NINE

Rudi

I didn't really want to go back to live with my mom if I must be completely honest. I would get a funny churning feeling in my tummy each time I thought of it. If I went back then how did I know that things would be all right? How did I know that she won't get sick again and I would have to be carted off to some stranger's home? How did I know that she was going to keep her promises of buying a house for us and getting a car and a dog? How did I know? I didn't want to hurt Uncle Ronnie and Aunty Pat by saying that I wanted to live with my mom and I didn't want to hurt my mom by saying that I wanted to stay with Uncle Ronnie.

Why did it have to be so hard?

I shouldn't have to choose!

But in the end I agreed to go back to my mom. She was my mom after all.

#

Saying my goodbyes to Uncle Ronnie, Aunty Pat, Sheila and Lorraine was hard. I would miss Sheila's stories a lot but most of all I would miss the stability, security and happy family times that I had whilst living there for the past two years. But of course I was not to know that at the time.

Mom had moved into a room at the Waverley Hotel which was just across the road from her shop which was very convenient. All her meals were provided by the hotel as well so she didn't have to worry about cooking. My first night back with my mom, I realised that I was to share a room with her once again. She said this was just temporary whilst she was looking for a house to buy.

It wasn't easy getting used to sharing a room with my mom once more. As I hadn't seen much of her over the last two years she felt like a stranger to me. In time I became more accustomed to her. But getting to sleep was a challenge. Mom kept the light on at night so that she could read and she smoked continuously so that the room became enveloped in a blue haze of smoke. It was hard for me to sleep so I eventually took my blanket and pillow outside and lay in the passageway in front of the communal bathroom. This didn't seem to bother her at all.

I felt confused and found it very difficult to settle. Every day after school I would walk up to Uncle Ronnie's house and the maid would give me a sandwich and a coke and I would take it and go and sit in the aviaries with the birds.

Just like I used to do.

It felt comforting. One day Sheila came home whilst I was sitting in the aviaries about to take a large bite of my sandwich.

'What are you doing here ragamuffin? You shouldn't really be here you know' she said kindly.

I nodded, my eyes filling with tears. I was suddenly overwhelmed. I couldn't finish my sandwich after that. As soon as Sheila went inside, I ran back to the shop where I spent the rest of the afternoon.

I never went back to Uncle Ronnie's house.

From then on, once I had finished school and eaten my lunch which was given to me at the hotel, although

I didn't eat very much because they gave me lots of vegetables which I pushed to one side, I would go straight to the shop and fiddle around in the basement with the tools that I had found there. Working with my hands was something that I really enjoyed and I was able to make use of the tools that I had discovered and make things out of wood. Quite successfully too, even if I do say so myself! It kept me busy. I made some coat hangers that my mother wanted as well as some dress stands for the shop. My proudest achievement was a wooden Nativity scene which I made at Christmas time and put in the shop window.

As I spent most of every afternoon in the workshop, I used to notice that the young African girl that mom employed to work in the shop used to come down to the room next door every afternoon with a rucksack on her back, then leave with it empty. One day when she had been down to the room next door I decided it was time to investigate. The room was off the workshop and used mostly for storage with shelves on the wall full of stuff and a small cupboard with a curtain around it that mom had put there with a kettle on top. Looking around I didn't spot anything at first until I looked behind the curtain and there I found an unopened bottle of gin together with numerous empty bottles.

My heart sank.

My mom was drinking again.

At the age of eleven going on twelve, I was well aware by then of what alcohol was all about and in thinking about it, I realised that my mother had had a problem with alcohol for quite a while.

And I had to ask myself ...

Was that the reason she had crashed the car twice?

Was that why we were taken to Aunt Sonja in Salisbury when she was 'sick'?

Was that why I was sent to live with Uncle Ronnie?

These were questions that I would never ask her and I never told her or anyone else that I knew she was drinking. It was my secret.

At school one day we were all given plastic money boxes in the shape of a rugby ball. They came from Barclays Bank and the teachers told us that 'money doesn't grow on trees' and if we want to be rich one day then we needed to save. So I proudly took my money box to show my mother and placed it on the top shelf of her counter at the shop. I was never given pocket money but I thought if I did some odd jobs then I could earn money to put in there.

Freddy was no longer in my class at school but I saw him at break time. I did not want to bring him back to the hotel because I was embarrassed that we were living in just one room so we didn't see one another over the weekends much. We did go to see the James Bond movie *From Russia with Love* at the Casino Theatre one Saturday which was cool.

'Why don't you come with me to boxing lessons after school Rudi?' asked Freddy one day at school.

'Wow! I would love that but I will have to ask my mom first,' I said. I couldn't wait to get home and went straight to the shop instead of going to have lunch in the hotel to ask mom.

'No, you can't go. Boxing is for poor people,' she said with a vehement shake of her head. I stood and looked at her for a moment, my hands on my hips and thought to myself that as it was afternoon, she had probably had a couple of gins already. I could normally tell that she had been drinking by the way she spoke. Hostile. Spiteful. This was obviously bad timing. I lifted my chin and walked out of the shop back to the hotel determined that I would go anyway!

Boxing was held in the basement of the local sports shop and was within walking distance of the hotel. I discovered that the lessons cost one rand a week. I couldn't ask my mom for the money because I knew what the answer would be! Defeated, I told Freddy that I wouldn't be able to go. The following day at school Freddy told me that his father had said that he would like to pay for my lessons every week. I was so happy.

I couldn't wait for my lesson which was straight after school in the afternoon. My mother would be at the shop and wouldn't miss me, probably wouldn't even notice that I was not there. I had never been to the gym before and I could hear the activity down below as Freddy and I and another friend from school, Kenny Matthews, descended the steps together. There was a punch bag hanging from a large hook in the ceiling where a boy of about my age was being tutored and I saw a couple of large balls on the floor which I was told were called medicine balls which were used to build strength. Freddy introduced me to the coach and he showed me how to put on my gloves. My hands felt strange and heavy but I soon got used to the feeling and enjoyed punching the hanging bag as hard as I could. It felt good. After that we were given skipping ropes and had to skip as fast as we could. It was very tiring but over the weeks as I became fitter, it did get a lot easier.

After a number of weeks of going to the gym we were told that there was going to be a competition. We were going to compete with other members of the club in a real boxing ring that would be set up in the town hall and our friends and family would come to watch. We would each only do two rounds but it would teach us how to face an opponent.

I was a bit nervous.

For two reasons.

I had never faced an opponent before obviously and now I would have to tell my mother. I knew that timing was important. I waited for the weekend when I could catch her early in the day but not too early that she was dealing with a thick head.

Taking a deep breath and with a swirly tummy and coming out with it all in a rush and straight to the point, I said 'I have been going to boxing lessons and we are now going to have a competition in the town hall and I would like you to come and watch,'

In typical reverse fashion, she just said, 'Oh I would love to come, Rudi.'

So that was that!

It was a shock to be hit in the face for the first time and I wanted to stop and cry but knew that I couldn't do that in front of everyone watching so I just had to carry on. I only lasted one round. My mother was sitting in the front row and I heard her cheering so that made me feel better. Over the next couple of months, with practice, I improved a lot and I eventually ended up qualifying to represent Margate in the junior championships and Freddy, Kenny and I, each won a medal. Boxing gave me a sense of achievement and although I only did it for a short while, the skills I learnt would become rather useful in the future.

I was still attending Cubs once a week as well as playing cricket at school and was very proud to be chosen, together with Kenny, for their first team to play against neighbouring Port Shepstone school who were our greatest rivals. Mom was so pleased when I made the cricket team as she said that my dad used to play cricket in England so cricketing talent must run in the family.

My life was busy with school of course, my boxing, cricket and Cubs and before I knew it I had been living at the hotel with my mother for about three months. Mom announced one afternoon when I was at the shop after school that we would be moving to a holiday flat on the other side of Margate. It was small and furnished with only one bedroom but had huge windows overlooking Margate tidal pool. I slept on a folding bed in the lounge away from mom's cigarette smoke that made me cough and so that the bedroom light did not keep me awake. Mom had bought loads of new expensive sheets, blankets and towels as well as some crockery. She said that 'you've always got to keep up appearances', whatever that was supposed to mean! I had to take a bus to school and Butch was on the same bus so we went into school together. My mother had opened an account at the Corner café up the road from the flat which was convenient for me as every day after school I would go to the café and get some fresh bread and a coke. I took the opportunity to get a comic at the same time because mom never thought of getting me one. Sometimes I would take my bread down to the beach and sit and eat it there. As we were so near the beach I spent a lot more time there and collected driftwood which I would eventually use to make lamps and pipe racks.

I did wonder though, when mom was going to buy a house for us like she promised. Although it was not something that I wanted to ask her. I wasn't brave enough.

#

Mom got a bee in her bonnet one Sunday and decided that she wanted to go to church and dragged me along. Not that she wanted to have a conversation with God however. That was probably the last thing on her mind. We had to walk quite a long way to the church which was on a hill about a mile away and she complained all the way that her feet were killing her. Well she would insist on wearing those ridiculous pointy high heel shoes. Throughout the service she would nudge me with her elbow and pass random whispered comments about people in the congregation. 'Look at that woman's hat. The one in the green dress. It looks like she's wearing a skunk on her head' Nudge, nudge. Or, 'He looks as if he has slept in his suit' pointing to a man whose suit jacket was all crumpled. Nudge, nudge. And then she would start to shake with laughter and start me off until eventually we would be laughing at each other, as silently as possible, trying to keep it in but failing, shoulders shaking and tears streaming down her face. Then she would have to cross her legs tightly because she said she had a weak bladder and she didn't want to have an accident. That would set me off all over again. Don't ask me what the people sitting near us thought!

Another crazy thing that she did was to decide one day that she thought it would be funny to steal some bananas from a field that ran right next to our block of flats. She used to put adverts in the *The Farmers Weekly* under a column called The Hitching Post so she could meet a male companion. She had a reply from one of her adverts from a man who she called the Major and after writing letters to one another for a while he came for a weekend visit.

The Major lived in Durban and he caught the Pulman bus to Margate. He was a tall thick set man with grey hair and a large handlebar moustache with impressive curled up ends that he enjoyed fingering. He was ancient of course. Let's face it, anyone with grey hair was ancient and most likely kept their teeth in a glass by their bed at night and used a walking stick.

On his first night with us mom thought she would like to provide him with some entertainment so decided to steal some bananas from the neighbouring farm. She made us all wear black and she called it Undercover Mission Unknown. I think the Major wore his suit. He wasn't keen on her madcap idea but mom convinced him that she needed him as he was a war veteran so had experience in these things. And in any case she needed him to carry the bananas.

It was dark when we climbed through the fence, mom all dressed in black, with a torch in the one hand and a bread knife in the other, looking nothing like the undercover operative that she was trying to portray, the Major stumbling along reluctantly behind. We walked along the rows of banana trees looking for a bunch that we could cut down. It was quite difficult in the dark despite the torch, but we eventually found a suitable bunch and mom handed the bread knife to the Major with instructions to cut it down. After much huffing and puffing the bunch fell to the ground and that was when we heard a shout. 'Oi! Who's there?'

'Ssshh', mom ducked down, stifling a laugh and needing to cross her legs to prevent an accident. 'Grab the bananas, Major and let's go,' she said, turning around and making off down the slope towards the fence. The Major followed breathing loudly with the heavy bunch of bananas on his shoulder eventually making it to the fence where he collapsed in a heap next to the bananas which he had dumped on the ground. He said he would prefer to be back in Italy fighting during World War Two. It was easier.

The following day I was sent to the shop to buy milk and butter but when I came to put the items on mom's account I was told that there was no more credit until she paid what she already owed. Back at home I told my mother but the Major said not to worry, he would come with me to the shop and buy what we needed. The Major not only paid for what we needed to buy that day but he very kindly paid mom's account in full which was very generous of him. After walking with him to the bus stop later that afternoon to catch the bus back to Durban and waving him off, I never saw him again.

Mom had met a couple, Liz and Hank Martindale who were on holiday in Margate from a place called Clocolan in the province of the Orange Free State. They had come into the shop to have a look around and had met my mother and they became friends straight away. That was the thing with my mother. She could make friends so easily. She just couldn't keep them somehow.

Mom and I were invited for tea at their flat one Saturday morning and they gave me the best raisin bun I have ever tasted. They invited us to stay on their farm which was just outside Clocolan, to give mom a break from the shop. Mom was really keen. A two week stay was planned during the school term, so when she phoned the school to tell them that I wasn't going to be at school for two weeks, Mr Stead, the headmaster insisted that mom take some extra work for me to complete every day whilst I was away. After arranging with a woman she knew, who she said really needed the work as she was bringing up two small boys alone, to run the shop in her absence, we were packed and heading off to the station in no time at all.

I had a ball in Clocolan. I loved everything to do with the farm. It reminded me of Uncle Arthur's farm and Lexington and the carefree time I had there, although this farm was a lot bigger. There was a huge dairy herd with an uncountable number of cows and there were also five horses and I was allowed to ride an old grey horse called Chummy. I didn't know how to ride a horse of course so he was ideal for me as he was eighteen years old and very docile and just ambled along. I rode him most days. The Martindales also had hundreds of merino sheep which they bred for their wool. I was sorry that I was not going to be there when it was shearing time so that I could watch.

The farmhouse consisted of two separate buildings facing one another. One building comprised the lounge, dining room, kitchen and study and then across the garden, the building opposite, housed four bedrooms and two bathrooms. I really didn't fancy having to get up in the middle of the night to get a drink of water from the kitchen though!

The Martindales had two children a number of years older than me and they were home schooled so Mrs

Martindale used to help me with my school work every day whilst I was there.

In the evenings, the adults would drink their gin and tonics and wine before supper and that would be when I was told to go and bath. The bath was an old metal tub with feet and the water was heated outside by using a Rhodesian boiler. The gardener lit a wood fire under the boiler to heat the water at about four o'clock each afternoon so I would need to bath at five otherwise the water wouldn't be hot anymore. The bathroom was very cold and there wasn't very much hot water so I would strip and speed wash and get into my pyjamas as fast as I could then hurry to the lounge so I could sit in front of the large log fire. Then at seven o'clock the maid would ring a bell and we would all go to the dining room for dinner. Time flew by and all too soon we were back on the train bound for Margate.

We had only been home for a couple of days when I began to feel unwell with a raging temperature and sore throat. I couldn't lift my head from the pillow and by the third day, mom decided that I needed to go and see a doctor and so made the appointment for that same day. When we got to the consulting rooms I realised that the doctor was Dr Johnston. Mom was very smiley and laughed a lot but I felt too sick to care really. As it turned out, I was put into hospital and I had to have my tonsils out. After staying in hospital for four days I was allowed home once more. By this time, including our time away in Clocolan, I had missed a total of a month of school., which of course didn't worry me particularly.

Mom had been acting weird. Ever since I came home from hospital she had been weird. She would either be super smiley and laugh at the slightest thing or she would be silent and grouchy. I think it was partly to do with the woman who was supposed to run the shop for her whilst we were in Clocolan. I don't think she ran it properly and I heard something about missing money. And partly because she had seen Dr Johnston again. I heard her on the phone to him a couple of times after I was back home from hospital and she was occasionally in a bad mood after these conversations. After one of my boxing competitions I complained of a sore stomach where I had been punched and she insisted on taking me to the doctor. There was nothing wrong of course.

Maybe she was just being cautious.

Or maybe she just needed an excuse to see Dr Johnston again!

Mom announced to me a couple of months later that she had to go to hospital in Durban again for an operation and she had arranged for me to stay with friends of hers, Peggy and John Liebenberg.

Here we go again! I felt like lifting my eyes to the heavens but I didn't for obvious reasons.

I know it wasn't her fault that she had to go to hospital but surely she could realise that it might be better for me if I were to go back and stay with Uncle Ronnie instead. I didn't know the Liebenbergs and it was just so unsettling.

After the initial unfamiliarity of living in a stranger's home once more, I settled down to some degree. Keeping busy helped me cope. The Liebenbergs owned a large joinery business and lived in a big house in Margate. Once again I had my own room. Mr Liebenberg was very good with woodwork and he had a fully equipped workshop at home. He spent a lot of time in his workshop with me after school showing me how to make lamps out of driftwood which we would collect from the beach and he also showed me how to make a pipe rack. I managed to make quite a few lamps and pipe racks during my stay and sold a lamp to Freddy's dad and another one to Uncle Ronnie. I tried to persuade Sheila to buy a pipe rack for Uncle Ronnie but she said he didn't smoke a pipe so that was useless. I decided that when my mom got back from hospital, I would put the money that I had made into my rugby ball money box that was sitting on the counter in the shop.

Mr Liebenberg also took me with him to the tennis courts on a Saturday afternoon where he played as he was a member of Margate tennis club. I would borrow a racket and hit the ball against the wall and sometimes if there were enough kids my age and a free court was available, then we would have a game. He continued to encourage me to play tennis and still took me with him on Saturday afternoons long after I had gone back home to my mother.

I stayed with the Liebenbergs for over a month. Nobody mentioned my mother so I had no idea how she was until one day I was told that she would be home the next day. I was quite excited to see her again and it wasn't long before we were back in the flat.

Jennifer had, during the time I lived with Uncle Ronnie, been living with my dad and his wife. She then left school and went to live in the YWCA in Durban and found a job with the bank. I had only seen her a few times over the past couple of years. She came down to Margate to visit mom one weekend with her boyfriend. She seemed very grown up.

I had now been living with my mother for almost seven months. We had moved out of the Margate flat briefly and shared a furnished room for about two weeks and then moved back into the same flat. I was not sure why, but I was pleased to be back in the flat because at least I could sleep in the lounge. Whilst she was in hospital in Durban, my mom had closed the shop. She said that she didn't want to get someone else to look after it like she had when we went to Clocolan, because you couldn't trust people to keep their fingers out of places where they didn't belong. But since she had been back, I noticed that she was closing the shop early each day and sometimes when I got home from school she was in bed. So I decided to go straight to the shop after school each day to help her out.

I, of course, knew that my mother had started drinking again so it was no surprise to discover a huge hoard of empty bottles in the little back store room at the shop. But what did surprise me was getting to the shop one afternoon after school and finding my mother sitting in a chair so drunk that she could hardly stand.

I stood and looked at her with unease. I had never seen her like this.

What on earth was I to do?

I decided to close the shop and managed to persuade her to walk home with me. She leaned onto me heavily as with difficulty we stumbled out of the door and eventually made our way along the pavement to the flat where she collapsed onto the bed. I breathed a sigh of relief that I hadn't seen anyone that I knew from school, although we did attract some side glances from people! Making sure that she had a glass of water on the table beside her bed, I returned to the shop for the afternoon to tidy up a bit. I wiped down the glass counter which was full of cigarette ash and emptied the ashtrays and in doing so I knocked my rugby ball money box to the ground. It bounced emptily along the floor. Puzzled I picked it up and gave it a shake.

My heart quickened.

Nothing.

Turning it over I saw that there was a big hole cut out the bottom. I sat down abruptly, realisation dawning. My money was gone.

I had my suspicions of who the culprit was!

I angrily went into the back store room and collected all the empty bottles and put them in a couple of cardboard boxes outside the back door for collection. I also found a half empty bottle of gin on the counter so without hesitation, I poured it down the sink. Mom would never know.

Feeling despondent, I returned to the front of the shop and continued tidying up gloomily. Sometimes I wondered what was the point?

There were a couple of customers who called into the shop that afternoon and I was very proud of myself for helping them with their purchases. At five o'clock I emptied the till and put the notes and coins into a bank bag together with the deposit book as I had seen my mother do before and after locking up for the night, I took it home. Mom was out for the count on her bed and as there was no food in the house I took myself off to the corner shop to get some chips for supper.

I couldn't ask my mother that evening about my empty money box of course. She often didn't surface before I

234

left home to catch the bus to school in the mornings either so I would just have to hope that she was not drunk when I came home from school the next day.

She wasn't.

Well, she wasn't *as* drunk.

She denied it of course. She said the maid took it. But the maid hadn't worked at the shop since before she had her operation and I know my money was there a week ago.

I was *so hurt*.

As if I didn't mean anything to her!

After that I continued to go to the shop every afternoon after school. Sometimes my mother was there but a lot of times she was at home in bed. I would then open the shop for as long as I could and collect the takings for the day and take it home for mom to complete the deposit book ready for me to take to the bank.

#

Mom announced a couple of weeks later that she had had enough of Margate and she was going to move to Clocolan and look for a job there and stay with the Martindales for a while. She said the shop had gone under. Like the hotel. It did spring to mind briefly about her promises to buy a house and car and for us to get a dog and I realised then, that it was never going to happen. I felt a bit downcast because I knew that I would miss Freddy and Kenny but the idea of going back to the farm excited me. I didn't want to have to move schools again especially to an Afrikaans school. I struggled enough with school in English as it was.

During the following couple of days Mom seemed a bit more cheerful. She packed all her recently bought linen, towels and odds and ends into a couple of large wooden tea chests, cluttering up the already limited space in the flat. She said that we would catch a train to Durban and then on to Clocolan in a week's time. Late one afternoon there was a knock at the door and I heard mom talking to Mr Stead, the headmaster from my school. My first instinct was to wonder what I had done wrong. But when he had left mom said that he had just come to say goodbye. I was so relieved.

For my last weekend in Margate, I had arranged to meet Kenny and Freddy at the beach outside the lifesavers' clubhouse to tell them that I was leaving Margate. I was dreading it as they were my best friends and I had just come to realise that I would probably never see them again. Ever. I think Kenny felt the same because after we said goodbye and he turned to walk back home I could see that he was crying which made me cry too.

#

After two days on the train we were met at the station by Mr and Mrs Martindale who drove us to their farm. It was great being back on the farm. Mom and I shared the same bedroom as before only this time I knew that I wasn't going to be returning to Margate. I used to get up early and go down to the milking shed and watch the cows being milked then bring back a small bucketful of fresh milk for breakfast. I took to riding Chummy every day after breakfast and if I went past the cow sheds out onto the road with sheep grazing in their pastures on either side, I would see a family of meerkats sitting up and watching me ride past. Then they would scatter and run into their holes in the dry red earth before peeking out again. They were so cute.

There had been no mention of sending me to school yet but my mother was planning on living and working in the town of Clocolan and had been searching the 'positions vacant' column in the newspaper every day for something suitable. Mrs Martindale would drive mom into town for her interviews and very kindly wait until she was finished and drive her back to the farm again. Mom would come back from each interview all bouncy which didn't last as the days passed and the telephone remained silent.

There was one day when Mrs Martindale had gone shopping in Clocolan and I happened to walk past the building with the row of bedrooms and saw my mother and Mr Martindale lying together on the bed. Mom said that they were just resting.

A couple of days later there was a telephone call for mom. I know that she was hoping that it was from one of the companies that she had had an interview with saying that she had got the job. But all I heard was my mom shouting and screaming. It was my Dad's wife Glenda, to say that he was in hospital and was likely to be there for some time and that she had stopped mom's monthly maintenance because there was no money. Mom was distraught and I think that she had rather a lot of wine that evening.

A few days later there was a loud shouting argument in the kitchen between Mrs Martindale and my mother with both of them screaming at one another. It went on for some time. I felt uncomfortable and went and sat in our bedroom wishing that they would stop. Mom eventually came to our bedroom and threw herself onto her back on the bed with her hands under her head looking at the ceiling. She stayed like that for a while then got up and went out, returning a couple of minutes later with a bottle of wine and a glass. She didn't go to the dining room for supper that evening and the following day she said to me that we were going to move to Pietermaritzburg and stay with friends of hers, Garth and Eunice Robbins.

Mrs Martindale drove us to Pietermaritzburg which took about five hours. It was a silent, uncomfortable journey bringing back memories of another journey leaving the farm in Hartley. My tummy was doing funny things and I was sad to leave the farm and knew that I would miss Chummy. All mom's boxes containing her precious things were left back at the farm never to be seen again. We were dropped at the Robins' house in the late afternoon and I was to share a bedroom with their son Peter. The Robins ran a well established funeral parlour in Pietermaritzburg which was right next door to the house where they lived. Peter was eleven, the same age as me and he said that he helped out at the funeral parlour. Not having any idea what a funeral parlour was all about, Peter said that he would show me around. When we got to the courtyard there was a coffin on a trolley to the one side and Peter said that I must go and have a look and reassured me that there was no one inside. So I went ahead and had a look and there was a dead body inside. I ran away and said that I didn't ever want to go back there again. Peter just laughed and said that he had seen many dead people.

The day we arrived in Pietermaritzburg mom said that we were going to the hospital to see my dad. Greys

Hospital was not too far from the Robins' house so we could walk there. My dad was in a private room in intensive care and he was lying on bags of ice and his face was very white. He was in a coma and I don't think that he knew we were there as he didn't open his eyes. We were not there very long when the nurse came in and asked us to leave. Mom went back a couple of days later and told me that he was out of the coma but he had lost his memory. She also said that she was not going to be getting any more money from him so she had to find a job and we would be moving to Park Rynie on the Natal South Coast.

So it was back to the train station in Pietermaritzburg the following morning to catch a train to Durban and then onwards to Park Rynie which was a small resort town with some pretty beaches, a small general store and a caravan park that was packed out during holiday season. Mom had found work at the small local Ocean Hotel that was hugely busy during the holidays but dead quiet otherwise. Once again we were in a shared bedroom which reminded me of the room we had shared at the Regent Hotel in Margate. It was now over two months since we had left Margate and my mother decided it was high time that I was sent to school. She enrolled me in the small local school which only had three classes.

My days at school in Park Rynie were horrible. When I started there I didn't have a school uniform to wear so I had to go to school every day in ordinary clothes. I stuck out like a sore thumb and everyone looked at me. I couldn't wait for the bell to ring at the end of the day so that I could get out of there. I was however chosen to play in the cricket team on the Saturday against Umzinto School. I knew that I played cricket well so I was really looking forward to the game although it did cross my mind that I didn't have any cricket whites to wear. However when I got home from school on the Friday my mother announced that we were leaving Park Rynie and going to live in Durban. I was disappointed as I really wanted to play cricket for my school and felt angry with my mom but I couldn't convince her that we must stay. Our suitcases were already packed and we went straight to the station where we caught the train to Durban. It seemed that my mother had lost her job at the Ocean Hotel. I had a good idea why!

We arrived in Durban in the late afternoon and it was almost dark with a light chill breeze coming off the sea. Mom marched straight over to the Royal Hotel which wasn't far from Durban station and booked us in. The Royal Hotel was a famous landmark in the central city and renowned for being a top international colonial hotel with an African twist. Our room was very luxurious with high soft beds and an en suite with a deep white bath and free soap and shampoo. Dinner in the dining room that evening was quite a posh affair and I felt rather self conscious in a crumpled shirt that I had tried to unkink by running my warm hands down the fabric a couple of times. Mom was dressed to the nines and I was only fleetingly anxious when she stumbled against the table next to us sending some wine glasses flying, before sitting down rather heavily in the chair opposite me. Fortunately the wine glasses were empty. The waiters were there in a flash and the incident passed without much notice from our fellow diners.

The following couple of days I was left to amuse myself which I was used to. Across the road from the hotel is the Durban Museum. I had never been to the museum before so I spent many a happy hour there. I also made friends with a boy of about my own age. His name was Mike Pike and he was staying at the hotel with his mom. We seemed to bond instantly and he invited me to come and visit him at his home in Matatiele during the school holidays. I didn't tell him that I wasn't at school at the moment.

We stayed at the Royal Hotel for three days. For most of that time Mom sat in the room all day and drank and then she told me that there was no money left. On the third morning she packed up our bags and we left the hotel and started walking slowly down the street towards the beachfront. She did not want to talk to me and she looked terrible. Apart from the fact that she hadn't even put her face on before she left the hotel which was *unheard* of, I mean she would *never* do that, she looked as if she hadn't slept for days. I was filled with a gurgling dread that I could not shake.

When we got down to the beachfront promenade, mom went to lay on the grass and I sat on a bench nearby with our bags. Durban beachfront in the 1960s was a busy and vibrant holiday destination all year round as the weather sat around a minimum of twenty five degrees at midday in the winter. The grass that mom was lying on was in front of the bench and it stretched down to a small wooden wall that separated the sand on the beach from the promenade. There were many people on the beach in their brightly coloured costumes, sitting and relaxing on blue and white striped deck chairs that could be hired for a couple of pennies. Everyone looked happy and carefree and sounds of laughter drifted up to the bench where I was sitting. I felt alienated from everything as if I wasn't really where I was. I sat there on the bench for the whole day. Just sat there. We had no food and nothing to drink. I felt helpless and wanted to cry.

It was getting dark and I was starting to feel cold as there was a chill in the air. Mom hadn't moved all day and I really didn't know what to do. A kindly looking lady with curly grey hair approached me and said, 'Hello, I'm Moira. You look as if you could do with a bit of help. Have you got anywhere to sleep tonight?' My eyes filled with tears and I shook my head, too full to speak. I saw another lady talking to mom and helping her up from the grass where she had been lying for ages not moving with her arm over her face.

'It looks like your mom might need a bit of help as well so we are going to take her to Kerr House where they will be able to give her what she needs,' said Moira 'And as for you young fellow, we will get you settled for the night into a hostel with some other boys your age and then we can sort out what to do in the morning.' Moira helped me to carry our bags and we moved off down the road towards what would be another temporary home.

Kerr House was established in 1951 as a temporary shelter for abused and destitute women and is a non profit organisation that does amazing work in the care of those women who need a haven from domestic violence and in giving those that need a helping hand an opportunity to get back on their feet. This is where they took my mom.

Moira handed me over to a lady from the Durban Child Welfare who ran the hostel who introduced herself as Mrs MacAllister. 'But you can call me Mac,' she said with a smile. The hostel was in a large double storey building that could have originally been a house and it wasn't very far from Kerr House where my mother was staying. The section that was to become my temporary home housed all the boys.

'Now you just follow me and I will show you where you will sleep tonight and where the bathrooms are as well,' continued Mac as she led the way up a curved wooden staircase to the first floor where we entered a room that had a row of six beds against the one wall, each with their own small table.

'This bed is yours,' she said as she placed my battered suitcase down on top of the blanket 'and through here is the bathroom. Why don't you have a quick face and hand wash for now and I will take you down to the dining room to have something to eat as I'm sure you must be hungry.'

I nodded. I was starving not having eaten all day.

The dining room downstairs was full of the noisy chatter of twenty young boys all sitting at a number of green Formica tables. I was shown to a table where three other boys were sitting, tucking into large plates of sausages and mash. My mouth watered. I pulled out a straight backed chair and sat down slowly, looking around the room.

'Here you go then young man.' A plate of food was put on the table in front of me the smell of fried sausages enticing and music to my stomach. I ate quickly as I was famished and I was allowed to have seconds. After a bowl of ice cream I sat back in my chair as full as a tick and feeling more comfortable.

It wasn't long after that, with heavy eyelids I was taken up to my room where I lay in bed listening to the unfamiliar sounds around me and wondered what my mother was doing before I fell into an exhausted sleep.

The following day Mac took me to the office downstairs, settled me in a chair and said, 'Well now, Rudi. Your mom is unable to look after you at the moment so you are going to stay here with us until the end of the school holidays. Then we are sending you to school in Bergville. It is a boarding school so you will live there during the term and come home to see your mother during the school holidays.'

'Where is Bergville? How ... how will I get there? T ... to the school?' I stammered.

'Bergville is inland past Pietermaritzburg, near Estcourt. We will put you on the train and once you reach Bergville there will be someone to meet you at the station to take you to school.'

That didn't seem too bad. I had been on a train a number of times so I knew what to expect.

But it was with dread that I thought about going to another new school. And a boarding school at that.

CHAPTER TEN

Joan

I opened the shop with a bang. I wanted to have an opening that Margate had never seen before and would remember for a long time. I wanted people to know that I was back. Joan Garden. Back with a bang!

With Dorothy and Bertha's business and personal connections in Margate, together with quite an extensive list of guests that I had come up with, I was able to send invitations to far more people that I had originally thought possible. Okay so maybe some of those who I had invited, probably wouldn't want to come. But still.

There was a catering company that was new on the block and I contacted them and ordered an array of exotic canapés and snacks all *beautifully* displayed on shiny silverware, which they delivered to the shop in the early afternoon of the official opening. There was a *mountain* of the most delicious chocolate-covered strawberries just waiting to be devoured and a large scrumptious meringue nest smothered in cream and passion fruit taking pride of place amidst a sumptuous collection of treats. The caterers provided luxurious lace napkins and fine bone china plates. And champagne. *Loads* of champagne served in the most divine crystal glasses. I hadn't felt this excited in *ages*!

A local lad who was an electrician set up a couple of strings of soft lights throughout the shop and it looked like fairyland.

It had all cost me quite a *bit!*

But at the end of the day ... ... .it was worth it.

I had planned on wearing the plum lace dress that I had bought in Hartley as I had only worn it once. But for some reason, I couldn't find it. I couldn't think what on earth had become of it. So I just had to go and look for something new. Something exotic. Something stunning. I came across this darling cocktail dress when I was in an upmarket boutique in Port Shepstone one afternoon. Just *darling*! It was red. And swishy. And red is my favourite colour as I have probably mentioned before. So of course I had to have it. No ... I was *meant* to have it!

The price tag made my eyes water.

Giving myself a shake, I just had to remind myself that I had plenty of money and I could buy what I want. So I bought a pair of shoes and a handbag to match as well.

Well ... why wouldn't you?

The opening evening was a marvellous success. It couldn't have gone any better. *So* many people turned up that I eventually had to send out to the bottle store for another two dozen bottles of their best champagne. Which went in a flash, I might add. I felt on top of the world in my new red dress which hung in soft folds from my shoulders. I was the centre of attention and I loved every minute of it. This was where I belonged.

So I decided there and then that I would have a cocktail evening at the shop at least once a month. Just for the fun of it.

#

I realised that it was time that I found myself somewhere to live as I couldn't stay with Dorothy and Bertha for ever. I had come to an arrangement with the Waverley Hotel which was just up the road from the shop, to rent a room long term for Rudi and I, in anticipation of his return. They would provide three meals a day and a bedroom for us both at a fixed rate which was rather a lot I must admit. But so what? At least I wouldn't have to worry about cooking food. Not that I didn't enjoy cooking but with Rudi expected to be coming home any day now and with me running the shop, it would just be easier. Certainly to begin with anyhow. Just until I started to look for a house to buy.

And to be honest I was quite *glad* to be leaving the sisters. I mean they were very *nice* and all that, very *sweet*, very *helpful*. But it just became a little too *much* with their constant 'do this,dearie' or 'it's a lot of money to be spending on décor, dearie' or even 'my you have bought a lot of stock. I do hope you will be able to sell it all, dearie'. Dearie this and dearie that. It was never ending!

And of course the sisters didn't drink. I know ... I know that I initially said that it was a good thing that they didn't drink because then there would be no temptation. But sometimes after a particularly busy day at the shop I just felt that it would nice to relax with a drink or two you know. And I knew that I could control it. So I had taken to buying the occasional bottle of gin and keeping it at the shop. There's nothing wrong with that now is there?

After about five months of running the shop on a day to day basis I discovered it was actually all rather *boring*. It *was* exciting at the beginning when I spent a lot of time arranging things beautifully on the shelves to their best advantage and changing the window display every week with a new theme that I would take *ages* mulling over. Deciding on what colour scheme I should have and what eye catching props I could use. It was fun! I made sure that I had fresh roses delivered once a week and placed them in a cut glass vase on the counter top. I did the paperwork meticulously and at the close of day I would total the takings and complete the deposit book carefully so it was all ready to be taken to the bank. I employed a maid who would come in every day to dust and clean the floors and windows and do any shopping for me that needed to be done.

Overall, the shop was reasonably busy but the stock wasn't turning over as quickly as I had expected. During the school holidays sunburnt families were strolling in and buying the odd thing here and there that caught their eye and lingering for a chat. But when the schools were once again open, Margate's streets were deserted of up country visitors and the footfall outside the shop was minimal. Sometimes I only had one person in the shop all day and then they didn't buy anything. So there was actually very little to *do*! It made for a long uneventful day with time hanging heavily on my hands. It was worse than watching paint dry! So just to help things along a bit I had taken to pouring myself a nice large gin just to while away the time. Although I did manage to wait until the afternoon so that I had something to look forward to.

Totts to Teens had been open for six months and I had been staying at the Waverley Hotel for almost three months when Rudi was allowed to come back to live with me. Eventually the Child Welfare had agreed that I was able to provide a home for him. It had been two years since I had lived in Salisbury and almost two years that

Rudi had lived with Ronnie Baker. It seemed much longer. I know I had promised him that I would buy a house and a car but I enjoyed living at the Waverley and I also enjoyed spending money. I reasoned that if I bought a house then all my money would be tied up. And that was the last thing I wanted to do.

Rudi was dropped off at the shop in the afternoon after school by Ronnie. He looked sombre. It was wonderful to have him back and hoping to cheer him up, I closed the shop early and we walked over to the hotel and I showed him where we would be living. I actually don't think that he was too happy about living once more in a hotel room. At night he used to take his pillow and blanket and sleep in the passageway outside the room as he said the light bothered him. But that was just too bad as there was nothing I could do. But I did promise him that staying at the Waverley was only temporary.

He had really grown up. I didn't see much of him in the afternoons for the first couple of weeks after he returned. I have no idea where he went. But then he started coming to the shop in the afternoons after school and would potter around in the workshop at the back.

A very friendly couple, Liz and Hank Martindale who were on holiday in Margate, came into the shop one day and we just seemed to hit it off. Hank was awfully handsome in a rugged sort of way and I couldn't help flirting just a little. They invited both Rudi and I to tea at their holiday flat one Saturday morning which I accepted without hesitation. I could tell that they had lots of money just be the way they dressed and they also mentioned that their two children would be going to private schools which I know costs a packet. When they left to go back home to their farm outside Clocolan, we exchanged address and telephone numbers and promised to keep in touch.

Going through the sales figures at the shop one day I realised that they were starting to look a bit bleak. Apparently the outgoings far exceeded the incomings, so my accountant said to me firmly one day. I hadn't stopped the monthly cocktail parties even though I was told it was an extravagance that the business couldn't afford. But they were something to look *forward* to even though they did cost a bit and didn't really bring in any new business. But I reasoned that once it was school holidays, then things would pick up again. So there was nothing to worry about. Although sometimes in the evenings after I had closed the shop for the day and made my way home, I would feel a bubbling of anxiety in the pit of my stomach when I thought of all the bills that still needed paying. But a nice large gin always eased my worries and I felt *so* much better.

When the schools closed for two weeks in October I was optimistic that the shop would get very busy and had ordered a number of gorgeous toddler dresses and rompers which I thought were so cute. I also stocked up on some teenage clothes as they always seemed to sell well. It wasn't really *necessary* to buy more stock but I had the rep come into the shop with all the newest ranges and they were so delightful that I couldn't resist. So I doubled the order. I mean ... I would still sell it. Eventually. And actually when all the stuff arrived I struggled to find place to put it all. But at least I didn't have to pay the supplier for three months.

In the meantime, I decided that we could no longer afford to live at the Waverley and I found a furnished one bedroom flat on the outskirts of Margate. It was a *lot* cheaper than living in the hotel so that was quite clever of me although now I would have to think about buying and cooking food. So for convenience, I opened an account at the Corner café up the road. I could then get all my food there and only pay at the end of the month. I opened an account at the chemist as well. Just for convenience. But the best thing was that I splashed out on some crisp new linen for the beds, lots of large fluffy towels with bath mats to match, an elegant bone china dinner and tea set and some stunning glasses that I just had to have. Then I came across this silver cutlery set with bone handles nestled in a hand carved ebony chest lined with blue velvet that was so divine that I bought it without even looking at the price. I just thought ... *So what!* I deserve it. I never spoil myself and it was just so nice to have my own home after so long even if it was not my own furniture.

October school holidays hadn't been as busy in the shop as I had hoped. It was fairly busy but I just did not make enough to cover what I had paid out for all the new stock. I felt a flutter of panic knowing that I would be needing to pay suppliers in a couple of weeks. Shrugging my shoulders and deciding that there wasn't much I could do about it, I poured a generous gin, enjoying the warmth as it spread through my body. Feeling *much* calmer and humming to myself, I closed the shop, went to the post box to collect the post and went home.

There was a letter from Liz Martindale inviting us up to their farm for a holiday. What a great idea. It couldn't have come at a better time. Without even thinking about it I wrote back straight away accepting her invitation. It would be good to get away for a bit. Although I thought that it would be better if the shop could remain open whilst I was away and Yvonne James sprang immediately to mind. Yvonne was local to Margate and I had got to know her after she had come into the shop a couple of times. Divorced with two small children to support, I knew she would jump at the chance to make a little bit of extra money. Feeling excited about my impromptu getaway I sat back, lit a cigarette and relaxed with another drink.

The following day after arranging with Yvonne to look after the shop in my absence, I phoned Rudi's school to let them know that he wouldn't be there for two weeks. I don't think Mr Stead was very impressed with my plan as he was quite reluctant to give permission and he insisted that I took work for Rudi to do every day whilst he was away. I almost told him that I didn't need his *permission* to take my own child on an educational *holiday*! But for once I held my tongue.

I thoroughly enjoyed my break in Clocolan with Liz and Hank. It reminded me a bit of Arthur's farm. We dressed up every evening for cocktails on the verandah which I loved and I realised how much I had missed it. Then a maid would ring a bell to announce that dinner was ready to be served in the large airy dining room. Everything was so elegant and tasteful. Even Hank. Especially Hank. With his thick head of dark hair, handsome square cut face and gracious manner, he cut an attractive figure. And I could never resist an attractive man.

I had made sure that I took quite a few bottles of gin with me, packed in with my luggage undetected underneath my clothes. One bottle was kept handy at the bottom of the wooden wardrobe so that I could have a quick mouthful when the urge arose, with the other bottles remaining in my suitcase until needed. This really seemed to work quite well and I was quite *proud* of myself for being able to make the bottles last the whole two weeks of my stay. I did manage to blot out that nasty persistent little voice in my head that kept telling me that I shouldn't be doing this.

Shut up!

Shut up! *Shut up!*

I am in control!

So what is the problem?

The Martindales had a beautiful home which filled me with envy somehow. They entertained effortlessly and the two weeks spent on the farm seemed to fly by. Fortunately for me Liz was busy home schooling her children before they were sent off to a private boarding school the following year so she offered to help Rudi with his extra school work. So at least he got it done.

We arrived back home mid-afternoon and I went straight to the shop as I was anxious to see how things had been going during our absence. Yvonne clearly wasn't expecting me as she appeared startled and flustered and couldn't wait to leave. Taking a seat uneasily behind the counter I started looking through the lists that I had asked Yvonne to make every day of each item sold. There weren't many at all which was a bit strange in itself. The bank deposit book told an even more pitiful story. After going through the list of items sold very carefully I realised that something was not right. I knew my stock. I knew what I had left on the shelves, in what colour and what size. So I knew that there were articles of clothing that were missing. Clearly Yvonne had been selling garments without making a note of the sale and pocketing the money.

I sat back stunned. And here's me thinking it was a good idea to get someone in to look after the shop whilst I'm gone. Fat lot of good that's done me! I'm worse off now than I was before. Shaking my head and not wanting to think about it anymore, I closed the shop and headed for the bottle store.

It was a couple of days later that Rudi became ill with a high fever. He said his throat was sore and he could hardly get out of bed. Feeling concerned I made an appointment to see the local doctor who just happened to be Michael Johnston. I had heard on the grapevine that Michael had remarried a year or so ago. She was fifteen years younger than him. A child! I would show him what he had missed out on. I would show him what a *real woman* was.

Dressing with the express idea of impressing Michael in a figure-hugging dress that I know enhanced my curves and fortified by a small gin that I knocked back in preparation for coming face to face with him once more, Rudi and I set off for the surgery, my stomach a flutter.

'Joan!'

His voice caressed my name. I looked directly up into his eyes and smiled my most beguiling smile. 'Michael. Its been a while,' I said holding out my hand. He took it and held it a fraction and I thought he was going to kiss it. Shaking his head slightly he dropped my hand and stood back, showing me the way into his office. After examining Rudi he said that he needed to be admitted to hospital to have his tonsils out rather urgently and that he would make all the arrangements. It was quite nice to have someone take charge for a change. Michael drove Rudi and I to the hospital where he was admitted and once he was settled for the evening Michael drove me home. I was so tempted to ask him in for a coffee but before I could he said, 'I need to get back to the surgery. Would you like a lift to the hospital tomorrow so that you can visit Rudi?'

'I would love that, thank you' And I floated up the stairs to the flat.

The following day Michael picked me up outside the shop in the afternoon as arranged. I had lingered in a bath that morning and dressed with extra attention in a bright yellow floral dress that I had bought just last week. It fitted me to perfection of course and I wore my new white sandals that showed off my brightly painted toenails. After spraying myself liberally with Blue Grass, which I'm sure would stir some memories for him, I was ready. Climbing into the front seat of Michael's car I leant over and gave him a soft peck on the cheek in greeting. He smiled briefly at me and we drove the rest of the way to the hospital in silence. I think that I felt more comfortable than he did.

Seeing Michael again had set my heart a flutter. All the pain of our destructive relationship and subsequent break-up was forgotten to be replaced by an intense longing to possess him. I know that at first I only wanted him to see what he had missed. But seeing him once more I realised that I wanted him. I knew that I could be irresistible so I deliberately set out to seduce him.

Rudi was much better. His fever was down and although his throat was sore which was understandable he was a lot more cheerful. I stayed a while and chatted to him until it was time to meet Michael. Three times he took me to the hospital to see Rudi and each time he behaved with utmost politeness. Once Rudi was home I knew that there would be no more car rides.

'Come in for a coffee. For old time's sake,' I said persuasively the last time he dropped me off at home. He agreed and followed me up the stairs into the flat.

'I think I would much rather have a glass of champagne,' I said going to the fridge and retrieving the bottle that I had placed there earlier in anticipation of Michael's visit. 'Let's celebrate Rudi's return home tomorrow. I'll grab some glasses.' Not giving him a chance to refuse I took two champagne flutes out of the cupboard and handed him the bottle to open. Michael poured our drinks and we walked through to the lounge and sat down. Raising his glass he turned and looked at me. My heart did a flip. The tension in the room was palpable. I smiled at him and took a small sip of my champagne not taking my eyes off his face. Oh how I've missed you. Missed your face. Missed your voice. Missed your kisses.

Taking a deep breath and hoping that I hadn't voiced my thoughts out loud, I came to a decision. Looking deep into his brown eyes, I put my champagne down on the table and leant over and took the glass out of his hand placing it next to mine. I stood up slowly and held out my hand which he took without hesitation and we walked through to the bedroom, Michael pushing the door closed behind him with his foot.

It was glorious, glorious, glorious!

'I never thought that I would be back with you Michael,' I said to him afterwards. 'This is something that I have never allowed myself to even dream about. It has made me *so* happy.'

I felt his sharp intake of breath at my words. Not having mentioned anything about his wife to me I just pretended that I didn't know that he was married. I felt it was up to him to tell me and to be honest, I really didn't care! I just wanted him. He sat up awkwardly and removing his arm from around my shoulders he turned to face me.

'Joan you are irresistible. You do know that, don't you? But I have to tell you that I have remarried and I am not going to leave my wife.'

The cad!!

'But you are happy to betray her!' My voice was rising 'and don't you dare tell me that this was a mistake' my previous resolve to not let it bother me that he was married had crumbled instantly.

What *was* I to him?

Just some plaything that he could discard whenever he had had enough fun!

I felt used.

I looked at him waiting for a response. He lowered his eyes and tried to take me in his arms. Pushing him away I swung out of bed, pulled on my silk wrap and walked out to the lounge taking deep breaths to calm myself down. Lighting a cigarette I inhaled angrily and stood in front of the large window looking out over the tidal pool the beauty of the morning lost on me. Although come to think of it ... I don't know why I was feeling so angry. I knew he was married all along didn't I? What did I expect?

But it became clear to me that I wanted more than the occasional furtive meeting.

I heard movement behind me but I did not turn around. Then I heard the front door close and I knew that he had left.

Bastard!

I walked to the kitchen and grabbing the champagne bottle, I had a couple of mouthfuls before I sloshed a generous amount into a glass and sat down and drank. Later on I organised a taxi to take me to the hospital to collect Rudi that afternoon and carried on drinking when I got home. Just so that I didn't have to think.

I didn't open the shop that day at all.

He phoned the following day. Apologetic. Ashamed of himself, he said. Not ashamed because he had run out on me. Oh no! Ashamed because he had 'given in to temptation' he said. As if *I* didn't matter!! As if I didn't have any *feelings* in the matter!

But he said that he wanted to see me again. The *cad*!

I said yes!

I was a bit like a moth to a flame really. I knew that I was going to be hurt but I did it anyway!

Because I *wanted* him!

Because I loved him.

Because I *hated* him.

But I knew that I would never really have him.

Over the following weeks I saw him a number of times. I should have been manning the shop that was going to the dogs, but the pull of Michael was too great. One day he arrived at the flat as usual when Rudi was at school and he said he had something to tell me. He said that he had to let me know that his wife was expecting a baby and that it was best that our relationship ended.

I just looked at him, my mind churning.

I was being rejected again. But this time I felt something else as well. Contempt! I was determined this time that I would not plead with him. I was *determined* this time to hold onto some kind of dignity.

Without a word I sauntered slowly over to the door, opened it and stood back looking at him directly in the face and slammed the door so hard behind him that I'm surprised the front of the building didn't collapse. But it helped.

Bastard!!

My body longed for the oblivion of a drink

I knew that I had to open the shop, but I wanted oblivion more.

Bastard!

I headed straight for the gin bottle and slugged back a good amount before putting it in my bag deciding to finish off what was left when I got to work. I polished it off within the hour. My wretched troubles were melting further and further into the distance. It was glorious. The only problem was that I didn't have any cash to buy any drink. But then I remembered the plastic rugby ball money box on the counter. I grabbed a knife from the small kitchen and cut a hole underneath the money box and took out what was there. Delighted to find that it would buy me more than a couple of bottles of gin, I headed off to the bottle store straight away absolutely thrilled with myself.

I had been so immersed in my up and down relationship with Michael that I had not been paying much attention to my health. After consulting a doctor it appeared that I would need to have a hysterectomy, sooner rather than later. The whole idea of another operation really irritated and depressed me. I was already feeling low anyway in the aftermath of losing Michael for the second time. I know I didn't really *lose* him as I never had him in the first place. But that is what it felt like. I felt like I had lost Joan too. That wonderful giggly, passionate, enticing, fascinating Joan.

No I wouldn't think about her!

Once again I had the problem of what to do with Rudi. I would *not ever* consider sending him to stay with Ronnie again, that is for sure. He had taken him away from me for two years. *Two years!*. And he had always been so disapproving of me that I would not give him the satisfaction. I decided to ask Peggy Liebenberg who wasn't a *friend* exactly. We didn't go out to tea together or tell one another our innermost secrets or anything like that. But we had seen one another socially and she had supported the shop and been to a couple of my cocktail evenings. So I thought that she wouldn't mind looking after Rudi for a while. I mean he's no trouble. No trouble at all.

The shop had to remain closed whilst I was in hospital. There was nothing that I could do about that. At least it was not school holidays and still reasonably quiet so I shouldn't miss out on too much trade. Rudi wasn't pleased when I told him that he was going to stay with the Liebenbergs but there was nothing that I could do.

My operation went smoothly and I was discharged from hospital after three weeks. I booked myself into a lovely hotel on Durban beachfront for another three weeks to recover my strength. Well ... why not? I needed the rest and I must say I felt *very* tired. But slowly I built up my strength again and six weeks later I was back in the Margate flat with Rudi.

Opening the shop for the first time after six weeks away was a bit uplifting actually. I spent the morning cleaning and dusting and rearranging things so that it all looked inviting. I had an appointment with my accountant in the afternoon and Rudi said that he would man the shop for me whilst I was gone. The outcome of my meeting was not good. I seemed to owe money all over the place. There were a number of suppliers that hadn't been paid, some of them for longer than six months and they were threatening to sue. Then there was the carpenter that I had hired months ago, to make some gorgeous bespoke cabinets for the shop, which looked stunning I might add. Well it seems that he hadn't been paid either. And not to forget the electrician who I had called back on a number of occasions to move the lights in the shop to focus on certain areas. I could have sworn that I had posted a cheque to him.

Calling in at the bank after seeing my accountant, I was confronted with the reality of my financial situation. There wasn't enough money in my account to pay all that I owed. And I don't think that the cheque from the Durban hotel where I had stayed for three weeks had come through yet either. That was for quite a big amount as you can imagine. Where on earth had all the money gone? Folding up the bank statement and putting it in my bag with the intention of going through it carefully that evening, I made my way home but not before I had called in at the bottle store to replenish my stock.

After a night spent tossing and turning despite a number of large gins, I made my way to the shop the following morning with the intention of getting my head around my bank statements. I'd had a cursory look when I got home last night but after the first gin I couldn't be bothered. I settled in the chair with a cup of tea and a cigarette and began to go through the figures. It made for sober reading and I felt sick. I had to acknowledge that I was in trouble.

I would have a sale I decided. At least that would shift some stock and it wouldn't matter that the prices were reduced because at least something was coming in. Feeling enthused I started going through the garments and marking prices down and creating special sales racks on which to place them. Then I put up huge red sale signs on the window and door and contacted the local newspaper to place an advert about the sale. I didn't think about how I was going to pay for the advert of course. Easter holidays were coming up shortly so that would be ideal to attract people into the shop. Why did I not think of this before?

The sale ran for as long as there was something in the shop to sell. A lot of stock moved I have to say, even those garments that weren't on sale were bought. But I was at the shop less and less. Sometimes I only went there in the late morning to open up and sometimes I only opened in the afternoon. There were times when it all seemed a bit too *much* and I would just stay in bed most of the day and not open at all. I couldn't see the point in opening the shop all day and sitting there bored out of my mind and nobody bothering to come in to buy anything. Even with the help of a bottle of gin.

#

There was nothing for it. I needed to get away from Margate. Again! The shop was going nowhere. Most of the stock had been sold, a lot of it for next to nothing I must admit. I had paid most of my outstanding debts and those that remained unpaid … well … you can't get blood out of a stone now can you? And there was just no more money! So there was nothing to keep me in Margate. All I had once more was my monthly maintenance money from Ian to live on.

Sitting in the half empty shop one day in a fug of alcohol, I had a brainwave. I would move to Clocolan. I could stay with the Martindales whilst I looked for a job in the town. *That's* what I would do. There must be loads of hotels there where I could find work.

Buoyed by my sudden decision I started making arrangements immediately the following day. All my lovely new things that I had so recently bought were carefully packed into a number of large wooden tea chests that I had managed to find at the local hardware store. Some of the linen had never been used and was still wrapped in its original packaging. Other than that, there wasn't much else. Only our clothes which wouldn't take long. Whilst I was busy packing one afternoon, I had a visit from Mr Stead, Rudi's headmaster, who made every effort to talk me out of moving to Clocolan. Or should I say, he tried to talk me out of moving Rudi to another school especially in the middle of the school term. He attempted to convince me that it wasn't good for Rudi to move schools again as he was settled and coping well apparently. I told him to mind his own business and carried on packing.

I went to the shop and had a last look around feeling a pang of regret for what might have been. Just a flash. Which I immediately squashed. Turning around I locked the door for the last time and dropped the keys off at the letting agent. We then headed off to the station to catch a train to Durban.

Liz Martindale met us at the station in the centre of Clocolan and helped me with the pile of tea chests and suitcases, loading them all onto the back of her large farm truck. It was good to be back on the farm actually and Hank looked even more handsome.

Over the following days, with Liz's help I managed to arrange a couple of interviews for work with various hotels in Clocolan. After setting off for each interview with high hopes of a positive outcome I was left disheartened and depressed when I was told each time that I had to be *tweetalig*. I had to be able to speak Afrikaans as well as English. Clocolan was an Afrikaans town. The schools were taught in Afrikaans. The books in the library were Afrikaans. The street signs were in Afrikaans. The police, the shopkeepers, builders, ministers, bus drivers, teachers. Everybody spoke Afrikaans. I didn't stand a chance of finding a job if I couldn't speak Afrikaans. Which I couldn't!

My gin bottle helped me cope.

So did Hank. We had been getting on so *well* Hank and I. We just seemed to be on the same wavelength and laughed at the same things. He would regularly have a word of encouragement for me and seemed to frequently be around the house during the day when I was there. He was awfully good looking and we would throw flirty banter back and forth continuously until it was banter no longer. Liz had gone to town and I was depressed about another rejection that I had received that morning. Failing to respond to his banter as I was so emerged in my thoughts, I felt his hand lifting my chin, my eyes meeting his. He kissed me gently and led me to the bedroom.

264

It didn't fix anything of course and I wasn't sure if I felt any better afterwards either. But it *was* nice to have Hank enthralled by me. It proved to me that I wasn't losing my touch. I was still appealing. Although when Liz got home later that afternoon I did feel a trifle bad but thought she would never find out anyway. So ...

One afternoon the phone rang out in the hall.

'Joan, there is a Glenda on the line who is asking for you,' said Liz. 'Goodness! That's Ian's wife. What on earth does she want?' I said puzzled taking the receiver from her.

'Hello Glenda' I said pleasantly 'This is a surprise.'

'Well it's not good news I'm afraid' her voice was soft but determined. 'Ian has been taken ill and he is in a coma at Greys Hospital in Pietermaritzburg. He has contracted encephalitis and I'm not sure of the outcome at this stage. But I thought that I needed to let you know that I can't pay any more maintenance payments to you as there is no money.'

'Wh ... *what*? You can't just do that' I exclaimed

'But there is no money, Joan. There is nothing that I can do.

'NO! NO!' I screamed into the phone '*You can't do that! What am I to do?'*

'I'm sorry, Joan. I just thought that I would let you know.'

'Well you CAN'T DO THAT. I am just going to have to speak to Ian myself! He won't allow that.' I slammed the phone down, shaking.

Reeling from the shock, I made my way outside onto the verandah, the sound of the bamboo wind chimes and the warm sun on my face feeling like a mockery to my inner turmoil. I blundered down the steps, battling to breathe and collapsed onto a garden bench.

I couldn't think straight.

I was numb.

They can't do that!

Surely they can't do that!

Can they?

What was I going to do? I can't even get a job!

I was still rocking from the news two days later when Liz called me into the kitchen, the expression on her face thunderous.

'What is this?' she asked holding up my yellow leather belt that I had worn a couple of days ago.

I reddened, realising that I must have left it in their bedroom. 'Oh you have found my belt!' I said with a smile recovering quickly.

'Yes, Joan. But what was it doing in *my* bedroom?'

'In your *bedroom*? Was it really? Gosh I don't have the faintest idea how it could have got there' I said warming to my theme.

'I have invited you into my home as a friend and you have betrayed me in the worst way possible. How DARE you take advantage of me. How DARE you LIE to me,' screamed Liz.

'I'm not ly … ' I started to say.

'Don't even bother to say another word. Hank has told me everything. You are a conniving thoughtless *drunk*. Poison. That's what you are. *Poison*. I want you away from my family. Away from me! And to make sure that you do leave here and never come back, I will drive you to Pietermaritzburg myself. I don't care where you go after that.' And she stormed out of the room leaving me dazed and light headed.

I walked to the bedroom that I shared with Rudi, opened the wardrobe and grabbed the almost empty bottle of gin. After draining the contents I threw the bottle aside and fell back onto the bed with exhaustion.

Stupid woman! It's not my fault that she can't hold onto her husband! And in any case, *he* started it! Yes I know that I flirted with him but it was all *harmless* and good fun. I can't help it if he took it a step further now could I?

After a while I got up and went through to the kitchen making sure that Liz was nowhere to be seen and found a bottle of wine and took it back to my room looking forward to the oblivion that it offered.

But the question still remained. What was I going to do now?

In a haze of alcohol I came to the conclusion that I must speak to Ian. He will sort out this whole mess with my maintenance money. Yes … That is what I must do. This was all Glenda's fault anyway! I was *convinced*. I knew that once Ian realised what had happened, he would have everything back to the way it was.

The following day, after rising late and feeling awfully thick headed I realised that I had to do something about accommodation for us in Pietermaritzburg. Fortunately I knew a couple Garth and Eunice Robbins, from my time in the hotel industry, who lived in the town. They were well known funeral parlour owners with a large successful family business. I was sure that they wouldn't mind putting us up for a week or two. Just while I sorted out my finances. Switching on my charm, I phoned them and told them that Ian had been taken ill suddenly and had been asking for me and that I needed a temporary roof over my head. They were ever so obliging. Feeling a bit more upbeat after speaking to Eunice, the remainder of the day was spent in a silent house. There was no sign of either Liz or Hank and I was sure that Hank was deliberately avoiding me. *Coward*! It takes two to tango as they say. Why does it always have to be *my* fault?

Early the next day we were loaded into Liz's car, a subdued Rudi in the back and we set off for Pietermaritzburg which was a good five hours drive away. It was an uncomfortable journey as you can imagine. I did not try and make idle conversation because I knew it would be met with silence. Throughout the journey I was fine tuning what I would say to Ian about my maintenance money when I got to see him in hospital. I was feeling quite optimistic actually. The whole thing could only have been a mistake.

After a long hot journey Liz stopped the car outside the large house which served as a residence on the one side and the funeral parlour on the other. She sat in the driver's seat looking straight ahead and didn't get out of the car to help us with our suitcases. Rudi and I were left on the pavement surrounded by our possessions as she drove off without a backward glance.

Bitch!

I was exhausted after the long drive and starting to feel very shaky and fidgety and the familiar pull for a drink was becoming increasingly stronger. I did not have much money left by this stage, so fuelled by desperation and anger at Glenda for putting me in this position, I decided to see Ian straight away despite feeling travel weary.

After being welcomed by Garth and Eunice, Rudi and I headed straight for the hospital which was within walking distance of where we were staying.

Ian was in a private room in ICU. He looked dreadful. Grey in the face. He was lying on his back with his eyes closed and was surrounded by packs of ice. I tried to wake him and talk to him but got no response. The nurses told me to keep my voice down. But I was in a bit of a state. I *needed* to talk to him. I needed to talk to him now. Didn't they understand!

We were only allowed in there for ten minutes then we were asked to leave. I was beside myself.

I returned to the hospital the next day and the next. There was no change in his condition until three days later when I discovered that he had been moved out of ICU to another ward and when I arrived at his bedside he was awake. I felt light with relief.

'Ian, I'm so glad you are awake. I really need to speak to you.' His blue eyes found mine and he gave a ghost of a smile. Not waiting for him to respond I ploughed on. 'Do you realise that Glenda has stopped my maintenance money. She can't do that Ian and it needs to be sorted out straight away. I have got to have that money to live on,' I finished vehemently.

Ian looked at me with a slight frown on his face. 'Who are you?' he asked in a soft voice.

'Ian! It's *me! Joan.*' For heaven's sake! Surely he knows me? I bent over him. 'You know who I am. Joan! Your ex-wife!'

'I'm sorry but I don't know you.'

'Oh don't be *silly,* Ian.' My voice rising. I wanted to shake him 'It's ME! *Joan!* You *know* me!'

'What is going on? We can't have all this noise in here,' said a nurse bustling in and looking accusingly at me. 'Mr Garden needs rest and quiet'

'Yes, but he doesn't know who I *am*!' I exclaimed, frantic now.

'It would seem that he has suffered some memory loss which is possibly permanent. Only time will tell I am afraid. But in the meantime he needs time to recover and I will not have my patients harassed in this manner.'

I was speechless. Memory loss! *Memory loss?* Not having any thought for Ian and what he was going through all I could think about was my money. Or lack of it! I turned around and walked out the room feeling wretched. What was I to do? Where on earth do I go from here? I was distraught.

On the way home finding myself walking past a café, I bought a newspaper. I had come to the realisation that I had no alternative but to go back to work and sooner rather than later. I had always in the past found work quite easily, except for in Clocolan of course, and this was no exception. Thank goodness I found a job straight away at the Ocean Hotel in Park Rynie. They were desperate to hire someone to manage the place before the start of the three- week school holidays which was just around the corner. It was a very small hotel which I would be in charge of which suited me. But at least it solved my immediate problem of accommodation and money. So a week or so later Rudi and I were on a train once more bound for the south coast.

As soon as I had arrived in Park Rynie and unpacked my suitcase I went into the small town and opened an account at the Corner café and as the bottle store was run by the same owners they allowed me to buy some gin on the account as well. I was so *relieved*! Shakily I left the shop and was hardly around the corner when I stopped and managed to sneak a couple of mouthfuls from the bottle, enjoying the warmth it offered.

Rudi was enrolled at the local small school. I sent him off there the day after we had arrived in Park Rynie. He was very reluctant to go although I think more so because he didn't have a school uniform and had to go in his civvies, standing out like a sore thumb. I was hit with a wave of *deja vu* remembering my first day at the convent that Aunt Rachel had sent me to and how nervous and out of place I had felt and realised that Rudi must be feeling apprehensive and awkward. I felt it was my fault. But not wanting to think too hard about that I had a few more mouthfuls of gin and the feelings of regret and shame receded until they were drowned out altogether.

As I was in charge of running the Ocean Hotel I had access to an unlimited amount of alcohol which I made full use of. Ok, so it wasn't entirely *allowed*. *Obviously*! I knew that. But if nobody saw and nobody found out, I couldn't see the problem. I befriended the Indian barman and gave him ten rand in the hope that if he did notice any drink disappearing then he would keep his mouth shut.

I had always thought that I was pretty good about deceiving those around me as to how much I was drinking.

I had always thought that I was perfectly in control.

I had always thought that I was managing my work with ease.

Yes, I know that sometimes I was a little *unsteady* on my feet. But who can blame me? If you had to totter around in my impossibly high heels all day the way that I did, you would also take a tumble every so often. I mean let's face it. Stilettos can be a blighter to remain upright in sometimes. So, I took a tumble ever so often. So what? That doesn't make me a drunk.

But I fooled no one.

Only myself.

After being employed by the Ocean Hotel for eight days, I was given my marching orders. Inebriated on the job I was told. I was *livid* let me tell you. I told them that I would not leave there until they had paid me in cash for the eight days' work that I had done otherwise I would go to my lawyers Allister Clarke and Son in Port Shepstone and then they would be sorry. So they paid me. It was just a threat on my part really. But it worked as at least I had some money now. Although once I was a bit sober I was well aware that I had no leg to stand on. But I was still livid.

Once again I had no roof over my head.

Deciding that I would head off to Durban as soon as Rudi came home from school, I packed our bags in readiness for the train journey. It took me five minutes. I only had two suitcases with me: A large sturdy dark brown one which I used for my clothes and a rather battered smaller case that I put all Rudi's things into plus some of my own. All my tea chests had been left in Clocolan. Then I took myself off to the store and bought two large bottles of gin on my account, of course, and packed them in my suitcase. My account would only need to be paid at the end of the month and I would be long gone.

Rudi arrived home half an hour later and I told him that we were off to Durban. He was quite vehement that he wanted to stay. Something about being in the school cricket team on Saturday. Well I just told him that he couldn't go and that was that and I didn't want to hear any more about it. Which I didn't.

By now addled by alcohol, and fuelled by bitterness and outrage, my thoughts were chaotic. I decided that I would just book into the Royal Hotel once we got to Durban. The *best* hotel in Durban. Yes! That is what I will do. That will show them. That will show everybody that I am not a drunk. *I'm not!*

In my reasoning going to a four-star hotel with very little money was the best solution. I was hell bent on a path to destruction by this point.

We arrived in Durban just as it was getting dark and made our way across the road to the tall building that was the Royal Hotel. After booking in for three nights and paying with a cheque upfront because that would at least leave me with some cash, we made our way to our room on the fifth floor. It was very luxurious. The deep pile carpet was soft and silky underfoot and the beds covered with exquisite turquoise down comforters looked soothing and inviting. All this was lost on me as my only need was to have a drink. Which I did, the moment I sat down.

I drank. Entering a world that I knew.

Entering a world that I craved.

A world that was warm and fluid with soft edges, smooth like a pain of glass.

For two days I just drank.

Until there was nothing left.

No alcohol.

No money.

No self respect.

On the Monday morning after a restless night and no other options available, I packed our bags and we left the hotel and walked slowly down West Street. Past all the lovely shops displaying their wares, past the City Hall and Durban Museum, past the Playhouse and Coliseum Theatres, past all these landmarks that made Durban the city that it was. I was oblivious to them. I didn't know where I was going. I just walked, a silent Rudi by my side. We eventually arrived at Durban Beach front and Rudi went straight to a bench to sit down and I sank onto the grass trembling with exhaustion. I don't remember eating much over the last three days. Actually, I don't remember much of the last three days.

I lay on the grass the whole day. On my back, my arm over my eyes to blot out the sun. To blot out the world!

I had no money.

No food.

No water.

I didn't know where to turn. I was in despair. I think I dozed at some point.

Joan Garden. Out with a bang!

CHAPTER ELEVEN

Rudi

I cried the whole night on the train as it rattled and groaned on its journey inland. I know that I was almost grown up now. I had turned thirteen a month earlier and perhaps I shouldn't have been such a baby. But I didn't feel thirteen. Although I didn't really know what being thirteen felt like. To me it felt the same as being six. My life was out of my control. Again! Hurtling along at breakneck speed into an unknown abyss. All I knew was that I felt scared and anxious.

I had been taken to Durban station by Mac and put onto the train that would take me to my new life in Bergville. I had been on a train before of course, quite a few times. But this time it was different. This time I was setting off all alone to go to some unknown town and worse still, an unknown boarding school that I was joining in the middle of the school year. The thought filled me with dread.

I had spent a good part of three weeks at the children's home run by the Durban Child Welfare. All the kids, mostly boys like me, were there on a temporary basis and a lot of them were in a worse position than I was although that didn't really give me much comfort at the time. It was school holidays so I was allowed to more or less do my own thing which I was used to. After settling in for the first couple of days I was told that I had a visitor. Walking into the reception office I saw my sister Jennifer sitting and chatting to Mac. Jennifer still lived at the YWCA in Durban and worked at a bank in the city. I ran and threw myself into her arms. I was so glad to see her. Jennifer said that she was going to take me to visit my mother.

From the outside, Kerr House looked much the same as its immediate neighbours. The building had a tired and slightly dejected air with paint peeling off the door and window frames in flaky curls, the unswept pathway full of dead leaves and discarded wrappers giving an impression of neglect. But inside was a complete contrast. The walls were painted in bright colours and sunlight streamed in through a large window above the staircase onto the old wooden floor. I heard the sound of some music playing coming from upstairs, together with soft laughter. There were a number of posters on the walls in the hallway together with a large notice board that had lots of papers pinned to it that were fluttering in the breeze that was blowing in from the open front door. The notice board reminded me of school. Through a door to the left of the entrance hall I noticed a couple of young children happily playing board games on a large shabby rug that partially covered the floor and I could see a wonky bookshelf up against the one wall, laden untidily with books of all sizes. It looked homely.

My mother came down the stairs to meet us. She was dressed in clothes that I had never seen before. An old unattractive coat of some murky colour that hung shapeless on her small frame and something she wouldn't have been seen dead in normally. She said that the clothes had been given to her as she didn't know what had happened to all her things. She was listless and subdued. But nice. I preferred her like this and not when she was nasty. I asked her how long she would be staying at Kerr House and she said she didn't know. I told her that I was being sent away to boarding school hoping that she would say that I didn't have to go if I didn't want to. But she didn't. She seemed lethargic and disinterested. She gave me a pat on the shoulder and a perfunctory kiss on the cheek when it was time to go. I left there with a heavy heart not understanding her indifference and not knowing when I would see her again.

#

The coach on which I was travelling on the train was full of children heading to Bergville boarding school for the start of the new term. They all seemed to know one another and I could hear them running up and down the passage outside my door, shouting out to one another and laughing. Mac had shown me to my own compartment when we got on the train and as soon as she left me there I bolted the door behind me and went and sat on the bench, my battered suitcase containing one change of clothes and a pair of shoes was on the floor by my feet. Looking out of the window I spotted a familiar figure walking along the platform. I scrambled up kneeling on the seat to unlatch the window clasp and push down the sash to open it. 'Mom!' I shouted, waving my arm rigorously, hanging halfway out of the window. 'Over here.' Her face lit up and she hurried over to the side of the stationary train where my compartment was situated, Jennifer in tow.

'Rudi! I'm so glad that we managed to get here in time to see you off,' she said out of breath. She was looking better than before although I could see that she was upset.

But I was pleased to see her and Jennifer too although I felt a bit tearful myself but tried not to show it.

The whistle blew and I hung out of the window waving as the train started moving slowly out of the station until I could see them no longer. I drew back and closed the window, leaning my head back against the seat confused and overwhelmed by my situation and I just cried. Thank goodness the train was moving faster by that stage so that nobody on the platform could see me. Wiping my wet face and nose with my hand I opened the brown paper packet that Mac had given me when I boarded the train. Padkos! There was a pack of peanut butter sandwiches on thick white bread and an apple to keep me going throughout the journey. These I placed on the small table in front of the window and settled back in my seat with a sigh, watching the changing landscape.

There was a sudden loud knock on the door and I almost leapt out of my seat with fright. With a racing heart I got up off the bench and heard muffled giggling from outside in the passage. Opening the door quickly I saw a boy and a girl running down the corridor giggling uncontrollably. Closing the door once more, I had just sat down when there was another loud knock. Again there was nobody there. I eventually decided that I wouldn't bother to open the door anymore hoping that they would tire of their game and leave me alone. It was quiet for a while and then I tensed as I heard whispering and more giggling outside the door. 'Hey! Baby new boy. We don't want you at our school you hear! You need to go back home.' Then another voice saying 'Yeah. We are in *charge*! Baby new boy. What we says, goes! You hear!' I kept as quiet as I could, glancing nervously at the door, so pleased that

I had pulled the blind down over the glass panel in the sliding door so nobody could see into the compartment.

'Go home new boy. We will get you at school. So go home. Go home' The chanting went on all night it seemed. I didn't sleep very well at all and I was up and dressed long before the train came to a stop at Bergville station early the next morning. All was quiet outside my door.

I got up and slid back the compartment door peering out into the passage. The train had stopped and there were sounds of activity outside on the station platform. I wasn't sure what to do but I knew that I had to get off the train so I picked up my suitcase in a sweaty hand and made my way out onto the platform. A bunch of children each with a suitcase in hand were gathered around a lady on one side of the platform. Looking apprehensively towards the group and wondering which of the boys were my tormentors, I walked slowly in their direction trying to appear as if I did this every day.

'Come on! Hurry up there!' A tall man in a khaki hat waved me impatiently over to the group. All heads turned in my direction and I felt the blood rush to my face, almost stumbling headlong into the bushes that were growing in a flower bed that ran the length of the station building. I heard a twitter of amusement and caught the whispered words 'new boy' in a voice that was familiar. I had heard it repeatedly during the night. I took a deep breath, lifted my chin and looked directly at the culprit.

His name was Allan Fouche, I was to discover. The school bully. He had a loyal ring of ruffian supporters who were an echo of himself and who would do a lot of his dirty work. He walked with an arrogant swagger followed by his side kicks and the younger kids used to scatter when they saw him approaching in the school-yard. He was thick set but short and over weight. His abundant red hair was coarse and untidy but easy to spot in a crowd and the scowl that greeted me seemed to be etched on his face permanently.

I looked away not wanting to provoke him and made my way shakily forward towards the group. I could feel his eyes upon me as we were led out of the station to an old Chevrolet truck with an open back into which we all climbed and settled down for the drive to school. There were eight of us on the back of the truck. There was no-where to sit other than the corrugated floor which was very uncomfortable as the road was gravel and rather bumpy. We all clung onto the sides of the truck to try and prevent ourselves from being thrown around too much and it was a blessing that conversation was impossible because of the noise. At least that kept Allan Fouche quiet. For the moment.

Bergville Primary School was a boarding school which catered mainly for children from broken homes and difficult backgrounds, providing education up to year seven or Standard five. There were some weekly boarders but these were for the most part children of local farmers who lived too far away to make the trek into school every day. I used to watch from my window with envy when they were picked up every Friday afternoon by some loving family member or other and taken home for the weekend. The school was in the small town of Bergville that was nestled in the foothills of the picturesque Drakensberg mountain range. We were driven to the hostel which housed forty boys and forty girls and was about a ten minute walk from the school itself. The truck came to a shuddering halt outside a clean looking red brick building. Grabbing my suitcase I tumbled off the back of the truck almost bumping into a tall lady with curly blonde hair who was holding a clipboard to her chest.

'Oh! So ... Sorry,' I said flustered.

'Well now,' she said stepping back and looking at me. 'You are not Rudi by any chance are you?'

'Yes, that's me.' I said with relief.

'I'm Miss Sharp. I'm going to help you settle in. So follow me and I will show you where your dormitory is.' I followed her in silence as she walked off towards the building and up a couple of steps to the open door. On either side of the entrance foyer were doors, one of which I could see opened up into a large dining room which as expected had lots of tables and chairs in rows. We continued up a flight of stairs to the first floor where the boys' dormitories were situated. There were four dormitories each with ten beds. Five beds along one side of the room and five along the opposite wall. I was shown to the second door and given a bed nearest the door.

'Now,' said Miss Sharp with a smile as she plonked my case on a bed nearest the door and proceeded to open it and unpack my clothes. Which didn't take long let's face it. I only had one pair of shorts, a shirt and a pair of shoes! 'This will be your bed.' She hesitated. 'I see you don't have a school uniform,' she said. I shook my head. 'Well that's not a problem at all. I will take you into Bergville which is five minutes away and buy you what you need.' Feeling rather important, I walked back downstairs with Miss Sharp and jumped into her car, an old red Volkswagen Beetle and drove out of the hostel grounds in a cloud of blue smoke that belched out of the exhaust. We drove to the local trading store where I was fitted for two sets of khaki shirts and shorts and two pairs of shoes, one black and the other brown. Miss Sharp also added a pair of white PE shorts and vest as well as a black blazer which I was told I would need as the winters can get pretty cold. Once we had driven back to the hostel Miss Sharp took me upstairs to Matron's office. Matron looked at me sternly over the top of her glasses.

'Right. Here is a towel for you. I need you to take off all your clothes and go into the shower cubicle over there and have a good wash all over including your hair,' she said not unkindly. I silently took the towel from her with panic. There was no way that I was going to take my underpants off. Pulling my shirt off over my head and wriggling out of my shorts as fast as I could, I got into the shower and pulled the curtain closed behind me with relief. I washed myself all over with soap that smelled awful but I didn't care really. Hoping that Matron was busy and wouldn't see me get out of the shower with my wet underpants still on, I opened the curtain slowly. But there she was ... waiting.

'Why are you still wearing your underpants?' she asked. I inwardly cringed and I wanted to roll my eyes. Resigned to the inevitable, I said, 'I am embarrassed to take them off because I am a teenager now.' my face reddening with discomfort. Matron burst out laughing and told me to get dressed in my school uniform but not before I had taken off my wet underwear.

Miss Sharp was waiting for me once I had finished with Matron and she took me back to my dormitory with instructions to pack my spare uniform into my cupboard which was by the side of my bed. Then we went downstairs where she left me in the prep room to amuse myself for the remainder of the afternoon. The prep room was the room that was used to do homework as well as any other quiet activities that we wanted to pursue. It was bright with white painted walls and a number of long tables with benches either side running the length of the room. There were a couple of boys in a huddle with a book between them and another group of boys sitting at a table talking loudly about what they had done in the holidays. My gaze flicked over them and I was relieved when I didn't spot any red hair.

'You must be new here.' said a voice behind me. Turning around I came face to face with a dark haired boy of about my own height who had a friendly open face and a sprinkling of freckles across his cheeks. 'Miss Sharp asked me to look out for you. I'm Allen. Allen Klue and I am in dormitory two the same as you,' he said. And then after a pause, 'Hey! That rhymes!' and he burst into laughter which set me off, helping to shed some of my melancholy. 'But you can call me Titch. Everybody does,' he finished.

'I'm Rudi. I've just got here today. Have you been here long?'

'This is my second term here. It's nice. Well nicer than home anyhow,' he said looking down. 'But come with me,' he brightened walking towards the door. 'I will show you around'

I immediately felt better and some confidence returned and it was with a lighter step that I followed Titch out of the prep room towards the dining room. It was a large room with a partition in the middle, boys seated on one side and girls on the other. There were a number of long wooden tables also with bench seats either side where we would sit and eat. Titch told me that each dormitory was allocated a table with the dormitory prefect sitting at the head keeping an eye on everyone. We peeked into the steamy kitchen where there were a number of huge pots on the stove boiling away furiously and through the haze I could see a buxom African lady standing at a table peeling a mound of sandy potatoes humming quietly to herself.

'What's for din dins Pretty?' asked Titch.

'For you small Bassie today is sausages,' said Pretty with a big smile

'Mnandi!' (nice) he responded.

Then we went outside to explore the grounds and Titch explained that we were allowed to be outside and do what we want after school and at weekends. The prep room we used every day for our homework hour and when it was raining we could go and sit in there and play board games or read if we chose. There was no such thing as television. He really took me under his wing even though he was a year below me at school we became firm friends throughout my time at Bergville.

We hadn't been indoors long when a bell went and all the boys started to gather their things and make their way to the dining room. I walked with Titch to the door of the dining room where groups of boys had formed four lines one for each dormitory. For the first time I saw the other boys with whom I would be living. A tall muscular man with military bearing strode into the room, a thick cane under his arm and immediately all chatter stopped. He was swarthy with untidy black eyebrows and a prominent nose, his silver rimmed spectacles glinting in the setting sunlight that was flooding the room.

His penetrating eyes looked challengingly at each boy in turn as he inspected the four lines. Titch nudged me with his elbow and whispered. 'That's Mr Van Wyk, the Housemaster. He's mean!' I glanced at him with trepidation, immediately looking away again wanting to escape notice. Mr Van Wyk indicated to us to file into the dining room to our allocated table which was already set with knives and forks and a large platter sitting in the centre overflowing with slices of brown bread and butter that we could help ourselves to if we needed to fill a gap. Once all four dormitories were seated at their tables Mr Van Wyk went and sat at the teachers' table which was at the other end of the room. Thank goodness!

The smell of hot cooked food wafted in the air and my stomach growled noisily. A tall African waiter whose name was Long John brought the food to the table placing a full plate in front of each boy. Then just as I was about to pick up my knife and fork one of the teachers stood up and said grace. Then we could eat. Bill Paton who was my dormitory prefect and who sat at the head of the table, told me that I had to finish everything that was on my plate whether I liked it or not. Which I didn't find difficult. I devoured what was in front of me I was so hungry. If I was still hungry I could always ask for seconds by putting my hand up in the air and Long John would come with another plateful. But after a couple of slices of bread and butter to help mop up the gravy I was full to bursting but still looking forward to pudding.

Normally after dinner every evening we would go to the prep room and do our homework for an hour but as classes only started the following day we were allowed to do what we liked until bedtime. We were in the prep room where I was chatting to some of the other boys in my dormitory when I heard a familiar red headed voice. Hoping that, as I was now wearing my school uniform like everyone else, I blended in so would escape his notice, I ducked behind a tall boy in an effort to remain undetected. To no avail.

'Well, if it isn't baby new boy,' Fouche said walking towards me the surrounding boys parting like the Red Sea at his approach.

'Come here baby new boy! O! Oooh! Look at you. Skinny aren't you?' he said looking me up and down, his words reminding me of Lizette's taunting which I had endured for a time. And look what happened to her!

'And look at your shirt full of food.'

I looked down in dismay to see a gravy spill on my new khaki shirt. I was mortified but more so because it had been pointed out in front of everyone.

'I think you might just need to join me on Saturday night in the boxing ring. Then I can give you a little *hiding*,' he said with glee, his face inches from mine. A bell went off and he turned and walked off to seek another victim no doubt, but not before he had flicked me across the cheek with his fingers.

'*Ouch*! That hurt!' I exclaimed holding my hand to my cheek and glaring at his retreating back.

'Come on,' said Titch. 'Just ignore him. It's bath time or you could shower if you like.'

With the attention off me and with the incident seemingly forgotten for the moment by the other boys, we all trooped upstairs to our dormitories. I was pleasantly surprised to see a Bible and a set of pyjamas laid out on my bed. 'Who put these here I wonder?' I muttered to myself.

'That would be Miss Sharp,' said Allen having obviously heard me. 'Get dressed straight into your jammies after your shower.'

But I didn't shower that first night. The bathroom was situated across the passage from the dormitories. One bathroom for forty boys so it could become a bit of a scramble. There was a row of toilets with half doors and opposite that was a row of showers which were open so everyone could see you showering. There were also three separate baths which had doors on thank goodness. I was *not* going to take my underpants off in front of everyone. So I had a bath. Under the row of wash hand basins were two large buckets of shoe polish with a brush resting on the lid of each one. One black polish and one brown. I was told that we had to polish our shoes every day before school. Black polish for school shoes and brown polish to be used on our church shoes. After bath time with everyone dressed in their pyjamas, Titch said that we had to stand at the foot of our beds and each read a verse from the Bible. My heart raced. I needed to find a verse that I knew or that was easy to read. Thinking quickly, I found Psalm 23 and put my marker there ready to turn to the right page straight away. I knew it off by heart so I could 'read' it without effort.

Mr Van Wyk walked in through the door slapping his cane on the side of his leg with a decisive crack after each step. 'Right, boys.' He pointed to me with his cane 'You can start.' Trembling I began to 'read' The Lord is my Shepherd' and I had only read a couple of sentences before he strode out of the room and I could hear his footsteps receding down the passage. We each continued to read in turn until Mr Van Wyk returned and said, 'Lights out and no talking' and I scrambled shivering into bed and drew the itchy grey blanket up to my chin rubbing my feet together to try and get warm. The lights went off and it was pitch black but that didn't bother me because I fell asleep straight away after an exhausting day.

I was woken the following morning by the loud clang of a bell ringing and the bright lights of the dormitory shining in my eyes. It was six o'clock and still dark outside and freezing cold. I bolted out of bed and dressed in my school uniform and black blazer with a badge on the pocket that eased my goose bumps. Breakfast was the same routine as supper and once everyone was ready we all lined up by the door in readiness to head off to the school building which was a ten minute walk away.

Walking along the crunchy rough path to school I breathed in air that was crisp and clear with a biting cold edge that swept down from the nearby mountains. For the first time I noticed the surrounding countryside. A quiet pink sky greeted the day and a couple of doves were cooing in harmony in the trees above the pathway. I saw a number of rabbits scurrying away over the frosty grass and then stopping to look back, noses twitching. The distant blue peaks of the Amphitheater were a majestic and imposing backdrop, that would greet me every day. Forever changing, yet the same. The path meandered along, eventually snaking past the principal Mr Hartman's low slung house where it widened slightly around a corner to the school buildings a short distance away.

Once we arrived at the school I was sent to a separate prefab in the grounds which I was told was going to be my classroom. To my surprise when I went in, there was Miss Sharp. She was going to be my teacher. I was so pleased.

During my first week at Bergville the district nurse arrived for her six monthly visit to do eye tests on all the pupils. Each dormitory would line up in turn outside Matron's office before we were called in individually to read letters off a board that was pinned to the wall. I could only read the top line. I was taken to an optician in Ladysmith where I had further tests and was then prescribed glasses. They were brown rimmed and rather thick and heavy and I did not like them one bit. They took a bit of getting used to but I must admit that I could see *so* clearly with them on. Even the blackboard.

Before I knew it my first week at boarding school was behind me. Once again, the everyday routine calmed me, gave me stability and a feeling of security. The school work didn't get any easier but it was awfully helpful being able to see. I really liked Miss Sharp and I found that I wanted to do well and I tried really hard.

Allan Fouche continued to plague me whenever he got the chance but I had made up my mind that I would rise to the challenge and agreed to box him on the Saturday night. I was nervous as I didn't know how well he boxed and he was bigger than me by a mile, but I knew that I had an advantage as he was not aware that I had boxed before. Once a month on a Saturday night a makeshift boxing ring was set up in a room off the boys' bathroom on the first floor. Mr Van Wyk was in charge of proceedings. There were a number of boys who were boxing that evening, all dressed in white PE shorts and vests and each completing two rounds of two minutes per round. Exactly the same format that I was used to when I was boxing in Margate, which seemed ages ago but *was* only last year. This was familiar territory and calmed my nerves a bit as I stood waiting in line to be gloved up. Allan Fouche was strutting around repeatedly hitting one gloved fist into the other and looking at me menacingly doing his best to intimidate me. I knew he was trying to scare me. Which he did, but I wouldn't let him see that.

Even though Mr Van Wyk's reputation was mean, I could see that he knew how to teach boxing. My heart plummeted somewhat when I realised that Fouche must have had some boxing experience. I watched the first couple of fights carefully and realised that actually, I could do this. I had fought opponents in the past who were much more skilled than what I was seeing here.

My turn seemed to come around in no time. I took a deep breath and walked into the ring and stood in front of Mr Van Wyk listening to the cheers of the boys as Fouche walked around the ring with his gloved hands in the air soaking up the applause as if he had already won his bout. His loyal sidekicks were shouting the loudest.

Mr Van Wyk called him over to stand beside me. 'Are you both ready?'

'Yes, Sir,' we answered in unison

'Right. On the first whistle you will touch gloves then take your stance. On the second whistle you will begin. Is that clear?'

'Yes, Sir.'

We touched gloves and stood back on the first whistle ready to begin. My nerves had left me completely by this stage and I was totally focused on what I was doing. The second whistle went, I could see almost straight away that this was going to be relatively simple. Fouche's gloved hands were hanging down by his waist leaving his head an easy open target. I immediately pounced and landed two quick lefts and a right to his jaw. As soon as he put up his hands to cover his face, I pummelled his midriff, varying the angles of my shots so that he was unable to block me fast enough to prevent the next blow. I could hear the words 'Go Rudi, go!' above the loud shouts and the noise of forty pairs of feet stamping in unison on the wooden floor. Fouche stumbled back and I followed him adding a few more lightning blows to the face all the while feeling in control of what I was doing and gaining confidence with each blow.

'Enough!'

Mr Van Wyk blew the whistle and jumped between us stopping the fight before I did any serious damage, then holding my arm up as the victor, he walked me around the ring. Fouche never landed a blow. The applause was deafening.

I almost wanted to bow.

I was *so* proud of myself!

I knew that I had defeated him good and proper! Fair and square! And in front of the whole school! Even Mr Van Wyk said well done! I couldn't stop smiling. I just knew that I wouldn't be bothered by Allan Fouche again.

From that moment ON I became one of the boys. A member of the pack! Everyone knew who I was and everyone respected me and some of the younger boys even looked up to me like a hero. It was a good feeling, a heady feeling and I felt like a weight had been lifted off my shoulders as I realised that I was accepted by everyone. Over time even Allan Fouche managed to hold a decent conversation with me although he was never my favourite person. I think I might have taught him a lesson.

#

Every school day at five o'clock we would have prep for an hour where we would have to do our homework or any extra school work that we had been given. During all my years at school I had never spent as long as an hour on my homework before. In actual fact I probably hadn't spent longer than ten minutes on my homework before. Because I couldn't be bothered for the most part. But here at boarding school I didn't have an option and actually by the time I left at the end of standard five my marks had much improved. Although whether that was from the prep hour or the stability of my circumstances, I couldn't tell. Prep hour was supervised by Mr Van Wyk and there had to be absolute silence. No talking whatsoever. I'm not too sure which part of 'No Talking Whatsoever' I didn't understand but Titch and I were whispering away obliviously one day when Mr Van Wyk strode over and whacked us both hard a couple of times across our backs with his cane. I gasped in pain and put my head on the table for the balance of prep hour and cried. Titch cried too. I didn't dare talk during prep again.

I had told anyone who would listen that I had an older brother. His name was Neil and he was in the Air Force where he flew Mirages. I had found a coloured picture in a newspaper of three Mirages in flight and I stuck it onto the inside of my suitcase lid. I circled the one plane and said that it was my brother's plane. Everyone was most impressed.

I had been at Bergville for a month when Miss Sharp came to me one day and said I could phone my mom. She gave me her phone number and a tickie which I would need to use in the coin phone in the foyer. I had been so busy trying to get used to my new life and dealing with different, sometimes difficult situations on a day to day basis that I never gave much thought to what mom was doing or where she was. Occasionally when I climbed into bed after lights out and all was quiet, my mind did flicker back to her but I always managed to push those thoughts away. I didn't want anything to interfere with my life in Bergville. I was feeling settled and I was determined to not let anything spoil my time here. It was with trepidation that I made the call.

Mom sounded cheerful and pleased to hear from me. She mentioned that she was still at Kerr House but that she would be getting a job soon probably in a hotel in Durban. She also mentioned that Miss Sharp was wanting to keep me in standard four for another year as I was struggling to keep up with the work. Mom had said no. I told her that I was very settled and enjoying boarding school and I was glad that she was going to get a job again. We said our goodbyes and I buried the conversation underneath as many activities as I could fit into my day.

Life in Bergville had settled down into a comfortable routine. During the week in the winter months there would be rugby practice after school. A couple of days after my boxing triumph I was approached by the rugby coach who asked me if I would like to come to practise twice a week. I agreed to try it out and was selected to play a match on the Saturday and was put in the position of flanker which I quite liked. Before the match the rugby coach said that there would be fifty cents reward for anyone who scored a try in the game. I scored a try during that game which helped boost my confidence no end. I'm still waiting for my fifty cents though.

Once a month on a Friday night we would have movies in the dining room. All the tables would be pushed back and the benches would be put into rows. Mr Van Wyk would set up a big projector and show the movies onto the blank white wall opposite. On Saturdays, as there were no classes, we were allowed to go into town to spend our pocket money. Every term parents would give the school R1 part of which we could use each Saturday morning to spend in Bergville. We would visit Mr Van Wyk in his office and ask for five or ten cents which he would then deduct from the one rand, keeping a tally for each of us in a little book labelled with our names. Then we would head off to Bergville Trading Store, the same store where Miss Sharp had bought my uniform from, and spend ages selecting what sweets we would have that week. Trading stores are the most wonderful treasure trove of places. They bulge with a huge diverse assortment of things, stacked from floor to ceiling. No matter what it is you want. You will probably get it there. From thick hairy blankets to motor oil, from bicycles to tins of beans, from china cups and saucers to screws and nails, footballs and cooking pots, ice creams, toilet rolls, magazines, welding goggles, plastic buckets and bread. You name it! It's on the shelf somewhere. It had a particular paraffin smell to the place. Because yes ... they sold paraffin there too. Just bring in your bottle and they will fill it up for you.

But we went there for the sweets. Apart from the more expensive chocolates and packets of sweets that were available to buy, what we were more interested in, was the row of large glass jars that sat along the counter top each filled with an assortment of brightly coloured sweets. Some like Chappies Bubblegum were individually wrapped in bright striped paper that I used to unwrap with hasty anticipation wanting to discover what colour the small block of gum was. Blue was the most treasured and pink the most common. Two for one cent they were. Printed on the back of each wrapper were 'Did You Know' facts which were always fun to read. Then there were the toffees. Wilson toffees. Oh my *dayz!* The best toffees in the whole wide world. I would put the whole square in my mouth and suck down hard, pushing it up onto the roof of my mouth with my tongue and continuing to flatten it as it became softer, swallowing the creamy sweetness that oozed out of the velvety toffee. Sometimes I would try and make it last all the way back to hostel without being tempted to chew it. There were round bright orange barley sugar balls, stripy humbugs with their distinctive flavour and marshmallow fish in three pale colours of yellow, white and pink, always fresh and melted in your mouth soft. We would make our choice according to how much money we had and the shopkeeper who very patiently helped us with our selection, would put our treasured sweets into paper bags for us to take home.

I loved going there.

I loved the fact that I had pocket money too.

Whilst we were in Bergville sweet shopping we often used to call on the Carnation factory which was further along the road from the Trading Store. The Carnation factory made tins of evaporated milk and condensed milk and probably other products as well. But all we were interested in were the tins of condensed milk. The manager there knew the children from the hostel. We had to dress in our khaki uniform at all times so we couldn't be mistaken anyway. We would stand at the gate and he would come out with some small tins of condensed milk without labels and hand them to us to take back to school. Once there we would pierce two holes in the top with an opener that we were given and then suck out the sweet milk. It was always a treat.

Another place that was important to go to during our Saturday jaunts into town was what we used to call the peanut factory. It wasn't a factory that made peanuts of course but I think that there were peanut or groundnut farms in the area. But lying just outside the big door of the warehouse was a huge pile of raw peanuts still in their shells. We were allowed to help ourselves to as much as we wanted. We just used to fill our pockets with as many as we could carry and munch them all the way back to hostel.

On Sundays it was compulsory for the whole school to go to church. After breakfast we would make sure that our knees were clean and church shoes shiny enough to pass Mr Van Wyk's inspection, don our blazers and walk down into town to the local church. Once we arrived at the church the minister had a roll call just to make sure that one of us hadn't ducked into the neighbouring bushes in order to get out of church. He used to call our names and we had to shout out 'present'. Titch always replied 'presents please' which I thought was so funny.

By now it was October and school closed for a week's break at the end of term three. Miss Sharp called me to her office one afternoon.

'Rudi as you know school will be closing on Friday for the October break. I have spoken to your mom and she has told me that she is now working and would love to have you stay with her during the holidays. How do you feel about that?' She asked.

How *did* I feel about that? 'I'm not sure' I replied hesitantly 'Will I still get to come back here?'

'Of course you will'

'Sh … .she can't run away with me, can she?' I knew it was a bit of a silly question but I suddenly felt so insecure and helpless and I knew that my life could sometimes change overnight and I didn't want anything to interfere with the life that I had found.

'She absolutely is not going to run away with you. And yes you will be coming back here and next year as well.' She finished, smiling reassuringly with a pat on my arm. Tears welled up into my eyes from *nowhere*. I turned my head and looked out of the window biting down on my lip. 'So Friday after lunch change into your civvies and pack what you need ready to catch the overnight train later on in the day. Leave your school uniform here so that it can be washed and ready for when you return next term. Your mom will meet you at the station in Durban.'

I turned and smiled broadly at her having had time to recover whilst she was talking. I wanted to hug her but just said, 'Oh thank you so much, Miss Sharp,' and left her office.

The train journey back to Durban was very different from the one that brought me to Bergville a number of months ago. This time I shared a compartment with Titch and had a lot of fun going from carriage to carriage seeing who was there and what they were doing. By this stage of course I knew everybody at the school especially the boys. We were all like family. We were soon pulling into Durban station where I spotted my mom and

Jennifer almost straight away. Mom was now working at the Lucian Hotel in Point Road not far from the beach front. We were sharing a room once again and I tried to block out the unwelcome surge of feelings that welled up threatening to unsettle me. It was all too inevitably familiar. Not welcome at all. But despite the occasional unsettling wave that came over me, I spent a pleasant enough week mostly on my own of course as mom was working. But I have to admit that I breathed a sigh of relief when I boarded the train for the return journey back to school. Back to my final term of standard four.

Summer was really making its presence felt during my last two months of the school year. The air was hot and dry and most afternoons around about three o'clock, menacing grey clouds would gather over the mountains and within half an hour there would be a torrential downpour together with loud sudden claps of thunder and lightning that forked threateningly across the sky. Fast forward another thirty minutes and the sun would appear through the receding clouds, as hot as ever, beating down on the surrounding countryside that had been washed sparkling clean of the day's dust.

I got involved with playing cricket. I was so proud to be selected for the school team batting fourth in the line-up. Not that I ever got a very good score. I didn't. But I enjoyed it anyway. As there was not enough cricket equipment to go around, we all had to share. This included the ball box which we used to remove after being dismissed and hand it nice and warm to the new batsman who was strolling onto the field.

It was now December and the school year was at an end. I had passed standard four. Just! By the skin of my teeth. But that didn't bother me. I was proud of what I had achieved after only being at school for six months that year. It was with high spirits that I jumped onto the back of the truck that was taking the hostel kids to the station to board the train once more for the return trip to Durban where I would spend the long summer holidays. Back to the Lucian Hotel where Mom was still working and back to the familiar but disliked room where I would be spending the next six weeks. I never saw her much at all during my time in Durban as she was always working but being on my own was something that I was used to and I just got on with things. Titch and I had worked out that we didn't live very far from one another in Durban so we ended up spending quite a lot of time together. I think Titch liked to get away from home a bit so we spent many a happy hour in the park and at the beach which was very crowded at that time of year. He also introduced me to Tea Room Bioscopes. These were known as bug houses. They showed movies all day long and there was often a double feature. The cost of a ticket was ten cents and for that price you were given a cold drink and you sat in chairs that had a small table in front and watched the movie from there. The tables and chairs were often dirty and sticky with spilt cool drink or bits of dropped food left behind from the previous occupants. But if you had nothing else better to do then you could sit there all day if you wanted to and watch the same movie, or two, over and over again. You could also buy hamburgers or hotdogs to eat, which we never did as we didn't have the money for such luxuries. And besides which, it was quite dark in there and you never knew what you might be eating! Even though the place was a bit of a dive it didn't bother my mother at all that I went there.

After many lazy days doing precisely what I wanted to do, it was time to pack up once more and head back to school. I did have a *smidgen* of unease when mom saw me packing my case and said to me, 'Oh, you're not going back there are you?'

'Of course,' I said as casually as I could. 'It's all been arranged.' Whether it had or not I had no idea. I just knew that Miss Sharp had told me that I would be returning to Bergville to complete standard five. And that was all that I needed to know.

I was happy to get back to school. It felt like coming home in a way. I was put back into dormitory two and appointed dormitory prefect. I was so proud. I would be in charge of the other nine boys and would have to keep them in control. I appointed Titch as my deputy and we chose beds that were screened off from the rest of the dormitory with a window in the area. As part of my duties as prefect I had to make sure that all the boys behaved well especially during mealtimes when Mr Van Wyk was quick to pounce on any small transgression. I had to see that the younger boys showered properly in the evenings, brushed their teeth and make sure that they cleaned their school shoes every day.

Titch and I decided that we needed to make some money. The latest craze at school was marbles. Both Titch and I were quite good at marbles and over the first couple of weeks at school we had accumulated rather a lot by winning them off other boys that wanted to take us on but didn't realise how good we were. We managed to sweet talk Moolla who worked at the trading store in town, into giving us some small paper packets. I felt that I must have inherited the art of the sweet talk from my mother but on reflection Titch had the gift of the gab and could talk himself out of the tightest corner so I guess that accolade should go to him. Moolla gave us a fist full of small packets, far more than we needed but I wasn't going to complain. We divided up all the marbles so that each bag held about twenty to thirty, depending on their size, giving the bag a couple of twists at the top to seal it. We sold the marbles back to the boys at five cents a bag. We were delighted with our entrepreneurship and were in the pound seats until marble craze came to an end to be replaced by yo-yos.

As it was still summer I continued playing cricket twice a week in the afternoons after school. Sometimes we went to towns in the area to play a match against other schools. At one of these games I was asked to do the scoring. I just said yes I would do it but I really didn't know much about how to score a cricket game. I was told to sit at the edge of the field next to the scorer of the opposing team. He seemed to know what he was doing so I just copied down on my score card exactly what he had on his. Needless to say the cricket coach was *not* impressed with me! At the time I felt really bad and a bit of an idiot really. I was never asked to score again. Obviously!

On occasional weekends one of the teachers would arrange an afternoon outing to the Tugela river which was about a fifteen minute walk from the school past the sports field. This was one of the few times that both boys and girls would be together. It was always good fun. We spent the afternoon playing in the water and would set up a zip wire slide to the other side and would whiz across screaming at the top of our lungs but loving every moment.

Soon the first term of school was at an end and the Easter holidays loomed ahead. Miracles of miracles, mom was still working at the Lucian Hotel. I don't think she was drinking any more and I heard her telling Jennifer something about meetings that she was going to although I wasn't quite sure what the connection was. I would be staying with Jennifer this holiday. She had a small flat in Durban and Mom would come and stay for a couple of days as well, as Jennifer was getting married. Johan her fiancé was a tall strikingly good looking young man who was a policeman at Durban Central Police Station. He grew up in Klerksdorp in the then Transvaal and his home language was Afrikaans. He also played club rugby and Jennifer fell for him hook line and sinker. It was very cramped for the three of us in her flat but it was fun being all together for the first time in years. One day I found a pair of handcuffs that Johan had left lying around so I said to mom to put out her hands as I wanted to try them on her. She held out her arms to me with her hands together and I clipped each handcuff onto her wrists and snapped them closed. Mom thought it was so funny. Even when I realised that there was no key to open them and we had to phone Johan and get him to come home to help us get them off, she still enjoyed the joke. Johan wasn't impressed as he came home late after a long shift and didn't have a key to open them so he had to try and pick the locks open which took ages. Mom had been sitting with her hands in handcuffs the whole day but she still saw the funny side.

Back at school the familiar routine kicked in once again. On the afternoons when I wasn't playing any sport I used to spend my time making all sorts of things. Together with a couple of other boys we made a kite once out of bamboo that was growing wild in the grounds of the school. The bamboo was used for the frame and newspaper for the kite itself. The tail was made out of ankle socks and seemed to work quite well. We were really impressed when the kite actually stayed in the sky.

Long John taught me how to make a guitar out of an old rectangular oil tin. He said he was an expert because he had made many before. He showed me how to cut a hole in the front of the tin, bending the edges of the hole back so that it was smooth and couldn't cut me. He helped me make a handle from a piece of wood that I pillaged had from a stack of empty tomato boxes that I found at the back of the kitchen. I used fishing line for the strings and I spent ages making up tunes. I had never had many toys so I really treasured my guitar.

It was soon time for the mid year holidays which were in July each year. I had brought my treasured guitar with me on the train journey home, excited to show off what I had made. Getting down from the train I saw mom waiting for me amongst the crowd.

'Good heavens, look at you. You look like a tramp! What on earth have you got there?' she exclaimed her first words to me painful and upsetting. My face fell. 'It … It's a guitar that Long John helped me make. Don't you like it?' I asked her. I think she could see from my face that I was hurt because she said quickly, 'Oh it's very clever' which wasn't very convincing!

My mother had changed jobs. She was now working at the Rio Grande Hotel which wasn't far from the Lucian where she was previously. I shared a room with her once again and I had to endure her cigarette smoke every night for three weeks. But as always there wasn't much that I could do about it. She seemed to be a lot happier and was quite a lot of fun to be with this holiday and I thought how I wished she could always be like that. One day she said she was going to a function and we caught a bus together to this old house on the Berea. Mom went into a room with other adults and the children were told to play in the garden. There was a girl by the name of Paula Scott who I met there who had come there with her dad. She was a big scruffy girl with long unbrushed hair. She was rather streetwise even though she was only nine.

'My Dad drinks too much beer and brandy then he gets nasty and starts to throw things around and sometimes hits us. He's scary!' She informed me candidly. 'He said he can't help it and so he comes to these meetings so that he can stop drinking. It's called AA'

'Oh! What's AA?'

'It's Alcohol Anamis or something. It's for people who drink too much anyway,' she said with authority.

It was only then that I realised that this wasn't a function at all. And on reflection I realised that Mom had not been drinking either, even since Jennifer's wedding and that must be why she was back to her fun self.

'So is your Dad different when he doesn't drink?' I asked her

'Yes. He's kind and he plays with my sister and me for ages and he doesn't even swear,' she said 'He's nice when he doesn't drink.'

I nodded. 'I like my mom when she doesn't drink too,' I said feeling a certain kinship with Paula as I recognised that she had a similar problem to me. I began to have a bit more understanding about mom and her drinking. It was not something that she had discussed openly with me at all. She was a very private person. I don't think she ever had any recollection of the time that she was so drunk that I had to walk her home from the shop and put her to bed.

When the meeting was over mom cheerfully called me to say that we needed to go and catch our bus home but no word was mentioned about the meeting. Other than going to a couple of meetings with her, I didn't see much of her as she was working as usual and I just did my own thing. Titch's family had moved out of the centre of Durban to an area above the city called the Berea so it was a lot more difficult for us to get together during the holidays. I had got to know a girl by the name of Cathy Fisher who was at my school and who lived just up the road from the Lucian Hotel. We became good friends during the holidays, spending time on the beach as usual and going to the funfair which always arrived in Durban during the month of July each year. I did see Titch once or twice during this time when we had arranged to meet at the bug house. Soon I was back on the train bound for Bergville sharing a compartment this time with Garth and Titch. I was telling Garth all about my holiday and spending time with Cathy and we both thought it was awfully funny to make jokes about what was between her legs. Well she was a girl and I was a fourteen-year old boy after all with hormones that were starting to make their presence felt.

'Oh! So you've got a girlfriend now,' he said with glee.

'She's my friend!' I said a bit annoyed. The next minute there was a knock on the door and I was happy to see that it was Cathy, hiding from some other girls on the train. She came in and sat down next to me.

'Rudi wants to know how big your thing is?' said Garth to Cathy innocently

'I don't understand. What thing?' said Cathy.

'The thing between your legs,' he said with a smirk

Cathy gasped and with a cry ran out of the compartment clearly upset and I could hear her sobs as she ran down the passageway.

'What did you say that for?' I said crossly to Garth, feeling terrible and wanting to go after her.

'Well there's no harm done. Just leave her. She was just being dramatic,' he said nonchalantly.

Later that evening one of the teachers came to our compartment to tell us that Cathy had spoken to her and she was going to report the incident to the headmaster. We were very subdued for the remainder of the journey.

It was almost a week later when I had thought that the incident was forgotten when it reared its ugly head once more. It was after lights out one night when I was just snuggling down to sleep when I heard my name.

'Garden! My office now!'

Scrambling up out of bed and running barefoot in my pyjamas I entered Mr Van Wyk's office to find Garth already there, standing shivering in the centre of the room. I went and stood next to him wondering what was coming.

'I have been informed about some very bad behaviour on the train over the weekend.' He said menacingly, walking up and down in front of us 'Boys don't talk like that about girls. Do you hear? **Do you hear me?'** he shouted 'You are both dirty little pigs. Dirty ... little ... pigs. What are you?'

'D … d … dirty little pigs,' I stuttered in panic.

'Dirty little pigs *who*?' he bent down glaring at us and was so angry that his spit flew into my face and I flinched rocking back on my feet.

'Dirty little pigs S… Sir.'

'I can report this to the headmaster and he will chuck you out of here' he snarled smacking his cane into the palm of his hand 'or I can finish it now with a good hiding. What is it to be?' Well I definitely didn't want the headmaster to hear about this as I didn't want to be sent back home, so I had to choose the other option.

'C … caning' I swallowed, 'Sir'

'Bend.'

I went first. Bending over and holding onto the edge of Mr Van Wyk's desk for support I closed my eyes tight in anticipation of the first blow. When I felt the first piercing sting from the cane as it whacked across my bum I cried out in shock wanting to stand up and rub away the pain. I gulped and held my breath for the following three strikes, cursing Garth for getting me into this.

'Get back to your dormitory. '

I stumbled back to the dormitory and climbed gingerly into bed, lying carefully on my side and cried myself to sleep.

I was black and blue for days afterwards.

#

In the middle of the third term we had an inter school sports day with the neighbouring towns of Estcourt, Colenso, Ladysmith and Winterton. It was held in Colenso so the whole school had to be ferried there by bus. It was planned to take place on a Saturday and I had been selected to run in the 200m race. I was dreading it so I decided that I just wouldn't go. On the Saturday of the event when everyone was lining up to get on the bus, I went back up to the dormitories to dormitory four where I hid in a cupboard. After a while I could hear one of the teachers walking along the corridor calling my name and I stayed as quiet as I could. Listening carefully for any more movement I eventually decided that it was safe to come out and I opened the cupboard door as silently as I could and stepped out. I was just making my way past my own dormitory when I came face to face with the teacher.

'Where have you been? Come on hurry up, the bus is waiting.'

'Oh I didn't know I had to go,' I said, which was a feeble excuse I know but the only one that came to mind under pressure.

'You have to go. Where are your white shorts?'

'I can't find them,' I said in a last ditch effort to wriggle out of it.

'Never mind. I have a spare pair. I will just have to pin a yellow stripe onto the sides of your pants, but I will do that when we get there. Come along.' I wasn't fooling her at all now was I?

I followed her dejectedly to the bus and climbed in joining the rest of the school. Colenso was about an hour's drive away and it wasn't long before we had reached the school and we all had been shown to where we would sit. The teacher came over to me with a white vest with Bergville on the front and a pair of shorts which had a yellow stripe pinned to each side. In no time at all it was time for the open 200 metre race. There were only two of us in the race. The two oldest boys from five schools. I came second which was nothing to blow my trumpet about. It was just so *embarrassing*.

The rest of the school year was spent pleasantly enough. I spent a lot of time out in the vegetable garden that was started by one of the teachers for those that were interested. I enjoyed seeing things grow although I think it was mainly being outdoors that attracted me. My school work wasn't bad and I really enjoyed history especially South African history which was part of the syllabus that year. Apart from the hourly prep in the afternoon which was for doing homework in, I did some extra learning over and above that. This really paid off because I got the top mark for history that year and won a prize. I had beaten the cleverest girl in the school, Ann Coleman who always came first in every subject. I was thrilled with myself.

I knew that my stay at Bergville school would soon be coming to an end. Most of the boys would be going to high school in Estcourt one of the neighbouring towns. It would appear that I would be going back to my mother in Durban. I had learned a lot since I had been at boarding school.

I had learned more than ever that I couldn't rely on anybody else other than myself to get by in the world.

I had learned that sometimes you've just got to do stuff that you don't want to do even though it might be hard at the time.

I had learned that I wasn't afraid of hardship.

I had learned that no one actually cared what I did most of the time.

I had learned that I could face anything and I would cope.

I had learned not to dwell on what had happened in the past as I couldn't change it.

I had learned to always look forward to tomorrow.

CHAPTER TWELVE

Rudi

It was with sadness and some trepidation that I boarded the train at Bergville station bound for Durban for the last time. The long December holidays spread out before me with nothing arduous to do, no school work … .*which was the best* … no boarding school showers … *they were the worst* … and no more school dinners. Which I quite enjoyed strangely enough. I had no idea what school I would be going to next or even where I would be living. All I knew is that I would be going back to live with my mother. Somewhere in Durban.

Mom had moved to a flat in Russell Street which was at the top end of the city away from the beach front. It was a very small one room furnished flat with three beds. But at least there was a table and chairs where I would be able to do my homework. That is, if I went to school which I suppose I would have to. Living with my mother once more was challenging. Every night she would sit and put her hair in blue spiky rollers and once finished she would wrap her head in a scarf and go to bed like that all night. I said to her that surely it was uncomfortable and she said, 'There is no beauty without pain'. Well I was so glad that I was a boy let me tell you! As usual she stayed up late smoking and either reading or playing cards with the overhead light on which was very bright. We couldn't afford such a thing as a bedside lamp. I pulled the blanket over my head in an effort to block out the light and slept in my manmade cocoon. Esme one of the ladies that my mom worked with at the pharmacy suggested to my mom that I go to George Campbell Technical High School which when I realised what it was, sounded right up my street. Mom took me to the school one morning during the holidays to register me there. It was a huge school, the biggest school that I had ever been to, the biggest school that I had ever seen actually. I felt quite intimidated and disheartened and thought to myself that I am never going to be good enough to get into this school. But whilst we were talking to the headmaster and when I heard the words woodwork and mechanics I brightened considerably.

I would be starting high school in the new year. January 1968. There was a regular bus which I could catch to the school which ran from town down to the beach front and back again and passed just outside our flat. Having missed so much school in the past which set me back two years, I would turn fifteen during my first year of high school. I would be the oldest in my standard every year until I left school. I didn't like it. It embarrassed me but there was nothing that I could do about it. Fortunately there were other boys who although they were younger, they were much larger and well built than I was so I didn't look obviously older.

Mom was happy. She still wasn't drinking and she was a completely different person. Much softer. She had a boyfriend too. His name was Don Scott and he often used to come to the flat in the evening for a meal and sit and chat to mom afterwards. She met him at the meetings that she went to once a week. Don had a white Ford Cortina which was all the rage at the time and he used to sometimes take us to the Tropicana Restaurant to have a bite to eat on a Sunday. This was a real treat as I hadn't often been taken out for a meal in my life. Don was a motor mechanic and worked at a garage a couple of miles from the flat. He loved all things technical and advised me that when it was time to decide what I wanted to do, then I should choose electrical. He had a big blow-up canoe which he brought to mom's flat over the weekends for me to use on Durban bay. It was a bit wobbly and unstable and sometimes when the wind blew even if it was just a little breeze, it felt like the canoe would flip over and I would be dumped in the bay amidst all the cargo ships. But it kept me occupied for a number of weekends.

I started my first day at George Campbell full of apprehension although I kept on reminding myself that this wasn't nearly as bad as being sent on the train to Bergville nearly two years ago. I caught the bus from the flat early in the morning and walked the short distance from the bus stop to the school. Mom and I had been shopping for my school uniform over the weekend and she had bought me one grey safari suit which I had to wear from Monday through to Friday without getting it too dirty. But at least I blended in with the other grey safari suited standard six intake. As all the standard six boys were in the same boat ... this was a first day for all of us ... I immediately felt my anxiety settle. The size of my class was a surprise to me. There were twenty four boys in total. Growing up in small towns for the most part, I had been used to half that. The subjects that we took were very different to what I had learned at primary school. Apart from English and Afrikaans which were compulsory, we did technical drawing, welding, basic electrical and working with a soldering iron. I had to buy a set of tools for technical drawing which came in a flat tin box. Things like a protractor, compass, dividers, a flexi curve, rubber and t square. I hardly knew how to pronounce them let alone use them. But I felt very important all the same.

I was chosen to play rugby for the under-fifteen side. The school gave me a second hand rugby jersey and socks from their stock but I had to ask my mother if she could buy me some rugby boots. I had spotted a pair on display in the window of a shop in town. I used to take a detour when I walked home from the bus stop then stop in front of the window and gaze at them longingly, imagining myself running onto the field in front of everyone wearing my new boots, all the time knowing that my mom could never afford such an expensive pair. She took me to a second hand shop where she bought a pair that were perfectly fine. I felt like a million dollars in my kit and couldn't wait for Wednesday afternoon practice.

I settled down reasonably well at High School. I was initially apprehensive about being teased because of my glasses. But I wasn't. Not at all. I enjoyed the different practical subjects which was a nice change from what I had been used to in Bergville and I seemed to cope with the work fairly well. One Friday morning I just didn't feel like going to school and got it into my head that I was going to bunk. I got dressed into my school uniform in the morning as usual, and put some clothes into my school suitcase to change into later. I walked confidently out of the flat after saying goodbye to my mother as if I was going to the bus stop. My plan was to go to the Plaza Hotel which was down the road and head for the cloakroom where I would change into my civilian clothes and wait there until the tearoom bioscope opened at nine. So instead of turning right when I came out onto the street, I turned left and hurried down the road towards the Plaza, looking back over my shoulder in case there was anyone that I recognised. Once I arrived I scuttled across the hotel foyer and made a beeline for the cloak-room banging the door loudly behind me in my haste to get inside. Heart thumping, I changed quickly, stuffing my school uniform into my case and turning down the toilet seat so that I could sit and wait out the time until nine o'clock. It was a long boring wait. Nowhere nearly as interesting when I had bunked in Margate that time when I lived with my mother at the Regent Hotel. At least I had a window to look out of then. And a toilet cu-bicle is not the most comfortable place to spend any de-cent amount of time in either. Eventually nine o'clock came and I slipped out, calmly walking out of the hotel and down the street towards the bioscope. I sat there and watched films the whole day and left just after two to go home as usual.

After roll call on Monday one of the prefects said to me that I needed a letter from my mother to explain my absence. So I knew that I was going to have to try and get a letter from her. But I left it hoping that they would forget and it would just go away. Which it did for about two weeks then I was called into the headmaster's of-fice one day and I just had to make the excuse that I had totally forgotten about it and that I would bring it in the next day. I was nervous all evening not knowing how to broach the subject with my mother. She eventu-ally said to me, 'What is wrong with you tonight? You are all fidgety' So I had to tell her that I bunked school two weeks ago and that the school was asking me for a sick note and I didn't know what to do. She just laughed at me and said, 'Well, at least you have made a girl pregnant!' And wrote me a letter. In typical Joan fashion, her reaction was unexpected. I was so relieved, but I never bunked school again.

My mother could be very kind, especially to animals and people who were worse off than her. There were two African men who were begging on the street on her way home from work one day. Instead of giving them money, she took them into a shop and bought them some bread, polony and some amaHewu which is a traditional African drink. I'm sure they thought Christmas had come early. She also befriended a young teenage girl who she brought back to the flat as she had nowhere to stay and said that she could sleep on the third bed. She had a very large tummy and my mother said that she was expecting a baby. When I got home from school in the afternoons she would be sleeping which made it very awkward for me as the flat was only one room. There would be a smell of sweet smoke in the air and I wished we had a fan so that I could blow it away and clear the air a bit. One night mom and I were woken by her screaming in pain.

'Oh my God!' said mom, 'she's in labour! Rudi go out to the call box and phone for an ambulance.'

We didn't have a phone so I rushed downstairs bare footed, in the pitch dark and ran to the call box on the corner of the street where I got hold of the emergency services. They said it would take an hour for them to get there. I ran back to the flat to tell mom and I could just hear screaming when I was walking back along the passage.

'Don't look,' said mom as I came back into the room and she was busy between the girl's legs.'She has given birth already. A lovely little girl. Can you grab me a towel Rudi please?' Mom asked calmly. The ambulance took about forty five minutes and they loaded her carefully into the interior and took her to hospital after mom doing all the hard work. It was quite difficult getting back to sleep after that but as it was already after four in the morning we didn't bother, but sat up until sunrise, mom endlessly smoking and drinking cups of tea.

I had noticed that Don hadn't been around to the flat for a while so as we were sitting in companionable togetherness, I thought I would just ask mom where he was. 'Mom, where is Don?' getting straight to the point.

'Oh him!' she replied with a dismissive wave of her hand as if it didn't matter, 'we don't see one another anymore.'

That is a pity, I thought. Mom was always happier when she had a companion.

It wasn't long afterwards when I came home from school one afternoon and aimed for the kitchen to make a sandwich for myself. Hollow legs as always. I dropped my butter knife on the floor and it bounced with a clang under the stove and bending down to retrieve it, I saw a bottle of gin on the floor between the stove and the cupboard. My heart sank. Here we go again. I was tempted to pour it down the sink, but didn't.

My first year at George Campbell had been going well. I seemed to be coping with most of the subjects and I would be writing my end of year exams in the next two weeks. During the last week of term, depending on my marks, I would be told which technical subject the teachers thought was most suited to me and that would be the

317

trade subject that I would take for the rest of my school days. I was hoping for electrical as I really enjoyed it.

It was early December and the last ten days of the school year. I was woken up early one morning by the sound of mom crying in pain. I bolted out of bed and went over to her 'What's wrong mom?' I asked a bit panicked.

'My legs. I can't move them and I have such pain,' she said.

'Can I rub them for you?' I asked not too sure what to do.

'No … I think I need a doctor', she said grimacing and clutching her legs.

'Hold on, mom. I will go and get Phyllis next door.' I ran out and banged on the neighbour's door until it was answered by Phyllis in her dressing gown. 'Why Rudi! Whatever is the matter?'

'It's mom. She's in pain and can't walk. Please come,' I said quickly.

We ran back to the flat where mom was still moaning in pain and with Phyllis's help we managed to get her up.

'You are going to have to get her to hospital. I will help you take her downstairs to the bus stop,' said Phyllis taking charge which was a relief. With Phyllis's help we got mom down the stairs slowly, one at a time, her legs buckling under her and hanging limply so that we had to hold her up under her arms to prevent her from sliding to the ground. She was a dead weight and Phyllis was breathing heavily by the time we got to the bus stop. She waited with me and helped mom onto the bus once it arrived. The bus driver very kindly drove right to the entrance of Addington Hospital and patiently waited whilst I struggled to get mom off the bus. I managed to get her the short distance into the hospital where I grabbed a wheelchair for her and pushed her through to the emergency section. We were shown into a cubicle with a bed and curtains all the way around. I helped mom out of the wheelchair and onto the bed where she collapsed in agony crying softly. Looking at her in alarm I wondered what on earth could be causing her such pain. A tired looking doctor with grey hair and brown rimmed glasses similar to my own, came into the cubicle.

'Hello. I'm Doctor Roberts. What seems to be the problem?' he asked as he examined mom. Mom was crying uncontrollably and didn't answer. 'She woke up in pain this morning and can't move her legs,' I told him. After he had completed a cursory examination he said,

'I'm not too sure what is wrong at this stage but we need to run some tests. I will give her something to ease the pain as well but I am afraid that she is going to have to be admitted straight away.'

'Will she be all right?'

'She is in good hands and I'm sure she will feel a lot better after she has had something to help with the pain. So don't worry,' he said kindly.

I nodded. 'I need to get to school as I am writing an English exam today but I will bring her some things later this afternoon,' I told him. I said goodbye to mom and hurried out. Feeling shaken up, I caught a bus back to the flat and got myself ready for school as quickly as I could. Ignoring my rumbling stomach, I grabbed my case and headed for the bus stop. Running from the bus stop into school I saw that everyone was already seated and almost ready to start when I burst into the exam room. I hurried to my seat feeling flustered and anxious, my tummy tight with nerves. Taking a deep breath to calm myself I turned the paper to start the exam and stared at words that danced in front of my eyes. It was very difficult to concentrate as I couldn't stop thinking of my mom and what might be wrong with her. Sweat prickled on my brow and down the side of my face in the airless room and I shifted uncomfortably in my chair thinking why did it have to be an English exam today of all days. Yielding to my fate, I did what I could and hoped for the best.

After I had explained to my teacher that my mom had been admitted to hospital that morning before school, I was allowed to go home straight after the English exam. At the flat I packed some things into a case for mom and made my way back to the hospital where I was directed to a ward on the fourth floor. It was a relief to see mom sitting up in bed and looking more relaxed and clearly no longer in pain. But not such a relief when the doctor told me that she was going to have to remain in hospital for some time as she had Guillain-Barré syndrome. In her case it had been a rapid onset and had affected the muscles in her legs and arms causing weakness and pain. She was in the right place for the best care that was for sure. I left the hospital with lots of instructions about what to bring for mom the following day and feeling a lot happier.

Phyllis knocked on the door almost as soon as I arrived back at the flat, wanting an update on mom's condition. She had never o Guillain-Barré syndrome. Well that made two of us although she was a lot older than me. A lot older than mom even. But there you go. She very kindly invited me to have a cooked evening meal with her every night whilst mom was in hospital. Fortunately mom had an account at Mr Stavros's café on the corner as well as another café up the road so I was able to get whatever I needed for breakfast and lunch.

It was strange staying by myself in the flat the first night. Not that it was quieter. It wasn't as we never had a radio. But just knowing that I was the only one there was so different to being alone in the flat during the day. But I was really self sufficient and just got on with things even doing my own washing in the bath. Now that I wasn't so worried about mom and as I was in the middle of exams I tried to use my time to put in some extra work for the subjects that remained. I took myself off to school each day and coped fairly well. When my exam results came in I had passed everything except English. Fortunately for me I was allowed to go through to standard seven but would have to rewrite English the following March. I felt as if I had been given another chance. I was also told that I would have to go into the mechanical stream the following year. I was devastated as I wanted to study electrical.

School was over for the year and Christmas was ten days away. Mom had told me that she had lost her job at the pharmacy and that we would have to be out of the flat by the end of December. So I spent some time clearing the flat and came across a number of empty gin bottles and one that was half full. Tutting in irritation, I poured it down the sink. Then I started packing our belongings into boxes which would be stored with Phyllis in her flat. We didn't have much so it didn't take very long at all. But looking around the flat stripped of all our things once again it felt rather forlorn and I did wonder uneasily where we would go from here.

There were no buses on Christmas Day, so I walked to the hospital which was a couple of miles away, through the city centre and along the deserted streets where all the shops were closed for the festive holiday, lights twinkling gaily in the windows and down to the beach front towards the bluff. It was a pleasant, flat walk but rather hot and very busy along the beach front with crowds of people having fun oblivious to the turmoil I was once again experiencing in my life. Mom was pleased to see me and delighted with her Christmas present of a pack of Rothmans cigarettes and a bar of chocolate. I had got it from the corner café and Mr Stavros kindly wrapped it up for me. I didn't tell him that mom had lost her job.

I had met up again with Garth my friend from Bergville who lived quite close to the beach front. I introduced him to tearoom bioscopes and we spent some time together there. He would be starting at George Campbell the following year one standard below me.

It was quite lonely staying in the flat by myself. Empty. The air felt different. Which it would of course as there was no cigarette smoke! But it was more than that. My mother was always such a presence, cheerful and chatty when sober, morose and silent when drunk unless she was challenged, then her rants would be loaded with vitriol and hostility. As I had to be out of the flat by the end of the month, I decided to ask Mrs Liebenberg if I could stay with her in Margate whilst mom was in hospital. She was happy enough to have me stay and we arranged a day when I would catch the train. I thought it would be more fun if I had someone to go with so I asked Garth if he would like to join me. I said he could tell his mother that my older brother from the Air Force would be there. Mom was pleased that I would be going to Mrs Liebenberg and said that she would phone her as soon as she could. After dropping off all four of our packed box-es with Phyllis and locking up the flat for the last time, I headed to the railway station. There I met up with Garth and we boarded the train for Margate.

Mrs Liebenberg was a little taken aback when two boys arrived at Margate station. 'Goodness, Rudi. You didn't tell me there were two of you,' she said with raised eyebrows.

'S ... .sorry Mrs Liebenberg. I really didn't think'

'No it's fine,' she said. 'Just double trouble' with a smile.

We had a ball in Margate, going to the beach that was packed with upcountry visitors every day, having a look at the amusement arcade which was such fun and generally running around entertaining ourselves. I met up with my friend Freddy and we had such a good time swimming and surfing. He was still at Margate school and his life seemed much the same. I envied him. Mrs Liebenberg had put rules into place for us. We had to be home at lunchtime every day for a cooked meal. We had to put our dirty washing in the laundry and hang our wet costumes on the line when we came home from the beach every day. Which was fine.

One day Mrs Liebenberg got a phone call from my mother to say that she had been discharged from hospi-tal and she was getting a lift down to Margate. When the car arrived outside the gate to the Liebenberg's house, I didn't recognise my mother. She was very thin and looked quite frail and she was wearing black iron callipers on each leg and struggling to walk. I rushed down to meet her and took her arm and helped her into the house. When we were alone she said that she had spoken to Gareth's mother who told her that he would be in Margate with my brother. 'I didn't know you had a brother Rudi,' she said. I blushed feeling embarrassed and told her that I had made it up but didn't tell her that it was something that I made up years ago when I was in Bergville. That was even more embarrassing. After that Garth wanted to go home so we dropped him off at the station to catch the train back to Durban. I felt a bit bad.

Mom and I stayed a week longer with Mrs Liebenberg then she drove us to Durban and booked us into the Plaza Hotel. I knew it well, especially the cloakroom. I enjoyed the breakfasts there and always remember the omelette with mince. It was my absolute favourite. Mrs Liebenberg stayed a couple of days to help mom look for somewhere to stay. They eventually found a furnished room out of the city in a large old house up on the hill in Mansfield Road. But this also meant that I would have to catch two buses to school and back again every day. After calling on Phyllis to collect our boxes Mrs Liebenberg dropped us off early on the Friday afternoon and made her way back to Margate.

Our room was on the ground floor of a large double storey house set back from the road with a separate entrance to the rear. It had its own bathroom although it didn't deserve to be called a bathroom. It was a small room at the back of our room which had a bare concrete floor and a hole in the ground at the far end. This had to serve as the toilet. It meant that you had to squat like a caveman! There was a shower rose at the end of a pipe jutting out from the wall over the toilet hole so that I had to shower hanging over the hole. And there was a basin. It was grim! The room where we would sleep had a hot plate, a small fridge, two beds and a table. Nothing else. Not even a chair. I would have to do my homework sitting on the bed. It would have to do or course. Sitting in a strange bare room once more I tried to be cheerful and helped mom unpack our belongings. It didn't take long. Mom was in a good mood and I know that she was happy to be feeling better. She still wore her callipers, especially on the left leg which seemed to give her more problems. And of course she wasn't drinking either. I just hoped that it would stay that way.

I would be starting the new school year the following week so made sure that I found my uniform and that it was clean and ready and that my suitcase was packed. Leaving very early on the first day of school as I was not sure of the buses, I walked to the bus stop to catch the bus that would take me into town. Then I got off in the centre of town and caught another bus to school. A rather roundabout journey but I got there in the end. I should have been starting the trade course that had been selected for me by the deputy head. But I had decided that I wasn't going to do mechanics that had been selected for me. I didn't like it as much as electrical. When the class split to go to the various trade courses, I just followed the boys who were going into the electrical side. It was never questioned. The teacher who put my name down for mechanics was apparently off sick so I got away with it. I never regretted my selection. A month after starting school I rewrote my English exam and this time I passed.

I had made friends with a boy in my class by the name of John Harrison. He lived about a mile away from Mansfield Road in a very good neighbourhood that had large double storey homes set in sizeable grounds. We would spend occasional Saturdays together on the beach then go to a movie in the afternoon where we would be picked up by his father who would drop me off outside the house in Mansfield Road. I never invited John in. I was too embarrassed. I had told him that my father was a doctor which wasn't all *that* far from the truth because both my grandfather and my great grandfather had been doctors. But I obviously hadn't learnt my lesson about making up stories but it was out of my mouth before I could stop myself. I hoped that it wouldn't come back and bite me on the bum.

Mom had found a job in a pharmacy in Florida Road which was in a bustling part of the Morningside area of Durban. It was tree lined and had many small traditional shops either side of the road. There was a local butcher, a greengrocer, bakery, chemist, tearoom and hardware store which all served the local community. It was far enough out of the bustle of the city to feel like the suburbs but close enough to jump on a bus and be in the city centre in fifteen minutes. A really nice place to work.

We had been living in Mansfield Road for over a month. By now I could read the signs of when mom had been drinking the moment she opened her mouth. Gone was the sweet, kind softly spoken mom. Her voice would be harsh, filled with bitterness and she could be horrible. She was a morose drunk. I kept well away. Since she had been admitted to hospital she hadn't been drinking and I was hoping that the time spent sober would help her to stay on the right track and keep clear of gin for a while. Unfortunately mom befriended our landlady, Mrs Biggs who had a particularly soft spot for gin herself and the two of them had started to get together on a Saturday afternoon after mom had finished work. They would sit in Mrs Biggs' kitchen drinking gins for the rest of the afternoon then mom would come home and drink whatever was there. Come Sunday there was more often than not, nothing left so she would give me a note to take to the emergency chemist with a request to buy a bottle of Sanatogen Tonic Wine and then spend the rest of the day drinking, finishing the whole bottle. This became a regular weekend routine.

A couple of months later I came home from school to find mom at home. She was drunk and she said that she had lost her job at the pharmacy. I wasn't surprised and actually *did* roll my eyes at her but she was too inebriated to notice. When she went to bed that night I rummaged in her handbag and took most of the money out of her purse and put it in my school bag so that I could at least stop her from spending it on alcohol. I wasn't sure how she paid the rent to Mrs Biggs but I was sure that the money would come in handy sometime down the line. The next day late in the afternoon Jennifer and Johan came to visit.

'Mom! Look at the state of you,' said Jennifer horrified by mom's unkempt appearance. Why don't we get you into rehab? Let's get you back to being the happy lovely Joan that we all love. Don't you think that's a good idea?'

Mom shook her head and lit another cigarette directly from the stub of the one before.

'Come on, Mom. You know you can do it. Do it for you!' Jennifer insisted persuasively.

Mom sighed and reluctantly agreed to be ready the following day when they would collect her at five. She had obviously given it some thought and decided that she did not want to go as when Jennifer arrived to collect her we had to carry her to the car and pour her onto the back seat, she was that drunk. I felt sick seeing her like that. Unfortunately the rehab centre would not take her in that state and we had to turn around and bring her back home again. A couple of days later mom seemed to have pulled herself together. She said that we would be moving back into the city and that she had got herself a new job at Henwoods Hardware store. I managed to gradually sneak most of her money back into her purse when she wasn't looking but I don't think she even noticed. I did keep R5 for myself though as mom never gave me pocket money and I needed to have *some* money for when I went to movies or the beach. But I was glad to be moving away. Apart from the grim bathroom, I didn't like Mrs Biggs.

We moved once again into a bachelor flat in the Durban city centre. The flat was in Acutt Street on the third floor and was accessed by an old birdcage lift with an interior of shiny wooden panelling. It was so slow that a lot of the time I used to run up the stairs and would be waiting at the flat door long before I heard the clang of the grate opening after it had arrived on the third floor. There was only one small room in the flat and one bed so my mother found a camp bed in a second hand shop and bought it for me to sleep on. As usual the bright light and mom's cigarette smoke troubled me and I struggled to sleep so I set up my camp bed in the kitchen every night closing the door to block out the light and minimise the smoke, although I could still smell it. It didn't bother my mother much that I slept in the kitchen.

Henwoods was a department store that had been open in Durban for many years. It had a very good hardware section and also a sports goods section. I used to go there often after school when mom worked there as I used to love to go to the sports section and admire all the new rugby and cricket kit that was on display. Mom also used to take me up to the canteen where she would get me a cake and a coke as a treat. That's probably the main reason why I went there so often. One day she said she had a present for me. She took me to the tools section, a boy's dream, and showed me an assortment of hand held power tools and said that as I was now sixteen I could choose anything that I wanted. So I chose a lovely Black and Decker drill which I thought would come in handy. She put it into a Henwoods bag and gave it to me to take home. It was only later that I realised that she never paid for the drill. When I asked her about it she just laughed and thought it very funny. It was during her time with Henwoods that she arranged a holiday job for me in the sports section. But it wasn't long after she gave me the drill that she told me that she was not working there anymore but had got a job at OK Bazaars, another large department store. With her knack of having the gift of the gab she then organised me a holiday job with OK Bazaars, fixing broken toys that customers brought back because they were not working. That was my first real job. After that I progressed to the menswear department. But now it seemed as if I had two jobs. One at Henwoods and one at OK Bazaars. I didn't want to go to Henwoods not after the power drill saga. And not after mom leaving there so suddenly and I had my suspicions why! So I said to my friend John Harrison that he could have a job at Henwoods for the holidays but he was going to have to go as Rudi. He agreed so he worked at

Henwoods as Rudi and I worked at OK Bazaars as Rudi. Because I was Rudi.

I'm getting as barmy as my mother!

I had completed standard seven passing with reasonable marks. Mom insisted that I remain in the academic stream for the following year even though I knew that it was not suitable for me. Standard eight would be my last year of formal schooling before I went into some sort of trade apprenticeship.

Mom didn't last at OK Bazaars. She was there only a couple of months when she announced that she was now working at The Powder Bowl, a chemist in central Durban. The Powder Bowl was followed soon after by Smith Street Pharmacy. During the time of mom's tour of employment, my schoolwork was not going well. Apart from the fact that I was in the academic stream which was totally unsuitable, the table where I did my homework in the flat had a wire mesh top so it was very difficult to write let alone write neatly. My writing was a handicap anyway. Eventually one of the teachers at school gave me a thin piece of board to cover the table so that at least I had a decent surface to work on.

Then we moved again. This time mom said she had a job as caretaker in a boarding house called Rose Garden Lodge in Glenwood. Glenwood was further out of town so the trip to school was a bit more long winded that before. At least we were provided with an evening meal every day. But once again I had to share a room with my mother. After living like that for a couple of days I discovered an old air raid shelter at the bottom of the garden. It was built of concrete and there were four steps leading down into the first room which led into another smaller room at the back. It was packed full of old furniture and junk. But it was nice and cool down there and I had an idea. I really hated sharing a bedroom with my mother and I had had enough so I asked the owner if I could stay in the air raid shelter which he agreed to as long as I cleaned it up. Excited, I roped in John Harrison and his brother Graham to help me and we spent the day clearing out the shelter and ditching some of the old stuff and packing the rest back into the small back room except for two wooden chairs which I thought I could make use of. Then we swept the floor and cleaned down the walls and it was ready. I moved my bed from my mom's room to the shelter and found an old tea chest which I used for a table. There was a light fitting in the roof where I used my newly acquired electrical skills to wire in a socket where I could plug in my precious transistor radio that I had bought with my first pay check from OK Bazaars. My very own space. I was thrilled. John and Graham were envious which I thought was a bit bizarre as they had a beautiful home and they each had their own bedroom.

#

I had failed standard eight which was depressing. I knew that I had been in the wrong stream. Mom asked the owner of the lodge what to do and he said that he knew a plumber who needed an apprentice to work for him and he came to see me. I didn't like him. I told him that I would think about it. But I knew there was nothing to think about. I didn't want to do plumbing and that was that! Mom was cross with me and said that she did not want to let the owner down. She was more concerned about letting the owner down than she was for me deciding on the correct career choice for my future. So what I *did* think about, was that I thought I would go back to school to get my standard eight certificate. Although there were still two more standards of schooling above standard eight to complete I would be content just with the standard eight. Mom was seriously not happy and accused me of letting her down and we had *words*. I didn't even bother to roll my eyes at her. I just told her that I would be staying with my sister for my final year of school. This time I went into the trade stream and I coped with the school work so much better.

Jennifer had moved to Sandown, a large block of flats opposite the old snake park on Durban beach front. She now had two small boys and together with her husband Johan, they lived in a two bedroom flat with a balcony overlooking the sea. I had a bed on the enclosed balcony. It was my own space. Best of all, George Campbell School was just up the road so I could walk there.

I noticed a new face at school one day: A scruffy looking boy with long brown hair which hung over his eyes and which looked so out of place amongst the short back and sides that was compulsory for all pupils at the time. He looked awkward and alone and was attracting sideways glances and snide remarks, particularly from the older boys. I immediately felt drawn to him knowing full well what it was like to be new and to stand out without meaning or wanting to. His name was Jerry Musgrove and he and I became firm friends and remain friends to this day.

That was a very stable year for me and I was really proud of myself when I passed with flying colours.

CHAPTER THIRTEEN

Joan

I am an alcoholic.

There!

I finally said it. I finally *admitted* it. It's what they expect you to say isn't it.

I am an alcoholic.

Satisfied?

#

I became aware of a light touch on my shoulder and a soft voice saying 'Here let me help you up off the damp grass and we will take you and your son to a safe place for the night.' I looked up into a kind face and immediately felt choked up and I couldn't stop my lips from trembling.

I felt utterly, *utterly* reduced.

Reduced to nothing.

Demoralised.

Shamed.

I allowed her to help me up, stumbling as I tried to encourage some life back into my trembling legs which by now were numb with cold and walked with her the fairly short distance to Kerr House.

'I am Carol and I am a volunteer with the Durban Welfare,' said Carol as we walked along the pavement. 'Your son will be taken to the children's home for the night and we will get you into Kerr House where they will look after you. Tomorrow we can chat to you about your situation but for the moment it's a hot bath and cooked meal for you and then bed. How does that sound?' She looked at me kindly.

I could only nod at her silently through my tears. I couldn't think straight. I felt so *tired*. I just wanted to sleep forever. We arrived at Kerr House and Carol took me straight to the bathroom where she ran a hot bath and after handing me a towel said, 'You go ahead and have a quick wash. I will leave some clothes on the chair just outside the door for you. Then come downstairs to the dining room where I will be waiting for you.'

Numbly, I took off my clothes and sank with a deep sigh into the warm water allowing it to flow over my shoulders as I lay back in the bath. I was suddenly over-whelmed by emotion and I sobbed and sobbed.

There was a soft knock at the door. 'Joan, are you all right in there?'

I don't remember giving them my name was my first thought. I realised that the bath water was cold. I must have been in there for a while. 'I'm fine,' I said foggily wiping my face. 'I'm coming out now. I didn't realise that I had been in the bath so long' I said by way of explanation. Drying myself slowly I wrapped the large towel around me as I opened the door to find some clothes folded neatly on a wooden chair. I didn't even notice what the clothes were to be honest, I really didn't have the brain power. In no time I was making my way downstairs to the dining room where Carol was waiting for me. After being given a wholesome meal of chicken stew and rice I was shown where I would be sleeping and left alone for the night.

I lay on top of the bed feeling comfortable after the bath and warm meal. It was the first proper meal I had

had for days. I really could do with a drink. But I knew that I wouldn't find one here. Exhausted, I slept.

I woke up the following morning still feeling exhausted. I didn't want to get out of bed. It was too much effort. It was an ordeal to *think* about getting dressed. What was the *point* in all this? I still felt numb. Out of it. I just wanted to sleep and never wake up. I just wanted everything to go away. I sat up in bed looking around vacantly and spotted the clothes that I had worn last night laying on a chair. Forcing myself up I got dressed slowly and made my way downstairs to the dining room. After a warm cup of tea and a bowl of porridge oats I felt marginally better. There were two other ladies in the room but I was so immersed in my troubles that I didn't speak to them at all.

'I hope you are feeling better today Joan,' said Carol as she walked into the room. 'When you are ready let's go into the office and I can take down some details from you.'

Carol ushered me into the office and explained what Kerr House was all about. A lot of what she was saying just went over my head to be honest as I was feeling so detached from everything. It was as if this was happening to someone else.

'Your son has been taken to a children's home up the road which I think I mentioned to you last night. Do you remember?'

I nodded.

'We will arrange for him to visit you in a day or two. I'm sure you would like that wouldn't you?'

I nodded once more.

'Good. So last night you told me that your name was Joan. What is your surname?'

'Garden'

'Okay, Joan. Can you tell me a little about how you ended up on the beach front where we found you?'

'I had a clothes shop in Margate that closed down and I lost everything and just after that my ex husband was taken ill and his maintenance stopped so I had no income. I thought that I could come to Durban and look for work but I ran out of money.' I said with effort giving her a scaled down version of events. I never mentioned about my drinking, because that wasn't the issue.

'That must have been awfully hard for you Joan,' said Carol sympathetically looking at me with such kindness that I felt myself well up. 'Where were you thinking of finding work?'

I swallowed. 'My ex husband and I used to own the Kingsview Hotel in Margate so I know the hotel industry well.' Feeling blank and clutching my hands which were trembling slightly I placed them into my lap so that she wouldn't notice. I needed a drink. 'Do you mind but I think I would like to rest now for a bit,' I said shakily. 'I'm struggling to think straight.'

'Of course. We can catch up later when you are feeling better. You go on up and I will bring you a cup of tea.'

I thanked her and stumbled blindly through the door to my room and slumped tiredly onto my bed. Exhaustion overwhelmed me. I heard Carol place the tea cup on the table by my bed and thanked her gratefully enjoying the warm sweet liquid. My head was woolly. I still needed a drink.

I spent most of the following two days either dosing or wandering around in a stupor not noticing my surroundings much. How had I come to this? How had I sunk so low? I now had nothing. *Nothing*! Not even my own clothes. I needed a cigarette. I needed a drink. *Any* drink!

On the morning of the third day Carol called me once again into her office.

'How are you doing Joan?' she asked kindly

I really want a drink I almost said. I knew my hands were shaking so tried to keep them out of sight and said, 'I'm okay, just struggling with a woolly head.'

Carol looked at me and said, 'When did you last have a drink?'

How did *she* know? The question threw me and I just looked at her unable to answer.

'I have had your file transferred over from Social Welfare and it seems the last contact with them was just under two years ago when Rudi was returned to you.'

I nodded numbly. Deflated. So they knew everything.

'Have you been drinking recently?'

'Yes.' It was pointless denying it. They had my life in black and white.

'Well the best thing is to get you started on a program as soon as we can so that it won't be long before you are in a good enough place to be able to go out and find work. It is imperative that you continue with the meetings Joan. Important for your overall wellbeing.'

I nodded not having words but wishing that this would just go away.

'But some good news,' Carol continued cheerfully. 'Rudi and Jennifer will be visiting you today so that's something to look forward to. The Child Welfare have decided that Rudi will be sent off to boarding school in Bergville to complete his primary school education and where he will have the benefit of a stable environment. This will give you the opportunity to concentrate on yourself and work towards getting better.' She closed the file and looked at me. 'It's a lot to take in I know. But it will all work out. Just remember, one step at a time.'

I nodded again trying to process what I had been told.

'Why don't you go and get ready? Rudi and Jennifer will be here to see you in half an hour.'

#

I tried to be cheerful, I really did. I tried to put a smile on my face and to look as if I was fine. For *their* sakes. I washed my hair and used some of the lipstick that was given to me to bring some colour to my face. But it was so *hard*! It was the last thing I felt like doing. But still. It was lovely to see Jennifer and Rudi.

'Mom, what are you *wearing*?' Jennifer asked her hand in front of her mouth trying to cover her smile. I had to laugh with her. It felt quite good. To laugh. I knew that I probably looked a sight but I didn't have much wardrobe choice now did I? Rudi was subdued and wide eyed and I could hear the trembled plea in his voice when he told me that he was going to be sent away to boarding school. A wave of guilt floored me and dammit I needed a drink! I just told him that he had to go. It was only later lying on the bed that I regretted my hasty words and I thought perhaps that I should have been more sensitive and gentle with him.

Helped by three square meals a day and the absence of any alcohol in my diet, I began to feel a lot better. Physically that is. I had been down this road before so I knew that I would start to feel stronger once I was eating correctly. And I also knew that when I felt better physically then I would cope better mentally. It was all too depressingly familiar.

I was given a chest of clothes to look through to choose something suitable for me to wear. To be honest there was nothing that I would choose ... normally ... .but I needed clothes so chose the best of what there was. Kerr House also supplied me with deodorant, soap, hair brush and cosmetics. I don't know what happened to my suitcase with all my things including my lovely, lovely dresses. I didn't want to think about it. I didn't want to think about my inheritance that had disappeared into thin air either. I didn't want to think about my shop that had gone under, my lost maintenance, Michael, Clocolan, Rudi being taken away for the second time! I didn't want to think about anything. Normally I would have a drink to blot out any unpleasant thoughts but I couldn't get my hands on any now could I? I was forced to face my demons.

Within a week of being at Kerr House, Carol had arranged for me to attend my first AA meeting. The meeting was held in a church hall in the centre of the city and was attended by about ten men and women. They were all strangers to me of course which somehow made it easier. I sat there on a wooden chair not opening my mouth and listening to the other people's stories and feeling so *angry*. White hot overwhelming anger! Anger because I shouldn't have to be there at all! Angry at Ian. Angry that I had lost my money. Angry that I didn't have a home. Angry that I seem to be on an endless treadmill and going nowhere. Angry, angry, angry! Once the meeting came to an end I leapt up and bolted for the door running down the steps two at a time to get away as fast as I could. I didn't want to be there. I just wanted to be left alone.

During the following couple of weeks at Kerr House I had a lot of time on my hands. A lot of time to think.

I had reached the stage where I was almost resigned to my fate. I knew that I had reached rock bottom. I mean, how much lower could I go? I had nothing! No roof over my head. No job. No money. No clothes. *Nothing*! I had to scrape myself off the bottom of the barrel and claw up with my fingernails to get out.

It was at my third AA meeting that a certain calm came over me and I realised that I was ready. Without hesitating, I stood up in front of everyone there and said, 'My name is Joan and I am an alcoholic.' That was the first time that I had said those words out loud. And it hit me hard to hear them. I sat down abruptly, unable to prevent the tears from pouring down my cheeks. Everyone clapped and said well done. It made me feel as if I had done something special, which I had. I had admitted for the first time to myself that I was an alcoholic. And that I needed help.

After that I went to meetings every week in a much more positive frame of mind and I have to admit, I felt stronger as time went on. Better in myself. More able to cope day to day until I reached the stage where I was ready to move on. Kerr House had been a sanctuary that had provided me with support and encouragement when I was in desperate need but I wanted my independence, to go out to work and earn my own money. After about eight weeks with the programme Carol agreed that I was ready to start looking for employment. As in the past, work in the hotel industry was relatively easy to come by and it wasn't a week later that I had secured a job running the Lucian Hotel in Point Road. With promises to keep in touch ... well obviously I had to, as Rudi was under the care of the Welfare ... I left Kerr house for my new job at the Lucian feeling positive and confident in my continuing state of sobriety.

The Lucian was a small hotel with only fifteen rooms but it was always full being in a prime position near the busy Durban beach front. It hadn't been too badly run in the past and with just a couple of changes here and there I had everything running smoothly in no time. It felt good to be active and busy again. It felt good to be earning money and being able to go out and buy some decent clothes that helped me feel like Joan Garden again. Not Joan the down and out, not Joan the drunkard. But Joan the undefeated. Joan the unstoppable. It felt good to have my own room where I could go and shut the door on the world. I'm not going to lie.

Soon it was school holidays and it was with great excitement that Jennifer and I went to the station to meet Rudi. He really seemed to be enjoying boarding school and spoke endlessly about all the friends that he had made there. He spoke particularly about a boxing match that he had been involved in early on in the school term. It was comforting somehow to know that he could stand up for himself.

Life carried on with me religiously attending weekly AA meetings and working at the hotel most days so that I didn't have much time to think. I still struggled to tame my demons and found it enormously difficult to accept my situation still feeling a certain amount of bitterness and anger at the world. Yes I know that I should be at the stage where I had accepted my situation. But I wasn't! I felt resentful. All the time! So staying alcohol free was a continuous challenge. Life was a continued struggle.

Rudi arrived in early December for the long Christmas holidays but as it was a very busy time of the year for me I didn't really get to see him much. I had been hoping that maybe he wouldn't have to go back to Bergville. But after one of my regular meetings with Durban Welfare I was disappointed to be told that he would remain there for another year. In the meantime Jennifer had got engaged. She was now nineteen and a really beautiful young lady. She had met a young man who was a policeman and she seemed very happy. They planned to marry in April during the school holidays so that at least Rudi could be there as well.

#

It has been 254 days since I last had a drink.

254 days!

I think that is a record!

Some days were easy. Some days were not so easy. Some days I didn't give alcohol a thought! Some days sneaky images crept into my head randomly and unbidden and the pull was as strong as a punch in the stomach and I could almost taste the fiery liquid on my tongue and feel the hot path as it trickled down my throat. That's when I knew that I had to be strong. Or busy. Or I phoned Don Scott.

I had met Don at AA. He was divorced and an alcoholic as well. So we had that in common! I know that's not an attribute that one would normally look for in a partner but he was nice enough and we were both on the same wavelength. Obviously! I could talk to him about my struggles with the bottle, depending on my mood, and of course he understood. And we would be able to support one another through the down times of which there were many. But you know me. I could never resist a good looking man anyway. And this was no exception. Although I have to confess that I was feeling just a *little* bit fragile, a little bit bruised shall we say. What with my recent episode with Hank. And of course Michael. But I used my charm as I was wont to do and we had a pleasant enough time.

I had worked at the Lucian Hotel for nine months and was becoming a bit bored so decided that I needed a change and found work at the Rio Grande Hotel which was in the same area. But overall I was finding it challenging working around alcohol every day, the familiar sour smell hitting the back of my throat causing me to catch my breath as I entered the bar area of the hotel. I couldn't avoid it. It was my job. The temptation was so strong, always there under my nose. It called to me. It pulled me. *Every day!* Do you know how *hard* it was to ignore that pull? How *hard* it was to ignore the chatter of budgies in my head? How *hard* it was to turn around and walk out of the room and force my mind onto other things? Do you have any idea? Ron did. Thank goodness for his listening ear and advice and thank goodness for the weekly AA top up meetings because at the time they were a godsend. I had been feeling so proud of myself for getting this far, for finally accepting that I was an alcoholic. I could see the light at the end of the tunnel. But I knew that if I wanted to continue to remain sober then I had to get out of the hotel industry once more and as I had done when I was in Port Shepstone, I decided to find work in a shop. Which meant that I would need to find a flat to stay in. I had always been good at turning on Joan charm and establishing rapport with people especially the hotel guests and I knew that there was a very well known pharmacy in the city centre that was looking for an assistant so without hesitation I applied for the position.

Because I hadn't been drinking ... *for 254 days* ... I had managed to save a bit of money whilst I had been working so I had the cash ready for a deposit on a furnished flat which I found in the city centre. It was only one room really with a glass partition where there was a bed and two other beds in the main room with space left only for a small table and chairs. The kitchen and bathroom were to the side of the entrance. It was very cramped but it would just have to do. Within a couple of days of moving into the flat I got the news that the job in the pharmacy was mine. My first unbidden thought was to go out and buy a bottle to celebrate which was what I would normally have done of course. But I bought a nice piece of fillet steak for myself as a treat. My favourite. Well *why not?*

My flat was a ten minute walk away from the pharmacy which was really convenient and at least I didn't have to fork out money for bus fare. It was with a spring in my step that I entered Murray's Pharmacy on my first day of work feeling as if I have emerged out of a long dark tunnel. Esme Pretorious, the assistant pharmacist met me at the door. Tall and slim with immaculate hair and make up, and dressed in a white pharmacist coat, she was a formidable lady that expected to be obeyed without question. She demanded the best out of her staff and I was a bit wary of her to be honest. I used to think of her as 'The Doberman' just to entertain myself on the side. But Murray's Pharmacy was a good place to work and overall I enjoyed my time there. Esme was very helpful in suggesting that I send Rudi to George Campbell Technical High School which I had known nothing about and upon investigation seemed to suit him well.

Don was becoming difficult. No, not *difficult* as such, probably more irritating really. He always persisted on arriving at the flat almost as soon as I got home in the afternoon, not even allowing me time to kick off my shoes and relax with a cigarette. Then he wanted to go out to the beach front or the movies and I was really not interested after working and being on my feet the whole day. He was just so demanding. It all came to a head one Saturday when I had just sat down and was putting my feet up after work, thinking about what to cook for supper, when in he strolled with that crooked smile of his wanting to go out. I was just so irritated and snapped at him to leave me alone for once. He snapped back immediately and called me a boring old hag and stormed out. I was relieved at first. But a week went by, then two and I didn't hear from him. He wasn't at AA meetings either. I never saw him again.

Three weeks after Don left I didn't go to AA. I just felt low and couldn't sum up the energy. On the one hand I felt rejected by Don. But on the other hand I felt responsible for his silent withdrawal from me and the programme. But I told myself that I would definitely go the following week which I didn't of course. I know ... I know! But I had taken a slight detour on my way home from work a couple of days ago, with no *particular* thought in mind, just for exercise, and I found myself walking past a bottle store where they were advertising gin at a reduced price. Well I couldn't pass that up now, could I? So I bought two bottles. Well it was a *bargain*! All the way home I was in two minds whether I should just dump the bottles or empty the contents down the sink when I got home. Then I was overwhelmed by the thought of that first mouthful and walked faster, knowing it was wrong, knowing that I was going to destroy all the hard work that I had put in to get to where I was.

Damn Don!

Damn him for disappearing just when I needed him!

By the time I got home I was in such a fever of anticipation that I was shaking and short of breath. I plonked the bottles on the table, poured myself a glass of water and sat down with a thumping heart, my head in my hands. Surely one drink will do no harm.

Did I really want to do this?

Yes!

Without further thought I grabbed a bottle and poured some gin into a cup and drank.

I'll just have one.

I can control this.

I know I can.

I've done it before you see.

I hid the bottles before Rudi got home as there was no need for him to know. I only drank half a cup that first time. I drank it slowly, feeling the smooth warm path of the liquid slip down my throat, savouring every last drop. After that, I did regulate it to a certain degree. I never drank in the morning before work and I was very good about not taking drink to work either. So the only time I had a drink really was when I came home in the evenings and at the weekend.

So you see. I *do* have the power to control it!

It was a couple of months later that I woke up suddenly early one morning with the most agonising sharp pains in both legs. What made it worse was that I was unable to move my left leg at all and only slightly move my right so I couldn't even get out of bed. My cries woke Rudi and he ran next door to call for help. I don't remember much of the journey to hospital as I was in too much pain. All I know is that we went by bus. It was such a relief when the doctor gave me an injection and I felt the pain fade away and I was able to think straight again.

I'd never heard of Guillain-Barré syndrome before. But that was apparently what I had. The doctor said that it could take anything from three weeks to six months to get better. I guess it's just the luck of the draw so I would have to wait and see. My legs were paralysed so I was unable to move at all. It was pretty scary lying in bed not knowing if and when I would be able to be back on my feet. It gave me plenty of time to think. Plenty of time to worry. I had lost my job with Murray's Pharmacy. I was only allowed one week's sick leave a year and clearly I would be off for a while. For heaven's' sake! Why? Why me? Why now? I had been with the pharmacy for almost a year and I was really happy there. So with no money coming in I knew that I would be unable to pay the rent on the flat and was told by the landlord that I had to vacate it by the end of December. I wasn't sure where I was going to go. Phyllis was really helpful and ensured that Rudi had a cooked meal every day so that was one thing less for me to worry about.

Jennifer came to visit me a couple of times. She was now living in Sarnia which was a suburb south of the city and quite far out. She still worked in central Durban and Johan drove her into town every day.

I was given physio every day which I suppose helped. Towards the end of three weeks I started to get some sensation in both legs and I was put into callipers and encouraged, with the nurses' help to practise walking. It was exhausting as my legs were not listening to my head and the callipers were really heavy and cumbersome. But I persisted every day. It *was* nice to be mobile once again even though it was a slow, painful process. I was told that I had to wear the callipers for as long as there was any paralysis in my legs.

Rudi, bless him, had packed up all our things from the flat into boxes and stored them with Phyllis next door. Actually I could do with a drink. Just thinking about where on earth I was going to go after I was discharged made me want to reach for a bottle. I mean … I had nowhere *to* go! When Rudi told me that he had arranged with Peggy Liebenberg to go and stay with her in Margate for a couple of weeks, I immediately realised that I could speak to her about putting me up for a while as well. Before I had thought of a plan Peggy phoned the hospital to speak to me and took the words out of my mouth and invited me down to Margate for a couple of days. It was such a relief. Soon I was discharged, still having to wear the callipers for as long as there was paralysis in my legs. Other than that I felt reasonably well and quite upbeat. It was just nice to be up and about again and I was so happy that my symptoms had disappeared as fast as they did. And of course the enforced three meals a day, even though they were hospital meals, together with the lack of alcohol, contributed to my general feeling of wellbeing. I had arranged a lift to Margate and within a couple of hours of being discharged I arrived at Peggy's house.

Just to let you into a little secret.

I didn't really need to wear the callipers at all any more. My legs felt quite strong and the muscle tone was almost back to normal. But they really helped to evoke sympathy so I pretended that I was worse than I really was. I thought it was rather clever actually. It was just a bit of acting really. Exiting the taxi with difficulty, Rudi helped me walk up the drive. It was awkward. And uncomfortable to walk on a slope but I got there eventually. Peggy was very helpful and sympathetic to my situation and I have to admit that I don't know what I would have done without her. She arranged to take us back to Durban primarily so that Rudi could return to school for the first term of the year and because there are a lot more job opportunities there for me. She booked us all into the Plaza Hotel and stayed and helped me over the following couple of days to look for accommodation for us both and also to scour the newspapers for a job. This was really kind of her but it meant that I had to wear the callipers every day whilst she was with us but I guess it was a good investment. We eventually found a room in Mansfield Road and Peggy kindly paid the first month's rent. The room was not the best but I couldn't look a gift horse in the mouth now could I? But it was a start.

It was a huge relief to get rid of the callipers. No, not get *rid* of as such, but just get them off my legs and move around normally again. I decided to hold onto them as they might come in useful in the future, you never know. Within a couple of days I had also secured a job in a chemist's a short bus ride away from where I would be staying. Work there was pleasant and Florida Road was a nice area to work in. More like a leafy suburb.

Myrtle Biggs, the landlady of Mansfield Road, was a heavy woman with a rotund face and ruddy complexion, her red painted mouth surrounded by numerous deep lines as she drew on the cigarette held permanently between her lips. Her substantial behind seemed to have a life of its own as she pulled her tight shift dress down over her rounded hips failing to cover the dimpled surplus of flesh at the back of her knees. She moved ponderously, shuffling forward, her thick ankles spilling over the tired slippers that she always wore. Despite her slovenly appearance she was a sharp businesswoman and owned two large houses on the Berea which she had turned into profitable income-producing bedsits.

The first month living in Mansfield Road went by in a flash. I was settled into my job at the pharmacy and had received my first month's wages. It was Saturday afternoon and the end of the month so I went across to Myrtle Biggs' house to give her the rental.

'Mrs Garden, do come in and take a seat,' said Mrs Biggs.

'Oh please call me Joan. I just brought your rental for the next month,' I said handing her a wad of notes and looking around the room and immediately spotting the gin bottle and glass on the table. I swallowed. 'You can count it if you like.'

Her pudgy hand reached for the money as she adjusted the cigarette in her mouth, closing one eye as the smoke drifted up past her nose and quickly counted out the notes. She turned and put the notes into a battered tin on the counter top.

'Thank you and you can call me Ma. Everyone does.' She smiled and sat gesturing for me to do the same.

My eyes kept on flicking to the gin bottle. I could feel my heart pounding in my ears. I hadn't had a drink now for two months, since before I became ill.

'Here. Join me,' she said as she poured a large gin and tonic and placed it before me.

I looked at her and smiled. 'Might as well. Cheers.'

I just had the one and took my leave but it left me wanting more. As it was Saturday afternoon all the bottle stores were closed until Monday. I thought of nothing else all weekend.

The following Saturday I bought a bottle of gin after work. The whole week I had managed to prevent myself from going to the bottle store so this felt like a reward somehow. I knocked on Ma's door just after two.

'Ta Da!' I trilled, holding the bottle up high when she opened the door.

'You are a girl after my own heart. Get yourself in here.'

We sat and drank and smoked for the rest of the afternoon and when I said that I needed to get home she insisted that I take what was left in the bottle back with me. So I finished it off at home. The following day was Sunday and I had woken up with an awful headache so took myself off to the emergency chemist which was within walking distance of the flat. Walking around the shelves I came across Sanatogen Tonic Wine. Picking up the bottle I saw that the wine was ten and a half percent alcohol. That will do! I bought two as well as some painkillers and walked home extremely pleased with my emergency supplies.

It was really quite tasty. I finished the bottle when I got home that Sunday and started on the next. On the Monday morning there was still about a third of a bottle left so I had some before work. Well it *was* a tonic with added iron!

From then on that became the routine of my weekends. Gin on the Saturday with Ma, then Sanatogen Tonic Wine on Sunday. More often than not I would have to send Rudi to the chemist with a note on the Sunday. If I bought it on the Saturday then I would finish it on the Saturday and still have nothing left for the Sunday.

The weekends started spilling over and encroaching onto the week days. By Monday mornings after I had drunk all the alcohol in the house I became desperate and sometimes I slipped out at lunchtime to the bottle store just around the corner from Florida Road pharmacy and bought myself a small gin. The first mouthful calmed me immediately. Really. It did. And I was able to continue with my day with the knowledge that it was there in my bag and the comforting anticipation of having a drink that evening lifted my spirits.

It couldn't continue like that of course without the wheels coming off somewhere along the line. And come off they did. I was fired. I was getting quite used to being fired by now. I went straight to the bottle store and bought a large bottle of gin and proceeded to work my way through it for the balance of the day to blot out reality. Jennifer visited me the next day after she had finished work at the bank. Her and Johan. She tried to persuade me to go into rehab and wouldn't take no for an answer and said that she would be back the following day to take me there. But I knew what that entailed and I just didn't have the energy. So I drank all the more. I do remember her coming back. It must have been the following day but I woke up in my own bed that morning so I'm not sure what happened.

Logically I knew that drinking did not solve my problems but made them worse. And I did feel a little *shaken up* with the thought of Jennifer wanting to take me off to rehab. I didn't want to go! But I also knew that I had to make some sort of effort to cut down and get myself another job. There were a lot more jobs available in the city centre so it was two days later that I had secured a job at Henwoods and also managed to get a one bedroom flat in the centre of Durban which would be very convenient for both Rudi and myself.

Henwoods was just another job. There was a nice canteen though which Rudi used to enjoy. And what was nice too was that I could open an account although I had to pay the whole lot back at the end of the month. I hadn't *stopped* drinking altogether but I was controlling it a bit more. I would have a large slug, or two sometimes, before I left for work in the morning but I was able to resist not taking any with me. I knew that it was too tempting and I had been down that road before anyhow. I'm not saying that the need to drink was any less. It wasn't. It was just that I knew if I had drink on me then I would not be satisfied until I had finished it. I did not work at Henwoods all that long. I actually overheard a couple of younger staff members whispering to one another that I was light fingered and that they thought that I was just an old soak. The cheek of it!

I mean I wasn't *old*!

But nevertheless their whispers seemed to have reached management and I was asked, very politely, mind you, to leave. So I found a job at OK Bazaars, another department store, in the women's clothing section. I had always loved clothes as you know so this was really my cup of tea, or more appropriately, my glass of gin, of which I had a couple to congratulate myself on after finding such a suitable job. I thoroughly enjoyed working with fashion again even though it was on the periphery but it was exciting to unpack the new stock and display the dresses and pretty blouses to their advantage. And of course I had the pick of the crop. I must say that for the first time in ages I felt a bit of interest in clothes again. For the first time in ages I was in the position to be able to buy myself some outfits once more mainly because we were allowed to buy on account and pay back over twelve months. So *handy*!

The bubble burst eventually. Our uniform was a red skirt and white blouse which I wore to work every day so the opportunity to wear all the lovely clothes that I had now acquired was limited. I hardly ever went out. The thrill and excitement of the new clothes soon wore off. Sometimes on a Sunday Rudi and I were invited to lunch with some friends that I had made whilst working at OK and other times we went to Jennifer's for lunch. Otherwise I spent every weekend at home, either reading or playing cards. This was by choice mind you but it felt so *depressing*. The gin helped. I felt that I had got it down to a fine art. The glow. I knew just how to maintain the depth of numbness that I needed. Once again that need for numbness spread into the week days and I eventually could not cope without a top up or two during the course of the day. After working at OK Bazaars for six months I eventually left. Well. Okay ... I was fired if you must know. But I was doing absolutely *fine*. It was only when one of my colleagues saw me having a quick sip and reported me that it all came tumbling down.

Nobody was even aware. It wasn't as if I was not doing my job properly or anything. Otherwise I would have quite easily have gotten away with it.

I found work as a manageress easily enough at a pharmacy called The Powder Bowl. I knew exactly what to do after spending nearly a year at Murray's pharmacy so I slotted right in. During my time at the Powder Bowl the unpaid monthly account for OK Bazaars continued to arrive on my doorstep with irritating regularity. I hadn't paid it since I had left their employment three months ago. Deciding on a plan, I dressed with care putting a calliper on each leg and made my way slowly to the store and up the lift to the accounts section. Walking over to the counter with difficulty and leaning on the wooden surface breathing rather heavily ... I was exhausted! Let's face it, it *was* difficult walking in those things ... I handed the young gentleman my account. 'I'm unemployed,' I told him 'and I can't pay this as I don't have any money.' Well! What do you know? It worked. They let me off and said that they would write the balance off. It was worth all the effort and I thought I was *so* inventive.

After a couple of months my job at The Powder Bowl came to an end as well and I found myself working at another pharmacy in Smith Street. It was my fourth job in under ten months. I really needed to pull myself together.

And pull myself together I did to some degree for a while. I decided to apply for a job as caretaker of a boarding house called Rose Garden Lodge in Glenwood, an area south west of the city. The owner, Joe, a captivating young man with a crop of thick blond hair which bounced back into place effortlessly when he moved, showed me around the property on that first day. He was utterly charming and had the most tempting *delicious* smile. But … no. No! He was far too young for me.

The boarding house itself was a large old double storey house with a classic 1920s frontage with some pretty wrought iron features. There were two floors, with three bed sit rooms and a shared bathroom, situated at the end of the corridor on each floor. There were a couple of maids that came in every day to dust and clean and to do a linen change once a week. An evening meal was prepared daily by a cook who also did the food shopping. It seemed to run well and my job was to supervise and ensure that it continued to operate smoothly. Joe called around regularly, sometimes just to chat. It *was* nice to have a young man enjoy my company for a change! I always made sure that I looked attractive and my make up and hair was meticulous. Just in case. Just because. I was given a room with a one plate stove and two beds to share with Rudi. Although Rudi had found an old air raid shelter at the bottom of the garden and I got permission from Joe to allow him to stay there instead. I hardly saw him after that except at supper time when he used to come up to the house for the evening meal.

One evening he came into the dining room looking glum.

'What's wrong?'

'I've failed standard eight,' he said softly

'Oh Rudi. What am I going to do with you?'

'Yes, but mom, I shouldn't be in the university stream. It's too hard for me!' he said vehemently.

'Well I don't know what to do!' I said irritated. 'Let me speak to Joe'

The following day when Joe arrived I mentioned Rudi to him.

'Why Joan, anything for you!' he said. I almost blushed. 'I have a friend who is looking for an apprentice. He can chat to Rudi and take it from there.'

Well Rudi wasn't happy. He said he would think about it. What's to *think* about! The man had offered him a job for heaven's' sake! I couldn't understand him. He said that he didn't want to do plumbing. Well I say that beggars can't be choosers! But he was quite adamant and decided that he was going back to school to repeat standard eight and he was going to live with Jennifer. because he wanted to be able to concentrate on his schoolwork. *Well!*

And that's just what he did.

Left me and moved out.

Left me.

Just like Michael.

Just like Charlie.

Like Don! Like everybody in my life!

He moved out and lived with Jennifer.

What on earth was I going to tell Joe. He had gone to *so* much trouble to set up this meeting for Rudi. And what did Rudi do in return? He had really let me down!

I had to have a drink. I had been going along quite nicely really. Until then. Concentrating every day on my tasks for the day, making sure that everything was sparkling clean and tidy. Taking time over my choice of outfit for the day. I mean it was so nice to have an admirer. To feel *valued*. Yes I know he was young and all that but it still made me feel good once again and gave me an incentive to dress up a bit you know. Thank goodness for my shopping spree when I worked at OK Bazaar as I now had much to choose from.

But as ever, feeling put out by Rudi's *unwarranted* departure, I turned once more to my only reliable source of comfort.

Throughout the following year whilst Rudi repeated standard eight living with his sister, I carried on regardless with my secret drinking. It was easy to hide as I only had the African staff to worry about and Joe's visits which were a couple of times a week. Rudi had in the meantime, managed to pass standard eight quite well actually and I arranged a job interview for him at the Electricity Supply Commission through one of my old contacts from my hotel days. Rudi was very pleased to be accepted into their apprenticeship program for the following year.

It was a couple of months after Rudi had started his apprenticeship that I had an unexpected knock on my door one Friday afternoon.

'Joe!' I said trying to hide my dismay. I was already well into the gin. 'How lovely to see you' I stammered.

'Well, Joan, this is not a social visit. Actually, it is a visit that pains me,' he said, a determined look in his eye that I did not like. 'I am going to have to ask you to go. I will give you two weeks to find alternative accommodation but your job here is finished. And I'm sure that I don't have to tell you the reason why.'

I was stunned into silence and looked at him aghast. Then shoulders slumped and dropping my eyes, I nodded. And he turned and walked out of the room. I sank onto my bed and reached for my bottle and without bothering to pour the liquid into a glass, downing what was left. I drank steadily, I think for about a week until Jennifer came to visit over the weekend. I had to tell her that I had lost my job and needed somewhere to stay. Jennifer just looked at me and shook her head. 'You can stay with me for a while as Rudi is on a course for three months in Johannesburg. But there will be no drink!' she finished sternly.

This I had to accept.

CHAPTER FOURTEEN

Joan

It was 1972 and I was fifty years old. God Almighty! I felt eighty! Staying with Jennifer was difficult. The need for a drink was unbearable some days. But without any money there was not much that I could do other than sweat it out. I wasn't easy to live with I know so I'm sure that it was a relief to Jennifer when, without much enthusiasm, I found work eventually as manager of the Grand Hotel in central Durban. I was depressed. I knew I was depressed but I dragged myself passively through each day always hoping that the next would be an improvement. I worked there for just on a year then I moved to the Waverley Hotel as a boarder and found work in the evenings between five and ten o'clock as a cleaning supervisor for Unilever in the head office on The Esplanade. This seemed to work quite well for me although living at the Waverley became expensive so I eventually moved to a small bedsit in Russell Street. I worked for Unilever for over a year then decided to take up another caretaker job offer in a block of flats in Manning Road just out of the city. After some months there in 1978 I moved yet again to a block called WestPoint on the Durban Esplanade where I was employed as a caretaker once more.

I liked the job of caretaker at WestPoint. I had a handy man at my fingertips by the name of Moodley who I could call on to do any necessary repairs or heavy work that needed doing around the place. I also paid him to keep his mouth shut about my drinking habits of which he was privy to. Moodley was a very good deputy and I could send him out on all sorts of errands, not least, keeping me supplied with alcohol and cigarettes. By this stage I didn't like to go out much but preferred to be at home where I could indulge in my habit without fear of prying eyes. Scotty, who lived in one of the neighbouring flats became a very good friend. We rarely went out other than occasionally to visit Jennifer or to Rudi's house in Westville for Sunday lunch over the weekend. Otherwise we would share a meal in the evenings and settle down together and watch some television. Scotty didn't drink but he was tolerant of my habit.

Throughout my adult life I had been dominated by my overpowering need for alcohol. I know that in the past I had been frivolous and reckless, self centred, impulsive and selfish. Full of regrets too. Many regrets. But I had to accept that Michael loved his wife more than me. Hank loved his wife more than me. Charlie loved his wife more than me. I guess like us all, I just wanted to be loved. Scotty loved me in his quiet caring way. In the end that was enough. That young sweet, fun-loving Joan was buried under layers of resentment, disillusionment and rejection. I know that I should have been a better mother. I know that I neglected Rudi often, not seeing much of him when he lived with me as I was too busy working or too busy drinking to give him much thought, with weeks going by without me having any recollection of events.

I understand that a lot of times in the past, choosing to drink was an emotional decision. But it built up to be a need. I never did go back to AA. I had just reached the stage where I accepted where I was at. I *wanted* to drink. There. Saying that almost felt like a confession. But I had surrendered to it. *I wanted to drink*. With an old practised hand I had been able to get myself to a level of pleasant intoxication and maintain it expertly. I said to Rudi once when he came to visit, that my only pleasures in life are my cigarettes and my drinking. I knew I had gone from riches to rags and I lacked the energy to come back. I couldn't battle the power of the bottle any more. I was tired. I'd given up you see. Given up and given in. Given up life. Given in to alcohol. It was easier.

It was almost a relief.

So I continued to drink, often forgetting to eat.

Often ... just forgetting.

CHAPTER FIFTEEN

Rudi

One of the advantages of Joan charm is that she knew a lot of people. She had contacts written down in her trusted address book that she had managed to keep with her over the years and not lose despite the number of moves. After completing my schooling and together with my friend Jerry Musgrove, going for a rather unsuccessful interview for a position as an apprentice electrician with Huletts Sugar, my mom contacted one of her connections, Alex Davidson who worked for the Electricity Supply Commission, to ask him if he knew of any vacancies. As it turned out, he was very conveniently in charge of all the apprentices for the Natal region and he arranged an interview for me. I was over the moon when he gave me a job as an apprentice electrician at Congella Power Station, starting in the new year of 1972. For once I had my mother to thank. She organised the interview for a job that would set me up for the rest of my life. I had just finished school and I was nineteen.

I successfully completed my apprenticeship with the Electricity Supply Commission after three years. My fourth and final year I was sent to Pietermaritzburg Distribution Department where I worked on overhead lines and substations. I never lived with my mother again after leaving Rose Garden Lodge but continued to live with my sister until I moved to Pietermaritzburg. There I stayed at a boarding house called the Pink Palace where I had a room with its own separate entrance. I painted the walls a brown colour which was the fashion at the time and I thought it very trendy and I bought all my own furniture making the place a home. From there I moved to my own flat leaving the many dismal furnished bedsits that were a feature of my growing up years, firmly in the past. I remained with the Electricity Supply Commission until 1991 during which time I had advanced to the Test Department which was responsible for the maintenance and commissioning of power stations and sub stations. I then opened my own electrical contracting company which I successfully ran until 2001.

My father had been admitted as a resident of Townhill Hospital in Pietermaritzburg from 1966 and I used to visit him regularly. He knew who I was and was always glad to see me, not least because of the sweets that I brought him, but he only talked about his youth, his cricket and his parents. He remained there for ten years and died in 1976 during the time that I was away on a compulsory military camp with the army on the border of South West Africa. Although he hadn't been much of a father to me during my childhood, one thing that he did give me was my UK birthright which entitled me to British citizenship enabling me to emigrate to the UK in 2001 after selling my business.

My mother continued to struggle with alcohol for the rest of her life. She would have occasional periods of brief respite but then it wouldn't be long and she would be back on the drinking treadmill again. She never looked after herself. It was as if she didn't care any more. She didn't eat properly preferring to smoke and drink. Although I tried to do what I could to help her, she would just wave me off and insist that she was fine.

She had countless store and chemist accounts and running tabs with many corner cafés for daily necessities wherever she lived, often moving from the area and leaving some unpaid. Or she would tell me that she was going to Greenacres or the chemist to 'explain my financial situation' and return home full of glee having successfully spun a tale of woe to the unsuspecting clerk in the accounts department and subsequently got away with not having to pay. I don't know what she told them but I'm sure she turned on Joan charm.

She had numerous affairs mostly during her younger days but still continued to have relationships as she grew older until she more or less settled down with Scotty although they never actually lived together. She didn't like to go out at all but preferred her own space, her own company. She died in 1986 from pneumonia at the age of 63. She had given up.

I spiralled into a deep depression for many months after she died. It took me a long time to accept that I had done all I could to help her stop drinking. I couldn't force her to eat properly. I couldn't force her to look after herself better. I couldn't force her to cut down on her 'packet of Rothmans a day' habit. And I certainly couldn't force her to stop drinking. The only person that could do that was herself. And Joan was having none of that.

I had grown to realise that although my mom's behaviour towards me a lot of the time was hurtful and indifferent leaving me feeling forgotten and unimportant to her, I had learnt that I couldn't blame her. It was the alcohol that was her first love and it brought out the worst in her.

But no matter what she said, no matter what she did ... I loved her.

She was my mother.

The End

EIN HERZ FÜR AUTOREN A HEART FOR AUTHORS À L'ÉCOUTE DES AUTEURS MIA KAPΔI
...RTA FÖR FÖRFATTARE UN CORAZÓN POR LOS AUTORES YAZARLARIMIZA GÖNÜL V
...ORE PER AUTORI ET HJERTE FOR FORFATTERE EEN HART VOOR SCHRIJVERS TEMO
...ZÖINKÉRT SERCE DLA AUTORÓW EIN HERZ FÜR AUTOREN A HEART FOR AUTHOR
...RAÇÃO ВСЕЙ ДУШОЙ К АВТОРАМ ETT HJÄRTA FÖR FÖRFATTARE Á LA ESCUCHA DE
...TEURS MIA KAPΔIA ΓΙΑ ΣΥΓΓΡΑΦΕΙΣ UN CUORE PER AUTORI ET HJERTE FOR FORFAT
...ARLARIMIZA ...VER ...RZÖINKÉRT SERCE DLA AUTORÓW EII
...OR SCHRIJVER ...RAÇÃO ВСЕЙ ДУШОЙ К АВТОРАМ ETT I

The author

Helen Garden was born and brought up in Durban on the east coast of South Africa, where she pursued a career in Financial Services. After moving to the United Kingdom and later settling in beautiful, pictur-esque Cornwall, she ran a successful holiday cottage cleaning business with her husband Hedley, until she took a well deserved retirement in 2023. She has always had a deep and abiding love of litera-ture and encouraged by Hedley's enthusiasm to document his difficult early years living with his mother in various parts of Southern Africa, she was inspired to write his story. She enjoys reading, gardening, creating culinary delights and spending time walking in the vibrant and varied Cornish countryside. She is an accomplished artist, and her undoubted love of the African landscape reflects in the majority of her work.